British Policy and the
Irish Administration, 1920–22

British Policy and the Irish Administration, 1920–22

JOHN McCOLGAN

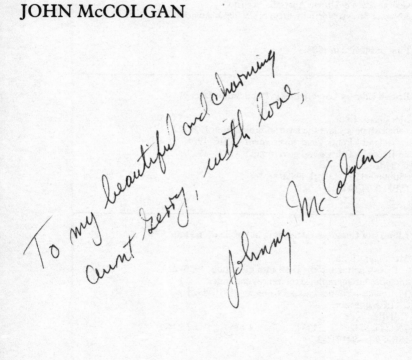

To my beautiful and charming aunt Gerty, with love,

Johnny McColgan

London
GEORGE ALLEN & UNWIN
Boston   Sydney

George Allen & Unwin (Publishers) Ltd,
40 Museum Street, London WC1A 1LU, UK

George Allen & Unwin (Publishers) Ltd,
Park Lane, Hemel Hempstead, Herts HP2 4TE, UK

Allen & Unwin, Inc.,
9 Winchester Terrace, Winchester, Mass. 01890, USA

George Allen & Unwin Australia Pty Ltd,
8 Napier Street, North Sydney, NSW 2060, Australia

First published in 1983.

British Library Cataloguing in Publication Data

McColgan, John.
  British policy and the Irish administration 1920–22.
1. Ireland – Politics and government – 1910–1921.
2. Ireland – Politics and government – 1921–1949.
I. Title
350'.0009415   JF429.I/
ISBN 0-04-941011-3

Library of Congress Cataloging in Publication Data

McColgan, John.
  British policy and the Irish administration, 1920–22.
Includes bibliographical references and index.
1. Ireland – Politics and government – 1910–1921.
2. Irish question.
I. Title.
JN1411.M32   1983   354.415   82-24429
ISBN 0-04-941011-3

Set in 10 on 11 point Plantin by Media Conversion Ltd., Ickenham
and printed in Great Britain
by Biddles Ltd., Guildford, Surrey

Contents

Foreword

Had I been invited a few years ago to draft an agenda for further research in Anglo-Irish history in the Treaty period, I would have listed two aspects in particular as still requiring systematic analysis, namely, the financial and the administrative. With the publication of Dr Mc Colgan's comprehensive inquiry into the transfer of administrative responsibility from British to Irish hands, the latter may now be deleted. His book not only fills a gap: it adds a dimension, one moreover that has thematic self-sufficiency while at the same time being complementary to studies recently made of the political, military, public opinion and other factors contributing to the shaping of the 1920–2 Anglo-Irish settlement. On both counts, the publication of Dr McColgan's work is to be welcomed. It is a pioneering inquiry almost wholly grounded on primary source material, much of it not hitherto critically examined and none of it, so far as I know, in this particular context. No one, it may be asserted with some confidence, will be able to write of the Treaty period comprehensively again without taking into account the questions Dr McColgan has posed or the answers to them that he has formulated. In that sense, this is one of those studies that widens historical horizons.

In times of revolutionary change the discontinuities are apt to be most evident at a high political level while a pronounced element of continuity may be preserved (and pass unremarked) in the administrative or executive sphere. This is not wholly fortuitous. A prospective successor authority, if far-sighted, will wish to ensure that the effective operation of the instrumentalities of government remains as little impaired as may be, so that they may continue to serve the same purposes, but for a different political master when power is in fact transferred. There was, however, in the Irish as later in the Indian case, one countervailing factor which rendered a sharp break in administrative continuity inevitable. It derived from the nature of the political transfer. When power passed in part or in substance from Britain to Ireland the natural line of succession would have been transfer in conformity with precedent and still continuing practice under the Union to a single central Dublin Castle administration. But the Government of Ireland Act 1920 was founded upon another premiss, that of a devolution of power not to one but to two co-equal successor authorities, one for the South and West, the other for the North (as contemporary parliamentary usage went) of Ireland with reserved powers, until agreed otherwise, remaining in the hands of the British government. The breach with continuity thus introduced was further compounded the following year when the Treaty settlement of 1921, with its principal feature the bringing into existence of the Irish Free State as a dominion, added a power and a status differential as between the two successor authorities. In conjunction, political division predicating the creation of a Belfast over and above a Dublin administration (with a consequent division of administrative manpower and resources) and the power differential (bringing into question the allocation of responsibility for services conditionally reserved to the British government under the provisions of the Government of Ireland Act 1920) opened the way to a series of complex manoeuvres by the three parties to this triangular situation, the purposes of which Dr McColgan elucidates and upon the outcome of which he has some novel reflections to offer.

The starting point of Dr McColgan's inquiry is a description of Dublin Castle administration as it was in 1920 when Sir Warren Fisher, Permanent Secretary at the Treasury and Head of the Civil Service, reported upon it in phrases unencumbered by qualification: 'The Castle administration does not administer . . . On the mechanical side, it can never have been good and is now quite obsolete.' Changes were recommended but, as Dr McColgan shows, haphazardly made, with a resulting uneasy equilibrium between the entrenched Castle régime and reinforcements sent from Whitehall. Among Northern Unionists there were fears lest the coming of the latter portended a more conciliatory British attitude towards Sinn Féin. One safeguard against such an eventuality was deemed to be the creation, openly when possible, surreptitiously when necessary, of a nucleus of civil government machinery in and for the six counties, the decisive move being the appointment in the first instance of an assistant under-secretary, Sir Ernest Clark, mechanically subordinate to the joint under-secretaries in Dublin Castle but in effect exercising a steadily increasing discretionary authority of his own. Not for the first or last time, from small beginnings large consequences flowed, the six counties in this case acquiring the nucleus of an all-important administrative base. Dr McColgan's reconstruction of this development is among the most illuminating and important parts of his narrative, the more so since outside the higher echelons of Unionist leadership in Belfast and at Westminster its significance was glimpsed but rarely fully understood either at the time or since. Dr McColgan places a high assessment on the price that was exacted for such oversight on the part of Sinn Féin. 'In contrast', he writes, 'with the South's failure to sabotage partition, Northern Ireland's desire to break all administrative connection with the South, where this was at all feasible, was fulfilled.'

While there is much in Dr McColgan's book on matters where high policy and administrative arrangements interlocked, there is a great deal also on more down-to-earth matters which were likely to affect civil servants in all sorts of ways. Were they to be 'directed' as to where they should work? Was a proportion of them, one-third was mentioned, to be allocated to Belfast? How and from where were recruits for the Northern Ireland administration otherwise to be drawn? From Britain or the six counties? What about the pensions of those who wished to transfer or to go (a matter of much concern to those involved, even if of indifference to others)? And what of facilities and equipment – the furniture, the typewriters, the reference books (even the ultimate destination of the old and dog-eared stirred momentary interest) without which a modern government cannot function? Were they to be divided or to remain in Dublin *in situ?* And at the last, with the detail disposed of, there is Dr McColgan's assessment of the contribution made by the large number of experienced administrators who transferred to the service of the Irish Free State to the establishment of settled, democratic government there.

While Dr McColgan's book will be of direct interest to students of Irish and Anglo-Irish history, it has also its wider relevance. I remember being asked early in 1947, as the day of transfer of power in India approached, whether I could advise on what had happened in the Irish case in respect of some of the matters mentioned above – pensions, allocation of equipment, and so forth. I had not, nor could I find, the necessary factual information. Now, as a result of Dr McColgan's research, it is not only available but placed in perspective. Furthermore it is of wider interest than one might at first glance suppose. In the last half-century power has been transferred in many states, in all continents. In most instances some at least of the same questions as in Ireland have arisen and provoked the same or similar reactions. Some relate, as in Ireland, to large issues, others to seemingly small ones. 'As usual', reported the last Viceroy of India in early August 1947, on the eve of partition and transfer of power in the sub-continent, division of certain mechanical office equipment was causing a 'complete deadlock', with the Indian Home Minister, Sardar Patel, 'flaring up' at the suggestion of a printing press going to the Pakistan capital at Karachi where there was only one. 'No one', Patel maintained, 'asked Pakistan to secede' and he had no intention of allowing them another press from India. Other parallels might be drawn on weightier matters – but this comparatively trifling example may serve to illustrate as well or perhaps even more realistically, than some larger ones, the sort of issues involved and the tensions to which they may give rise, especially when transfers of administrative responsibility come to be effected in association with partition. Amid the rhetoric that precedes national revolution and the violence that attends it, it is easy to overlook the dependence of a modern state upon experienced administrators and the equipment without which they cannot effectively function. Of this Dr McColgan's book is a timely reminder in a particular and significant historical setting.

NICHOLAS MANSERGH

Preface

The administrative history of Britain's disengagement from the government of Ireland in 1920–2 has yet to be investigated fully. Documentation on the transfer and partition of executive powers, especially in the year 1922, is considerable, and only a minute fraction of these archives has ever been used in historical writing. With the aid of some of these records this book addresses the political role of the mechanisms of British withdrawal from Ireland. More specifically, it attempts to analyse the function of administration and administrators in some of the major political maneouvres of statesmen who worked on the Irish question in this period. It is hoped that the purpose and intent of British policy in this period will become clearer, now that it is examined in the hands of such English civil servants as Sir John Anderson, A. W. Cope, A. P. Waterfield, Lionel Curtis and Sir Ernest Clark; and as examined in the light of how bureaucratic machinery was manipulated to suit the purposes of such politicians as Walter Long, Sir James Craig, Lloyd George and Michael Collins. Admittedly, the story told here is episodic, an eclectic navigation of political and administrative issues arising from varyingly distinct developments. Yet, the episodes here dealt with – the reform of Dublin Castle, the creation of a Belfast branch of the Irish government, the forging of partition in the Government of Ireland Act 1920, the transfer of powers and division of government organizations, etc. – document a consistency of purpose in British policy. All demonstrate how administrative apparatus was used in pursuance of political objectives on the two great issues of the Empire and Ulster. They provide, it is hoped, a fresh understanding of British withdrawal from Ireland, partition, and the formation of new states with native governments.

All errors and inaccuracies of this work are my own. I ascribe its virtue in large part to many other people to whom I have incurred debts of gratitude in the years of its making. First on the list of my creditors are the custodians of the archives on which the book is based. Archivists are far more than mere handmaidens of historical researchers. Their unique expertise in the management and appraisal of official records and in the preservation of historical documentation will have to be more widely recognised, if current administration is to run efficiently, and if past experience is effectively and adequately to serve the present and the future. I therefore wish to express an historian's thanks and indebtedness to the staffs of the following institutions: the Public Record Office, London, where the great bulk of research on this book was serviced efficiently and patiently for many months among the treasures and charm of Chancery Lane (shortly before the opening of the new building at Kew); the House of Lords Record Office whose indexing aids and preservation techniques should serve as models to other repositories; the Public Record Office of Northern Ireland whose modern, purpose-built repository houses the rich archives of the government of Northern Ireland and whose staff are justly enthusiastic about its holdings; the State Paper Office of Ireland whose staff never failed to go out of their way to be helpful; the National Library of Ireland whose massive research materials on Ireland and friendly and helpful staff played an immeasurable part in the secondary source grounding for this work; Harvard University's Lamont Library whose microfilm collections of British Cabinet records helped to fill gaps created by research omissions I committed in London; Boston College's Bapst Library and the Boston Public Library, both of which hold impressive Irish book collections; and finally and by no means least, the University College Dublin Archives Department, where the highest professional standards have been applied to processing the invaluable archival collections of early Irish Free State ministers, and where my friends on the staff taught me much about archives and showed me a hospitality over the years that I cannot hope to repay.

Among my other creditors are people whose involvement with my work, encouragement, advice and criticism have been crucial to its fruition. It is a privilege to be in such a debt to Professor P. N. S. Mansergh of St. John's College, Cambridge. As extern examiner in the work's thesis stage, Professor Mansergh provided constructive criticisms that facilitated significant improvements in substance and approach. He has now paid the book the exceptional compliment of writing its foreword and has thus greatly enhanced its value. R. Dudley Edwards, Professor Emeritus of Modern Irish History at University College Dublin, I mention with affection. Professor Edwards has never failed to place at my disposal his great mind with its labyrinth of historical insight. His interest in my work, his moral and professional support and encouragement, his pedagogical guidance and his valued friendship are among the most important reasons why this book is written. Dr Ronan Fanning, author of the monumental history of the Irish Department of Finance, supervised the doctoral thesis from which this work developed. His energetic competence and inspirational guidance provided the driving forces needed to push along the efforts of slow and deliberate research. Professor T. Desmond Williams was another source of strength and inspiration. To him I am grateful for many kindnesses, sage counsel and helpful encouragement. As academic advisor to the Trustees of the T. P. McDonnell Historical Scholarship Fund, Professor Williams has an additional and pre-eminent claim on my gratitude. To the Trustees of the fund I am indebted for their generous grant toward the book's publication. I wish to mention in particular Mr D. W. Pain, Trust Officer at the Bank of Ireland who has ably represented the Trustees as manager of the Fund. I wish to thank, too, my publishers, and particularly Mr Keith Ashfield and Ms Gillian Chandler for their patience and competence in guiding the work into print. My family I mention with love and gratitude for their loyalty and support during long periods of separation in the course of this work. Many more people have had an inspirational effect on my efforts. I mention in particular my friend Miss Kerry Holland who has supported and encouraged me in countless ways and to whom I owe much. Others include the late Mr Ernest Blythe, Dr Patrick Buckland, the late Miss Maire Comerford, Dr Kieran Flanagan, the late Mr Michael J. Gallagher, Mr Louis Gogan, the late Professor E. R. R. Green, Mr Marius Harkin, the late Reverend Martin P. Harney, S. J., Dr Michael Hopkinson, Mr Frank Litton, Dr Sheila Lawlor, Professor Donal McCartney, Miss Valerie McGuile, Dr Deirdre McMahon, Mrs Julia Mullen, Mr Peter Mullen, Dr Leon O Broin, Mr Coleman O'Callaghan, the late Mrs Nora Reddin, Mrs Jean Rowlands Tarbox, and Mr Oliver Snoddy. The list is hardly exhaustive and I apologize to those who have been unjustly omitted. I include finally, however, and not the least, all the people living on the island of Ireland. They were for many years my mentors and taught me much about their country and more. I wish them peace and well-being.

J. J. McC.

Dorchester, Massachusetts
Christmas Day, 1982

TO MY PARENTS
and to
THE MEMORY OF ANDREW F. LEONARD

1 Dublin Castle, 1920

The administration of Ireland through the Chief Secretary's Office at Dublin Castle ground to a halt in 1920. That the intensity of the Irish separatist movement could paralyse the apparatus of British government in Dublin was the consequence of both the organisational deficiencies of this apparatus and the irrelevance of its policy to political developments in Ireland. Both anomalies had been developing hand in hand for some time. The decades after the land war of the 1880s had witnessed 'a policy of drawing the teeth of the Irish executive' on the part of both major British political parties; by the time of the Home Rule crisis of 1912–14 and the Easter Rising of 1916 Dublin Castle retained neither the mettle nor the resolution to confront Volunteer armies or to hold in check revolutionary movements.[1] The oft-quoted remark of the Hardinge Commission reporting on the causes of the rising deserves repeating again: that the Castle system was 'anomalous in quiet times, and almost unworkable in times of crisis'.[2] In 1916 the view was shared by the Prime Minister, Asquith, who felt that the Castle

> in itself and in what it represented . . . no longer provided a basis for the administration and government of Ireland. He contemplated the disappearance 'of the fiction' of a chief secretary, the appointment of no successor to the lord lieutenant – the vice-royalty having become 'a costly and futile anachronism' – and single British ministerial control of Irish administration operating with the help of an Irish advisory council.[3]

But when Lloyd George's negotiations with Sir Edward Carson and John Redmond failed in July 1916, the problem of the Irish administration, and indeed of the Irish question as a whole, was shelved yet again. The half-hearted repression which followed in the wake of Augustine Birrell's disgrace, the failure of the Irish Convention of 1917–18, and especially the bungling and backfiring policies which created what became known in Ireland as 'the conscription crisis' all bolstered the influence of Sinn Féin and the Irish Volunteers and led to the ascendancy of the separatist movement.

For the remainder of 1918 and throughout most of 1919 British policy in Ireland remained essentially undefined and confused because of age-old party differences and because the government were not prepared to give the matter their full attention. Having swept to victory in the 1918 general elections outside the north-east, Sinn Féin MPs met at the Mansion House on 21 January 1919, formed Dáil Eireann, declared independence and provisionally constituted a republic. Yet, these events were largely ignored by a British government preoccupied with the whole range of enormous internal and international problems arising in the immediate postwar period. When from 1919 the shooting of policemen and escalating IRA activity forced the attention of a reluctant Cabinet back to the Irish question, the hard-liners prevailed. Coalition Liberals, such as H. A. L. Fisher, Christopher Addison and E. S. Montagu, pressed for a conciliatory Irish policy, arguing that as Sinn Féin had the moral support of the Irish population it should not be proclaimed.[4] The Cabinet majority, however, were blind to the distinction between expressions of moderate Sinn Féin opinion and increasingly numerous acts of violence. A reactionary administration in Dublin Castle therefore felt it had a free hand to pursue a generally repressive policy. By September 1919 not only Dáil Eireann and the Volunteers, but also Sinn Féin, Cumann na mBán and even the Gaelic League were declared illegal.[5] The result was the increasing alienation of moderate Sinn Féiners and other nationalists who initially opposed IRA attacks and who might have worked with the government towards a settlement, and perhaps averted hostilities, had the government instituted conciliatory initiatives.

Contemporary observers frequently blamed the deterioration in Anglo-Irish relations between 1916 and 1920 on the Dublin Castle executive. In October 1917, after the death of the hunger-striker Thomas Ashe as a result of force-feeding, the journalist C. P. Scott remarked that Dublin Castle was embarking 'on a course of provocative action directly opposed to the government'.[6] Two years later his view was the same. 'There was beyond question', he warned H. A. L. Fisher 'some malign influence in the Irish administration which *did not want* [Scott's italics] a settlement and had again and again conspired or at least succeeded in preventing it. You cannot trust your own government. He listened and more or less acquiesced, but it needs a good deal more than that to put a bridle on the Irish executive.'[7] However, the Castle would not be bridled, essentially because its more conservative and repressive elements had the support of the Tory majority in the Cabinet. A key figure representing this support was Walter Long, a hard-line Unionist, who pulled considerable weight on the Irish question.[8] In his diary the Cabinet Secretary, Tom Jones, records a revealing incident concerning Long. In January 1919 Viscount Haldane, who had been chairman of the machinery of government committee in 1917–18, arrived in Ireland and found the Viceroy, Lord French, 'very worried in the midst of some thirty-six departments, many of them hardly on speaking terms with each other'. Haldane offered to head a similar committee for Ireland to include 'an

Ulster man and de Valera himself', the purpose of which would be to 'work out some scheme of administration for Ireland, on the assumption that there would some day be some home rule act and some good will behind it'. But when the proposal reached Long, the latter's reply – according to Jones – was "'to go to Hell" or words to that effect'.[9] Long, although generally in accord with French's hard military line, did not concur with the more liberal political outlook[10] held by French and Haldane. Moreover, on questions concerning the Irish administration, Long seems to have taken his advice from the assistant under-secretary, Sir John Taylor,[11] a classic martinet in both the political and administrative sense, about whom we shall soon learn more. Thus, if there was a 'malign influence' in Castle administration, it was buoyed up by hard-line anti-nationalist elements in the Cabinet, of whom Long was a prime example.

It would seem, then, that the British search for a settlement in Ireland at this time was pursued not by means of attempting to conciliate Irish nationalists, but rather by attempting to conciliate different sections of the Cabinet. Only in the latter part of 1919, when the world war was a year ended, when the traditional gaps between Conservative and Liberals over Ireland, though far from resolved, were sufficiently narrowed, was a Cabinet committee appointed to examine the Irish question and recommend the details of a new policy. The continuing preponderant influence of the hard-liners was reflected in the appointment of Walter Long to the chair of this committee, the deliberations of which eventually led to the introduction of the Government of Ireland Bill in early 1920. For some time to come the government's political and military policies would continue to reflect confusion and dissension, but at least it was beginning to pay increasing attention to Irish problems. And now in the early months of 1920 the dramatic upsurge in guerrilla activity, the assassinations, the evacuation of police outposts on a large scale, the supplanting of British authority in local government and jurisprudence by Dáil institutions, the popular support for prison hunger-strikes, all had a significant impact on the government. Not that it became convinced that it should expedite a speedy settlement by reconciliation with the nationalist population, but at least it was moved to inquire as to what was wrong with the existing state apparatus in Dublin. The on-the-spot action which the British believed would rectify the situation was threefold: to install new personnel at the top – a new Chief Secretary, Sir Hamar Greenwood, a new GOC for the army, General Sir Nevil Macready, a Chief of Police, General H. H. Tudor; to reinforce the military strength of the army and of the police, the ranks of the latter being filled by ex-servicemen recruited in England (the ruthless Auxiliaries and the notorious Black and Tans); and to revitalise the bureaucracy of the Irish executive in the

Chief Secretary's Office, whose effective action up until this point had been brought to a standstill. The strengthening of police and military may have been a welcome development to Castle reactionaries; but they could not have been pleased with the coming of young progressive English civil servants with twentieth-century political ideas. Rather suddenly it seemed as though the influence of Walter Long had come to an abrupt end in Irish administration. But, as we shall see, the efforts of the new reformers would not be sufficient to avert a horn-locking struggle between Irish nationalists and the Tory-dominated government that wore on for another eighteen months.

The Fisher Reforms

The reorganisation of Dublin Castle in the spring of 1920 was a victory for the Viceroy, Lord French, who had complained of the need for administrative reform since 1918.[12] After Macready arrived in Ireland in early April, one of his first actions was immediately to support French in his long-standing plea. 'Before I had been there three hours', Macready wrote to Walter Long on 23 April,

> I was honestly flabbergasted at the administrative chaos that seems to reign here . . . His Excellency appeared to me to have been forced into an entirely false position, and to be made to do the work of a departmental junior. The whole idea seemed to be that no one would take responsibility, even in small matters; and I was with him on several occasions when he was called upon to do things which honestly amazed me.[13]

The occasion which revealed the Castle's shortcomings to Macready was the Mountjoy hunger-strike, which Macready saw as a protest against the arbitrary removal of certain established privileges of political prisoners by Dublin Castle. His memoirs recall that 'Sir J. Taylor, the assistant under-secretary, endeavoured to throw the blame on the governor of the prison, but there was little doubt that the fault lay in Sir J. Taylor's office, where work was centralized to a degree almost unbelievable'. It was quite plain that 'no effective action could be taken in Ireland until the civil administration was placed on a more businesslike footing'. Immediately he wrote to London to 'ask that a small committee of experts in office administration might be sent to overhaul the various departments in the Castle'.[14]

The 'experts', who arrived in the first week in May, were led by Sir Warren Fisher, Secretary to the Treasury and chief of the United Kingdom civil service. He was assisted by R. E. Harwood, also of the

Treasury, and Alfred W. Cope, a former customs detective, currently second secretary to the Minister of Pensions and shortly to begin a key role in Anglo-Irish political relations in the next two years. 'In the twinkling of an eye', so went the lyrical account of a contemporary Castle official, they 'had settled the office reorganisation, even those portions of it which [they] had not seen, much less grasped. They came, they saw, and then they disappeared as promptly as they came, leaving not a wrack behind. And men wondered whether things were to resume the old course, and gossip was busy with the name of a possible new assistant under-secretary'.[15]

The opening paragraph of Warren Fisher's report to Austen Chamberlain on 12 May pronounced a concise and condemning verdict upon the Castle system: 'The Castle administration does not administer. On the mechanical side it can never have been good and is now quite obsolete; in the infinitely more important sphere (a) of informing and advising the Irish government in relation to policy and (b) of practical capacity in the application of policy it simply has no existence.[16] In the Chief Secretary's Office, the investigation of which was reported on separately by Cope and Harwood, it was apparent that the inadequate size of staff during the period of political turbulence and deficiencies in office procedure had led to administrative chaos. Little could be done about the obsolescence of procedures during the crisis until certain individuals were removed from positions of power and staff was strengthened with officers of sufficient competence and numbers:

> We are strongly of opinion that if the government of the country is to be exercised through the civil power, a drastic re-organisation of the chief secretary's office is required, and that if this is to be accomplished and satisfactory assistance to be given to the chief secretary, the introduction of new and additional personnel into the department is urgently necessary. The establishment of the office is practically on the same basis as would suffice for normal times, and is totally inadequate to meet the demands made upon it under present circumstances. It is undesirable to assign to it a permanent addition of staff which might be redundant when normal conditions are restored, but it is essential that it should at once be strengthened against the present emergency, and this can most effectively be done by seconding a small number of suitable officers from English departments. This would allow of a convenient and temporary re-arrangement of the work dealt with on the administrative side.[17]

Also, what the Chief Secretary's Office badly needed was a whole new attitude toward the position of under-secretary, as well as an individual really capable of carrying out its important duties. 'The prevailing conception of the post of under-secretary', Fisher observed,

who *should* be the principal permanent adviser of the Irish government in civil affairs – appears to be that he is a routine clerk. This is due to obvious causes amongst which are (a) the personality of some of the occupants of the post and (b) the attitude of some chief secretaries.

The position at the present moment is seemingly that no one in the chief secretary's office, from the under-secretary downwards, regards himself as responsible even for decisions on departmental papers, let alone for a share in the solution of difficulties in the realm either of policy or of execution.

The chief secretary, for his part, appears to be under the illusion that a civil servant – even though he has the position and emoluments of permanent head of the Irish administration – is entirely unconcerned with the exploration or settlement of the problems which the Irish administration exists to solve.

So long as these notions continue, the attainment of merely perfection has next to no value. For with the chief secretary skied on Olympus and his top permanent official hewing wood in the remotest valley the natural expectation is that the essentials must suffer. . .[18]

The inference from the above observations is that the under-secretary should be a man of marked ability and force and of long general experience, and that the proper conception of the duties of the post should be adopted. If the latter condition were ignored, the right man could not be expected to be got for the post or to remain in it.[19]

The investigators regarded the existing under-secretary, the Rt Hon. James MacMahon, as falling 'considerably short of the requirements now generally demanded of a permanent head of an important department. His failure to assert his authority over his immediate subordinates shows him to be lacking in strength of character, and we do not consider that his general ability is outstanding'.[20] MacMahon, formerly Secretary of the Post Office in Ireland, had been appointed under-secretary at the Castle in 1918 (according to Sir Henry Robinson, 'much to his dismay').[21] The then Chief Secretary, Edward Shortt, seems to have insisted on his appointment 'as a concession to the Catholic Hierarchy, with whom he held close relations, and in order to conciliate the home rule party, with whose political aspirations he was in sympathy'.[22] Once appointed he was unable to prevent the assistant under-secretary, Sir John Taylor, from usurping the great bulk of the under-secretary's duties. Indeed, Macready had reported MacMahon to be 'very anxious' for Fisher's arrival 'as I fancy he finds his administrative difficulties considerable'.[23] 'Quite clearly', stated Fisher, 'the post is inadequately held during the present crisis. Mr MacMahon is not devoid of brains, but lacks initiative, force and driving power. Neither by temperament nor by training is he ready for responsibility; his conception of his functions conforms to the traditional Irish limits; and he has had no experience of running a big show or of shaping policy.'[24] At the same time Fisher saw the advantages of retaining MacMahon. He was a nationalist and a Catholic, and his loyalty to the Crown went unquestioned (except perhaps when defined by Ulster Unionists who were not happy to see an Armagh Catholic nationalist in the highest post in Dublin Castle); and his popularity made him 'something of an asset' to the Irish government. Cope and Harwood thought 'it would be impolitic to remove him' even though his nationalist associations 'may, in other respects, have impaired his usefulness'.[25] Rather than having him replaced, Fisher recommended keeping him as a propaganda asset and appointing a dynamic, competent figure, preferably Sir John Anderson, Chairman of the Board of Inland Revenue, as compeer to MacMahon to carry out the more important duties of the under-secretary:

> The alternatives open to the government in these circumstances are (a) to retire MacMahon or (b) to retain him but to place alongside him a man who will fill the bill and has the necessary tact to use and manage him. The one quite impossible thing to do was done by the Irish government when they retained him as nominally sole undersecretary but authorised his subordinates to short-circuit him.
>
> The inclination of my judgement is to keep Mr MacMahon (who would mature for retirement if desired in about eighteen months) as under-secretary and to appoint a joint under-secretary (pro tem) in the person of a picked man seconded from London. The argument for retention which Sir Nevil Macready uses is that Mr MacMahon's appointment is a source of satisfaction to the Roman Catholic hierachy and I think there is some force in this provided Mr MacMahon is not treated by his superiors as outside the pale of any confidence, as the only effect of this must be to offend the hierachy . . .
>
> For the additional under-secretary, Sir John Anderson, KCB, chairman of the board of inland revenue, would be quite admirable and would rapidly acquire the real control.[26]

Fisher's first reports made an impression on Austen Chamberlain. In a cover note recommending to Bonar Law and Lloyd George that they take time to read the reports, Chamberlain told his colleagues he 'was prepared for none too satisfactory an account of the Irish administration, but [the reports] disclose a condition both of administration and staffs which is worse than anything that I had anticipated'.[27]

Not only did Fisher decry the abysmal lack of administrative efficiency, but he also stressed the need for the Castle to take on a new political outlook, liberal and sympathetic to moderate nationalist aspirations. A further reason why Fisher wished to keep MacMahon as under-secretary was that he 'sincerely holds views more in keeping with 20th century sentiment than those expressed by the ascendancy party and the supporters of indiscriminate coercion, and so far as it counts, his advice would be on the side of judicious moderation'.[28] Fisher, himself a convinced and zealous liberal, was as much disturbed about the unbending, narrow arch-conservatism pervading the Castle, as he was about its gross inefficiency. In a supplementary report to the Cabinet, dated 15 May, he saw the existing government in Ireland (with the exception of Macready)

as almost woodenly stupid and quite devoid of imagination. It listens solely to the ascendancy party and (previous to General Macready's arrival) it never seemed to think of the utility of keeping in close touch with opinions of all kinds. The phrase 'Sinn Féin' is a shibboleth with which everyone not a 'loyalist' is denounced, and from listening to the people with influence you would certainly gather that Sinn Féin and outrage were synonymous . . . In fact the ruling cast reminds one of some people in England – mainly to be found in clubs and among retired warriors and dowager ladies – who spend their time in denunciation of the working classes as 'socialists' without ever condescending (or indeed being able) to analyse what they mean. But here such a performance is academic; it has not led and is not likely to lead to the proscription of the Labour Party or movement as illegal. But in Ireland the Sinn Féin party – representing the great majority of Irishmen – had been proclaimed as an illegal organisation! Imagine the result on public opinion in Great Britain of a similar act by the executive towards a political party (or the women's suffrage movement)!

By all means proclaim organised murder and outrage, whether it is the outcome of hooliganism or of a topsy-turvy kind of patriotic fanaticism; but this would aim at the isolation of the murder etc. gang (or gun-boys as General Macready calls them) from the rest of the community, whereas the Irish government by refusing to discriminate and by using the label 'Sinn Féin' to cover murderers and criminals on the one hand and everyone whose political persuasion it dislikes on the other is simply antagonising the majority and inducing it to view with indifference the campaign of outrage.[29]

He thought there was still time 'to isolate the murder gang' from the moderates of Sinn Féin. If 'wisely treated', developments among the nationalist population, such as the establishment of Sinn Féin land courts, could be turned to advantage. Even the Volunteers, he went so far as to suggest, could be regularised as an 'Irish militia'. Acts of 'stupid violence' by government forces under the Defence of the Realm Act were 'calculated to drive to extremism the moderate (i.e. numerically preponderant) elements in Sinn Féin; and the indescribable folly of proscribing Sinn Féin as a political creed . . . is capped by the blunders of brute force'. All this would 'inevitably lead to a condition requiring martial law', unless government in Ireland was placed in the hands of wiser counsel.[30]

The government, in response, never showed any sign of being moved by Fisher's case for a conciliatory policy. However, they were sufficiently impressed by his arguments for *administrative* reform to give him sanction to bring to Ireland a team of talented officials from British departments, led by Sir John Anderson. Anderson, regarded at the time and for a long while afterwards as perhaps the most competent official of the entire British civil service, arrived in Dublin in May to take up the duties of joint under-secretary with James MacMahon. A widower of two weeks at the age of 38, he is said to have welcomed such a task absorbing his full time and attention as well as smothering personal grief.[31] The hard-working, highly-strung A. W. Cope was made assistant under-secretary at the recommendation of Fisher, and the witty, debonair Mark Sturgis assumed, in effect, the duties of a joint assistant under-secretary, but was referred to as Anderson's private secretary, apparently in deference to the sensibilities of Cope.[32] Other officials on the new Castle team loaned from London were G. G. Whiskard and L. N. Blake Odgers from the Home Office, N. G. Loughnane from the Ministry of Pensions and T. D. Fairgrieve from the Scottish Office.[33] Most of the officials seconded to Dublin Castle generally appeared to be of a political hue similiar to Fisher's. Cope, in particular, became especially dedicated to the conciliation of Sinn Féin and his direct contacts with that party are said to have been instrumental in bringing about the negotiations and truce of the summer of 1921. One of their new Irish colleagues in the Chief Secretary's Office saw them as 'officials who had no axe to grind, no stake in the country, whose future careers did not lie in Ireland, and who therefore could afford to act independently. Sinn Féin distrusts politicians. It was hoped that the olive branch, when held out by a civil servant would prove less of a scarecrow than when the visage of a chief secretary smirked above it.'[34]

The official who wrote these words, G. C. Duggan, and his assistant, Joseph Brennan, were first division clerks in the finance division who impressed Harwood and Cope favourably. Both were to enjoy distinguished careers in the future: the former in Northern Ireland as assistant secretary in the Department of Finance and later comptroller and auditor-general; the latter in the Irish Free State as permanent secretary in the Department of Finance and, from 1927, chairman of the Currency Commission. Duggan, Brennan and C. M. Martin-Jones (another first division clerk and an Englishman who had spent all his civil service career in Ireland) were kept on – quite possibly as much because of their 'twentieth-century sentiments' as their ability as civil servants. Indeed, the new Castle team should be seen in contradistinction to the officials who were replaced.

The Purged

The key officer in the Castle had been the assistant under-secretary, Sir John Taylor. By all accounts Taylor had an enormous capacity for work, but was prone to centralise everything into his own office. A cold, resolute, conservative and humourless man, bitter at having been passed over for the under-secretaryship in 1918,[35] he was exceedingly unpopular and to some extent may have been used as a scapegoat for the many deficiencies of Castle rule. In the hands of both Taylor and the principal clerk, W. P. J. Connolly, Cope and Harwood 'found an undue concentration of both important and unimportant work', their methods being 'such as to deprive their immediate subordinates of any initiative or authority in handling matters for which they should properly be responsible'. Both had been government servants for about forty years. Connolly was 'hopelessly out of date and inefficient', and his retirement the investigators urged 'as a necessary preliminary to any successful reorganization of the department'.[36] This would involve the unfortunate man's removal to England for his own safety: the branch of the office in which he worked dealt with 'criminal matters and the suppression of the Sinn Féin movement', and because of this association he had been resident in Dublin Castle since the assassination of Alan Bell in March.[37] In September he transferred to the Irish Office in London where he remained until retirement on his sixtieth birthday in March 1921.[38] The recommendation to retire Taylor was phrased in less abrupt and more respectful terms, the investigators insisting that his unpopularity was apparently not 'due to any defect of character or personality, but to his personal association with certain duties which the office has been called upon to perform'. Still, they believed that it would be 'unfair to induce Sir John to remain if he is desirous of retiring, and even if he is disposed to remain it would, without any disparagement of his work as a distinguished official, be in the public interest if a change were now made'.[39] In fact, Taylor, who had been dealt a blow in April when Lord French ordered the release of the Mountjoy hunger-strikers, was away on leave when he learned of his 'retirement'.[40] He later made attempts to be retained in the civil service, but was refused and awarded £3,000 gratuity in the 'special circumstances'.[41]

No other officials are mentioned in the reports of the Fisher investigation, but it is possible that other persons were removed from the scene because of incompatibility of view with the 'new brooms'. Samuel Watt may have been such a person. A year later in 1921, Watt would become permanent secretary in the Northern Ireland Department of Home Affairs under the hard-line Unionist minister, R. Dawson Bates. But in 1920 he was an assistant principal in the Chief Secretary's Office. In early June he was transferred 'on loan' to the Admiralty in London.[42] The Admiralty was a department for which Sir Edward Carson had been minister in 1916–17 and Sir James Craig, who was to become Northern Ireland's first Prime Minister, was currently parliamentary under-secretary. Watt may have been the first Irish civil servant of a long line to leave Dublin departments on the route to Belfast in the next two years.

One other victim of the Dublin Castle purge is worth discussion: 'Pouf!', went the gleeful headline in the *Freeman's Journal* on 27 May, 'out goes another Castle light!', announcing the removal back to Whitehall of Maurice Headlam, the Treasury Remembrancer.[43]

The Fisher Reforms – the Treasury Dimension

Headlam was in charge of a small Treasury office in Dublin Castle with the quaint title of Treasury Remembrancer. The financial system of the Irish administration was awkward and roundabout, a 'dilatory and cumbersome' practice as Headlam himself described it.[44] Official procedure was for Irish departments to submit their financial requests to the Treasury in Whitehall, who returned these to the Treasury Remembrancer who, in turn, sent them back to Whitehall recommending approval or rejection. In practice, shortcuts were found, the more direct, informal methods of personal communication being facilitated by 'the advantage of belonging to the Kildare Street Club'.[45] But in the emergency of 1920 this style of 'government by continuous conversation'[46] would be superimposed upon by a larger staff with greater and more immediate powers. Sir John Anderson, in addition to assuming the under-secretaryship jointly with MacMahon, was given the same financial powers in Ireland as those of the Secretary to the Treasury in Britain.[47] Combining both the administrative

and financial function of the Irish administration under one person –
though at times producing the odd spectre of Anderson requesting funds
in one capacity and refusing himself in the other[48] – was an
extraordinary step and underscores how serious British officials regarded
the administrative emergency in Ireland. The Treasury's office at
Dublin Castle now became a fully fledged 'division', with authority to
make decisions on important matters officially and on the spot. The new
division, Treasury (Ireland), became operative from 25 May 1920 and
was responsible 'for all questions relating to expenditure' by departments with headquarters in Ireland, including 'matters relating to
establishment as well as supply'.[49] The Irish work of several
Whitehall divisions thus became consolidated under Treasury (Ireland).
As in the case of the Chief Secretary's Office, officials were specially
seconded from England to carry out duties under Anderson's authority.
These officials included an acting principal secretary, A. P. Waterfield,
and two principals, B. W. Gilbert and W. T. Matthews. Together with
their colleagues in the Chief Secretary's Office they administered what
one authority has called a 'super bureaucracy' similar to administrative
innovations in other ministerial departments to cope with emergency
situations arising from the world war.[50]

As in the case of the Chief Secretary's Office, the political dimension of
the reform in the Treasury Remembrancer's office becomes clear when
examining the official who was replaced. In his *Irish Reminiscences*,
published many years later, the existing Treasury Remembrancer,
Maurice Headlam, recalled how one day in May 1920 Warren Fisher and
John Anderson visited his office and 'talked generalities'. When Headlam tried to warn them of an official they were about to see, suspected by
Headlam of being a Sinn Féin informant, his guests 'looked down their
noses, and one of them said I ought not to say such things'. Only
afterwards did Headlam learn from MacMahon – as an unpleasant
surprise, it seems – that he had been relieved of his duties in
Ireland.[51]

Headlam had been Treasury Remembrancer since 1912. His *Irish
Reminiscences*, published in 1947, serve equally well as a eulogy of Irish
fly-fishing and an elegy for the demise of coercive government in Ireland.
He admits in the book to having lobbied the parliamentary opponents of
the government on the Irish question during the Home Rule crisis of
1912–14 and at other critical stages of the government's Irish policy. He
felt justified in publicly expressing his staunch and consistently pro-Uni-
onist views because 'the ordinary civil service rules about taking part in
politics did not apply in the Irish case, which was not politics but flagrant
disloyalty to the crown whose servant I was'.[52] G. C. Duggan, in his
unpublished memoirs, has left an orthodox civil servant's condemnation
of such licence. 'Surely', says Duggan of Headlam's rationalisation,

this is a most dangerous dictum. It is the duty of a civil servant to point out to his own minister whither he thinks government policy is leading, but surely, if he finds that he can make no headway, it is not then open to him to lobby the opponents of the government? Such a course of action can only breed distrust between ministers and their senior officials. Moreover it leaves a civil servant free to choose his loyalties, to determine himself the point at which it is open to him to use official knowledge to thwart the government of the day . . . If Headlam's views are accepted, then they can be equally used to justify the action of those civil service colleagues of Mr Headlam who conveyed secret official information to their friends in the Sinn Féin party. Maurice Headlam was an English conservative . . . opposed to any change in Ireland and prepared to go to any length to retain the status quo. His book leaves a bad taste in the mouth of any ex-British civil servant.[53]

The departure from Ireland of Taylor, Connolly and Headlam was to the great relief of Duggan and Brennan. For a long time both had been living uncomfortably under the oppressive thumb of Taylor, who in complicity with Headlam, effectively prevented them from performing the more responsible functions of their jobs. Again, Duggan:

Taylor was hand in glove with the diehard representative of the Treasury in Ireland, Maurice Headlam, the Treasury Remembrancer . . . I foolishly thought that, when departments put forward proposals for new financial expenditure, it was part of my duty to examine them on their merits, discuss them with the promoting department and advise the Treasury on the views of the chief secretary. I was soon disillusioned. The document was merely to be copied and sent on with a covering letter 'for consideration', or even (occasionally) for 'favourable consideration', and nothing more, and that was what I was paid for doing. The Treasury next returned this letter to the Treasury Remembrancer at the Castle attaching any relevant files and the latter then settled directly with Taylor what was to be the fate of the proposal. As both were cheese-parers, and both were opposed to the policy of killing home rule by financial bribes there was little that got through the net.[54]

Relations were particularly bad between Taylor and Brennan, who later in life described Taylor as 'a loathsome character, bigoted and anti-Irish'.[55] The coming of Cope and Waterfield was doubtless a breath of fresh air, and for the next two years provided both young Irish officials with the experience which prepared them for the positions of the leading administrators they were to become under autonomous governments.

The New Dublin Castle and the Political Question

The political outlook of the new Castle bureaucracy was far removed from the Unionism of the Taylors and the Headlams and fundamentally in tune with the idea of Irish self-government within the empire. But the political views of civil servants and the policies they are obliged to implement are different matters. It was plain that, more than sympathetic officials, what was needed was a new government policy if there was to be a speedy settlement. The *Freeman's Journal* sounded the warning to the new officials:

> There is only one cure for Castle misrule. Abolish the Castle. Tinkering is no good. That has been tried before. New patches on the rotting texture have not made the garb of alien and undemocratic rule any more pleasing to Irish eyes . . . The advent of one or two well-intentioned officials has never done more than for a time to steer the governmental ship clear of the more egregious blunders, and that only for a short period. Being wrong in its fundamentals, the system soon returns with all its old viciousness and futility fully restored.
>
> Asquith and Lloyd George in moments of honesty and clear-seeing have declared that the root evil is the withholding of the right of self-government from the people. With English statesmen, however, it is a long cry from the mouthing of democratic commonplaces to their application where the freedom of Ireland is concerned.
>
> Yet the truth is plain for every honest man to see. There can be no peace between the Irish people and the English people so long as the latter permit this country to be governed through Dublin Castle.[56]

In the first few weeks of their administration the new English officials felt that their policies were having a favourable impact on public opinion in Ireland. They were sure that a climate had been created in which a quick settlement could be brought about if only the British Cabinet would respond generously on the political question as a whole. But it is doubtful whether their work could have reversed the dramatic upward spiral of revolutionary activity in the summer of 1920. And, in any case, the zeal, competence and ideals with which Anderson, Cope and Sturgis seemed to have changed the face of civilian administration at the Castle overnight in fact were not of sufficient influence to win over an indecisive, inert and still mainly hard-line Cabinet.

After arriving at the Castle, Anderson and Cope found that their views on the political question generally fell into line with those of MacMahon and W. E. Wylie, the law adviser to the Irish government. All believed Dominion Home Rule to be a feasible and effective settlement provided immediate action was taken on the part of the

British government. A letter from Cope to Sir Warren Fisher on 16 June 1920 captures the hope of the Castle officials, the challenge that was before them and the awareness of imminent failure without the support of a conciliatory government policy:

> Both Wylie and MacMahon tell me they are convinced that people are holding the opinion that the Castle is improving. I hope it is true. The chief secretary's office is a 1000 times worse than I imagined. Anderson is satisfied there is some improvement and that the offices show that a spring clean is in operation.
>
> The team you have gathered together for us is working splendidly. Brennan and Duggan now smile and I shall soon be happy – but only so far as office machinery goes. As far as the country is concerned, *now* is the time for action; 'soon' may be too late.[57]

But the weeks passed and no such government action was forthcoming. Rather, the anti-Irish stance of the government was seen to be maintained as the military continued to file into the country. This perception was reinforced by the government's threat to close down Irish railways in response to the ban by trade unions on the movement of munitions; by Walter Long's concessions in the House of Commons to Sir Edward Carson which strengthened the Ulster grip on the Government of Ireland Bill and enhanced prospects for partition; and by police and military reprisals against the property of civilians in Fermoy, Lismore and Tuam.[58] Calls had come for a Dominion Home Rule settlement, but the failure of the government to respond led Anderson to state that government inertia had practically nullified the beginnings of *rapprochement* with the Irish public generated by the Dublin Castle reform, and that it was the reason why 'outrages', which had let up in May and June, were once again on the increase in July. Urgently did he plead with the Chief Secretary, Hamar Greenwood, on 20 July to have the Cabinet act swiftly in taking a conciliatory line towards Ireland while there was still time to salvage what goodwill in Ireland the British government still enjoyed. On his arrival two months before, he began,

> the ordinary machinery of civil administration in the chief secretary's office, Dublin Castle, was practically non-existent. No business that was not urgent was being attended to and business which had become urgent was disposed of in very many cases without proper consideration. The general state of this office, on which the whole civil administration of the country should pivot, was really incredible . . .

The increasing level of violence and Sinn Féin influence, he believed, was irrelevant:

It is not necessary for the purpose of these notes to set out in detail the measures taken during the short period of two months that has elapsed towards the re-establishment of an effective organisation. Enquiry would show that much has been done: much undoubtedly remains to be done. But in any case no practical results could yet be apparent from spade work of this kind, and any conclusions as to the state of the administrative machine that might be drawn from a comparison of statistics of outrages or of any other manifestations of Sinn Féin power are bound to be absolutely illusory.

On the other hand, there is, I believe, ground for holding that during the first few weeks of the present regime the political situation showed signs of improvement. Outrages of the grosser sort decreased in number; there were indications that the conscience of the Roman Catholic Church was stirred; and the beginning of an attempt on the part of the Sinn Féin leaders to stop murder and other crimes of violence seemed to be traceable. All this synchronised with a succession of political rebuffs in America, with an unexpectedly hostile attitude on the part of labour in England, and incidentally with the visit of the Catholic bishops to Rome. During the last few weeks the tide has set in the opposite direction. It is impossible to come to any certain conclusion but I believe that the early improvement was due in some measure at least to an idea that the reconstituted executive stood for a more generous policy. I believe also that within the last few weeks that idea has given place to a conviction either that the original idea was unfounded or that the attitude of the cabinet does not correspond with that of the Irish executive, and that we see the result in the increased hostility of the local press and more recently in the recrudescence of outrage on a scale hitherto almost without parallel, and indirectly in the stiffening of the attitude of labour.[59]

Though he believed that the recent outrages demanded 'firm measures', he was certain that repression alone was no solution; there were not 'the instruments at hand' to ensure success. Any coercion necessary 'should be accompanied by a declaration of policy and an appeal to moderate opinion in Southern Ireland which will create an atmosphere favourable to suppression of crime and prepare the way for an ultimate settlement by consent'.[60]

On 23 July, Anderson, Cope, Wylie and MacMahon brought their views before a conference of Cabinet ministers in London.[61] The united front presented by the 'experts', who argued for an end to coercion and the introduction of Dominion Home Rule, had the support of Macready and impressed both Winston Churchill and Lloyd George. The latter put out feelers to his die-hard colleagues, commenting that it was 'very significant that two such able civil servants as Sir John Anderson and Mr Cope agreed broadly with Mr Wylie', and warning that 'the view of the experts was a very serious factor, and, if known to the public, it would be impossible to go on with the Government [of Ireland] Bill'. He remarked that 'the Commander in Chief agreed in the main with the diagnosis of Mr Wylie, and Sir James Craig accepted Mr Wylie's summary of the situation as substantially true'. But the die-hards remained duly unimpressed. 'I accept his diagnosis', retorted Craig, 'but not his remedies'. The Ulster Unionist Attorney-General for Ireland, Denis Henry, afterwards to become Lord Chief Justice for Northern Ireland, believed the Castle officials had overestimated the number of 'righteous Sinn Féiners' and that 'the bad element in Sinn Féin would seize on any new statement by the government, and any Sinn Féiners negotiating would be shot'. Walter Long agreed with this point because 'experience showed that from the days of O'Connell'. Moreover, if such concessions were made to Sinn Féin 'the reaction of the Unionist party in the House would be more determined even than in the case of the Amritsar incident'.[62]

The Castle officials heard only one or two voices of qualified support. Churchill 'was quite prepared to go much further than the government bill' provided it did not appear to be a victory for Sinn Féin; but he also wanted to 'raise 30,000 men in Ulster by whom the authority of the crown could be vindicated not only in Ulster but throughout Ireland'.[63] Less compromising support for the Castle's proposal came from the Southern Unionist, Lord Curzon, who regarded the 'arming of Ulster' as a 'fatal suggestion'. He 'was in favour of getting into touch with the responsible leaders of Sinn Féin, of keeping the Home Rule bill still before the commons, and then of remodelling the bill later in the light of a conference with the Sinn Féiners'. But like Lloyd George he was aware that 'the difficulties turned around Ulster'.[64]

In the end the hard-liners prevailed. It was clear that they would consider no settlement beyond the terms of the Government of Ireland Bill while armed opposition in Ireland remained at large. Lloyd George listened to the Castle group but was only too well aware of the right wing which dominated his coalition Cabinet. He seems to have felt instinctively that the Ulster problem was the key to a most expeditious settlement from the British viewpoint. Questioning the Castle officials on the Ulster dimension, he was told that Sinn Féin might accept Dominion Home Rule with the six counties excluded, but would never agree to a Belfast Parliament. Thus with no prospects of eliciting an agreeable bargain from Sinn Féin on the question of Ulster, it would be futile for Lloyd George to approach his numerically preponderant Conservative colleagues on the proposal of Dominion Home Rule.[65] Thus, fundamentally, the government stance remained unchanged: splintered as the Cabinet view was, it could only fail to adopt bold measures on any definite line of policy or fixity of purpose. The only government response to the challenge of the Irish question in the summer of 1920 was a new measure of limited coercion, the Restoration of Order in Ireland Act, passed 9 August. Stopping short of martial law, the new law clothed the military with extra judicial and police powers. In so far as there was any political policy, it remained the suppression of crime and the implementation of the Government of Ireland Bill.[66] Walter Long still held the reins.

So disheartened was Warren Fisher with the Cabinet's drift towards yet more repression that he ceased to believe in the utility of civil government in Ireland. The Restoration of Order in Ireland Bill, now before Parliament, would have the effect of making it no longer safe for the English officials in Ireland to reside outside Dublin Castle's walls; and in another long memorandum to Austen Chamberlain two days before the Act was passed Fisher advocated considering their withdrawal from Ireland, because under such conditions they would lose the goodwill built up among the Irish public since their arrival and would no longer be able to work effectively.[67] Twisting this argument slightly to suit their own perceptions, the Cabinet dismissed it, stating that the 'efficiency' of the officials would not be affected 'to the degree which has been anticipated'.[68] Again they could not come to a bold decision between peace and war, between civil administration and martial law. Rather they strengthened their hand with the cards of coercion while at the same time attempting to maintain the appearance of the Irish problem as a matter for police action – a situation requiring the maintenance of civilian administration. Also a competent team of administrators would have its role to play sooner or later when Irish armed resistance was worn down and the nationalists came round to British terms, and when an Act of Parliament establishing native government had to be implemented in its practical aspects.

One plausible reason why the Dublin Castle initiative did not work politically in the short term was that it contradicted the Cabinet's Ulster policy. It is possible that, had the Cabinet come out in favour of Dominion Home Rule even as late as the summer of 1920, their officials in Dublin could have achieved some sort of détente with moderates and possibly split the nationalist movement. Warren Fisher had been convinced that the public had changed their attitude towards the Irish government and 'the Irish majority interpreted the substitution of personnel as evidence of a new orientation of British thought'.[69] And Anderson, not at all the liberal idealist of the ilk of Fisher, Cope and Sturgis, but rather a hard-nosed utilitarian who sought out the most effective and practical means of carrying out policy regardless of personal feelings, believed the same. On the other hand, the Irish question was new to Anderson and his men. Though they wasted no time in grasping the political climate of Dublin, it might be reasonable to suppose that their perceptions of conditions in Belfast and the Ulster dimension of the Irish question had not had opportunity to develop. Even if there had been no Tory intransigence on the questions of law and order and Ireland's constitutional status, and détente with moderate nationalists indeed could become a *via media* to peace, would a really bold initiative against Ulster Loyalists be on the cards? Given the make-up of the British Cabinet, this is very doubtful. The commitment to Ulster of the Tory majority in the Cabinet was sufficient to place Dominion Home Rule outside the bounds of practical (British) politics in 1920. It was perhaps the great weakness of the position of the Castle group in their first weeks in Dublin that they lacked appreciation of the peculiar circumstances in the north-east of the country and the impact of this on the Irish question as viewed by the Cabinet. Sturgis and Cope never learned to sympathise greatly with the Ulster Unionists; but Anderson was to show that at least he had come to grasp the reality of the North when he invited Sir Ernest Clark, an English Revenue Board official, to become special assistant under-secretary in Belfast.

Notes

1   R. Hawkins, 'Dublin Castle and the Royal Irish Constabulary (1916–22)', in T. D. Williams (ed.), *The Irish Struggle, 1916–26* (London, 1966), p. 167.
2   *Report of the Royal Commission on the Rebellion in Ireland*, Cd 8279, HC 1916, *Parliamentary Papers*,vol. 11, p. 171.
3   N. Mansergh, 'The Government of Ireland Act, 1920: its origins and purpose', in J. Barry (ed.), *Historical Studies*, vol. 9 (Belfast, 1974), pp. 23–5.
4   C. Townshend, *The British Campaign in Ireland, 1919–21: The Development of Political and Military Policies* (London, 1975), p. 24.
5   ibid., p. 10.
6   T. Wilson (ed.), *The Political Diaries of C. P. Scott, 1911–28* (Ithaca, NY, 1970), pp. 308–9.
7   ibid., p. 379.
8   In May 1918 he was given chief responsibility for Irish affairs in the Cabinet (see Townshend, op. cit., p. 47) and headed the Cabinet's Irish committee during the conscription crises (see PRO CAB 27/46).
9   Townshend, op. cit., p. 22.
10 ibid., p. 34.
11 ibid., pp. 26, 33.
12 ibid., p. 13.
13 Macready to Long, 23 April 1920, HLRO, Lloyd George papers, F/34/1/19.
14 Gen. Sir C. N. F. Macready, *Annals of an Active Life* (New York, 1925), Vol. 2, pp. 446–9.
15 'Periscope' [G. C. Duggan], 'The last days of Dublin Castle', *Blackwood's Magazine*, no. 128 (1922), p. 148.
16 Report of Sir Warren Fisher to the Chancellor of the Exchequer, 12 May 1920, HLRO, Lloyd George papers, F/31/1/32.

17   Cope–Harwood Report attached to ibid.
18   Here Fisher parenthetically made the following comment with reference to Macready: 'During the past few weeks the unsoundness of the prevailing Irish system has been somewhat disguised in consequence of the appointment to command the military forces of a man who would be admirably equipped to play the dual role of Under-Secretary and GOC. But this is incidental'.
19   Fisher Report, op. cit.
20   Cope–Harwood Report, op. cit.
21   Sir H. A. Robinson, *Memories: Wise and Otherwise* (London, 1923), p. 264.
22   Macready, *Annals*, pp. 448–9.
23   Macready to Bonar Law, 4 May 1920, HLRO, Lloyd George papers, F/31/1/20.
24   Fisher Report, op. cit.
25   Cope–Harwood Report, op. cit.
26   Fisher Report, op. cit.
27   Chamberlain to Bonar Law and Prime Minister, 12 May 1920, cover note to Fisher Report of same date.
28   Fisher Report, op. cit.
29   Further memorandum by Sir Warren Fisher to the Chancellor of the Exchequer, Lord Privy Seal and Prime Minister, 15 May 1920, HLRO, Lloyd George papers, F/31/1/33.
30   ibid.
31   J. W. Wheeler-Bennett, *John Anderson, Viscount Waverley* (London, 1962), pp. 44, 56, 58.
32   Townshend, op. cit., p. 80.
33   Wheeler-Bennett, op. cit. Wheeler-Bennett says that Fairgrieve came from the Privy Council Office, but an official source indicates he was on loan from the Scottish Office. SPOI, index and register of CSORP for 1920, reference to [removed] file CSORP/1920/17677.
34   'Periscope', op. cit. pp. 149.
35   ibid., p. 138; Robinson, op. cit., p. 265.
36   Cope–Harwood Report.
37   Bell, from Banagher, King's County (Offaly), had been a resident magistrate in Lurgan, County Armagh until coming to Dublin in late 1919 with the special assignment of tracing Dáil Eireann loan accounts in Dublin banks. Michael Collins's 'squad' dragged him out of a tram in Ballsbridge on his way to work on 26 March and shot him dead. In his younger days as an RIC constable Bell had been engaged on a similar assignment against the Land League, and had personally arrested the American journalist and land reformer Henry George in Athenry in 1882. See *Freeman's Journal*, 27 March 1920; R. Fanning, *The Irish Department of Finance* (Dublin, 1978), pp. 23–4.
38   Cope to Waterfield, 28 May 1921, SPOI CSORP 1921/2602/30.
39   Cope–Harwood Report.
40   'Periscope', op. cit., pp. 146–8.
41   Fisher to Taylor, 4 August 1920, PRO T 158/1.
42   SPOI, index and register of CSORP for 1920, reference to [removed] file CSORP 1920/17321.
43   *Freeman's Journal*, 27 May 1920.
44   M. Headlam, *Irish Reminiscences* (London, 1947), p. 57.
45   ibid., pp. 57–8.
46   A quote attributed to George Wyndham, Chief Secretary 1900–5. See R. B. McDowell, *The Irish Administration, 1801–1914* (London 1964), p. 31.
47   Treasury minute 23123/20, 25 May 1920, copy in CSORP 1920/16963.
48   Wheeler-Bennett, op. cit., p. 59.

49 Questions relating to supply were to be 'referred for advice and consultation to the Treasury division primarily concerned'. See Treasury (Ireland) draft notice, 22 December 1920, PRO T 158/2.

50 Hawkins, op. cit., p. 171.

51 Headlam, op. cit., pp. 215–17.

52 ibid., pp. 196–7; see also pp. 62–3, 189.

53 G. C. Duggan, extract from an unpublished work entitled 'The life of a civil servant'. I am indebted to Dr Leon O Broin for providing me with a copy of this.

54 ibid.

55 Fanning, op. cit., p. 6.

56 *Freeman's Journal*, 28 May 1920.

57 'Extract from a letter dated 16 June 1920', enclosed in Warren Fisher to Lloyd George, 17 June 1920, HLRO, Lloyd George papers, F/17/1/2.

58 See *Freeman's Journal*, June–July 1920.

59 Anderson to Chief Secretary, 20 July 1920, HLRO, Lloyd George papers, F/19/2/14.

60 ibid.

61 See 'notes of a conference with the officers of the Irish government', CP 1693, 23 July 1920, PRO CAB 24/109. See also the complementary notes for this meeting in T. Jones, *Whitehall Diary, Vol. 3: Ireland, 1918–25*, ed. K. Middlemas (London, 1971), pp. 25–31.

62 Jones, ibid. Conservatives and Unionists defended the actions of General Dyer, removed from his command in India after the Amritsar incident of April 1919 in which his troops fired on a crowd threatening to riot and killed 379 people. The Tories and Unionists apparently favoured similar remedies for unrest in Ireland and India.

63 A foreshadowing of British policy for establishing the special constabulary in Ulster later in the year.

64 Jones, op. cit.

65 See D. G. Boyce, 'How to settle the Irish question', in A. J. P. Taylor (ed.), *Lloyd George: Twelve Essays* (London, 1971), pp. 151–2.

66 See Townshend, op. cit., p. 103.

67 Sir Warren Fisher, memorandum to the Chancellor of the Exchequer, 7 August 1920, PRO CAB 21/207.

68 Cabinet conclusions 48(20)(4), 13 August 1920 (extract), PRO CAB 21/207.

69 Fisher memorandum, as note 67.

2   The Creation of the Chief Secretary's Office (Belfast Branch)

Though they failed to persuade the Cabinet to adopt conciliatory Irish policies, the English officials who came to Dublin in May 1920 may be judged by their ability and ideological inclinations to have been the sort of men best qualified to implement whatever policy the British would put forward when they were ready to come to terms with the nationalist South. However, in ensuring a smooth transition to Home Rule under the Government of Ireland Bill, were they the most appropriate people to deal with the Unionist North?

The large Unionist/Protestant populations of the north-east of Ireland had been watching developments in 'the south and west' with growing alarm. As raids and assassinations increased in fury and number in Cork, Limerick, Tipperary, Clare, and Dublin, tension grew in Ulster's urban ghettos. The Sinn Féin movement, active politically in the North as in the rest of the country, soon stepped up its military activity as well. By the middle of May 1920 co-ordinated series of raids began on unoccupied police barracks and tax offices. The *Belfast Newsletter* decried that 'the rebels . . . now . . . are trying to prove that they are as powerful in Ulster as they are in the other provinces' and were 'as ready to commit murder in Ulster as they are in the south and west'.[1]

Politically, Ulster Unionist opinion was growing impatient with the British. It had neither asked for nor desired the Government of Ireland Bill and only acquiesced so long as 'Ulster' was not obliged to be ruled by a Dublin Parliament. And it condemned what it saw as passivity on the part of the British in the face of increasing 'Sinn Féin' political crime. The *Newsletter* lamented that 'a government with a strong Unionist representation in it', did not have

a clearer appreciation of the Sinn Féin ferment than to imagine that such a policy could have any effect other than to aggravate the evil that is at the bottom of the situation. We can in some measure understand a politician of Lloyd George's mentality, and with his inborn inclination towards the nationalists' demand for self-government, inclining towards a temporising policy with Irish treason and rebellion, but we cannot understand ministers like Bonar Law and Walter Long agreeing to such a policy until they have been driven to depart from it by the very desperateness of the situation to which it has brought Ireland.[2]

The reform in Dublin Castle hardly allayed Loyalist fears. As early as 1 April Ulster Unionist leaders got wind of an imminent shake-up in the Castle in which Sir John Taylor, the Assistant Under-Secretary, T. J. Smith, Inspector-General of the Royal Irish Constabulary (RIC), and Sir Henry Wynn, the Chief Crown Solicitor, were to be removed.[3] Bonar Law 'at once told Carson that there was nothing whatever in this', and suggested to Lloyd George that the rumour 'had emanated from the Irish government simply for the purpose of making trouble'.[4] Yet, from some 'high official source' the *Belfast Newsletter's* London correspondent continued to elicit leaks about 'changes at Dublin Castle – a weeding out, as it were, of permanent officials', which, he claimed, had already begun with Sir John Taylor's holiday. Furthermore, he wrote on 23 April, this development was connected with 'a new policy' on the part of the government 'with "conciliation" as its keynote, to pave the way for home rule'. The under-secretary, James MacMahon, now 'has the government's confidence and may be expected to loom large in Irish administration in the near future'.[5] A few days later, Bonar Law again denied – this time in Parliament – that Taylor had been dismissed, insisting he was only on leave of absence.[6] He was supported by Denis Henry, the Attorney-General for Ireland, who claimed on the very eve of Sir Warren Fisher's visit 'that in fact the expert or experts sent over were concerned only with "reorganization of the chief secretary's office in order to give early effect to the recently approved recommendations of the civil service National Whitley Council". It was, he [Henry] suggested, a reorganisation common to all government departments.'[7] The *Newsletter's* reporter remained sceptical; and after the events of the following weeks (described in the last chapter) he could say that his prophecy had been fulfilled:

In Parliament and without, Bonar Law has a reputation for sincerity to maintain, but this won't do it. His reply of April 26 may have been accurate to the letter, but the effect – if not the intention – was to mislead. As a matter of fact, not only had Sir John Taylor's retirement and Mr MacMahon's recovery of ascendancy been decided on at the time I wrote, but the change in policy now in operation – which was also forecasted – had been determined.[8]

The deteriorating situation in the summer of 1920, both in Ireland as a whole, and more pertinently in terms of the Derry and Belfast riots, served further to alienate the Northern Loyalists from the new Dublin

Castle executive. Derry had experienced serious rioting in the week of 16 to 21 May, but this was only a prelude to the vicious and bitter fighting from 18 to 24 June, in which nineteen people were killed. The role Dublin Castle played hardly spoke well for its new expertise. Appeals for troops from city magistrates were ignored for some days, and not until 24 June did General Carter-Campbell receive authority to intervene and restore order. To show that they really were concerned MacMahon, Anderson, Tudor and Wylie travelled to Derry on 25 June, but were greeted none too warmly for their belated response. The Unionist magistrates present blamed 'Dublin Castle authorities for flouting the opinion of the city's representatives when they appealed for troops to free the citizens from the reign of murderous terror . . . ' Had troops been sent when asked for, 'many lives would have been saved and much suffering avoided'. There was a feeling, the Castle officials were told, 'that the Irish government were allowing things to drift'; and 'the people of Derry had no faith in what Dublin Castle would do'. In its editorial on the following day, the *Newsletter* assailed MacMahon, in particular, for his comment in Derry that 'a peace based on force would not be a lasting one'. Making reference to the military measures which quelled the recent riots, the *Newsletter* held that 'all peace is based on force'. It seemed, then, to the Unionists that Dublin Castle, in following such a fallacious principle in its policies, could hardly be relied upon to protect them from the Sinn Féin menace.[9] On 17 July the *Newsletter* stated that 'the patience of the British people, as well as that of the loyal people in Ireland, is becoming exhausted, and they will insist on the administration of the country being placed in competent hands'. Citing a report in the *Daily News*, that Macready, Greenwood and Anderson would resign if the government decided on martial law, the *Newsletter* commented that at any rate 'the state of the country has not improved since they came to it'.[10]

An even more ominous sign of Ulster Unionist estrangement from the Irish administration was the suggestion, now being put forward publicly, that the Loyalist population themselves should organise to undertake responsibility in the enforcement of public order. In the House of Commons, at the height of the Derry riots in June, the Unionist MP, McGuffin, asked the government whether it was

prepared to accept the assistance of loyal volunteers to aid in the restoration of law and order, and whether in this connection the government has received an offer from the Ulster ex-servicemen's association to place at its disposal 3,000 trained officers and men, who in view of their special knowledge of the country and their loyalty to the crown, would be of signal service at the present time in dealing with the disloyal forces in Ireland.[11]

A few days later the Ulster Unionist Council's standing committee passed a resolution calling on the government 'to protect the lives and property of the loyal inhabitants of Ulster . . . without further delay by means of the forces of the crown, failing which to utilise and recognise the services of the Loyalists of Ulster to assist in preserving law and order in the province ...'[12] Sir Edward Carson, who was sent a copy, promised that while he thought the government ready to protect the Loyalists, he agreed that the Loyalists might have to organise to protect themselves – with or without government approval:

> I believe the government are prepared to give all possible protection; but I can assure the council that should it become necessary, by reason of the inability of the government to carry out the essential duties of government, I shall not hesitate at any cost – with the cooperation and under the control of the government if they allow it, and if not, on our own responsibility – to organise our people for defence against those whose crimes are ruining Ireland, and making our country a byeword amongst civilized nations.[13]

By this time Loyalist paranoia was being whipped up to new heights of frenzy. More than 8,000 Catholics, refusing to submit to the degradation of signing pledges of non-association with Sinn Féin, were expelled from jobs in the engineering and linen industries. Soon, Loyalist vigilante units were forming all over the north-east, an example being set by a group in County Fermanagh, whose successful defence against an IRA attack in the village of Lisbellaw was much noted. In mid-July, the assassination by the IRA in Cork of Colonel Smyth, the controversial RIC divisional commissioner for Munster[14] – and a Banbridge man – was instrumental in sparking off three days of riots in Belfast which left seventeen dead.[15] Worried lest Loyalists at the local level should pass beyond the Unionist Party's own control, Sir James Craig assigned Colonel W. B. Spender the task of resurrecting the Ulster Volunteer Force (UVF) in order to harness Loyalists' militant energies.[16] Simultaneously he began to press the Cabinet for official recognition of the UVF as an imperial force. The idea appealed to Churchill and to Lloyd George, but was bitterly opposed by Anderson, Wylie and Macready – Macready reportedly threatening resignation over the issue.[17] But in a matter of weeks the position in Ulster grew so serious that the British felt compelled to take active steps to conciliate the Loyalists. The assassination of another Ulster Protestant police constable, District Inspector Swanzy, in Lisburn, touched off riots in that town on 22 August. These spread to Belfast where after eight straight days of spectacular violence 31 people perished and over 200 were wounded 'more or less seriously'.[18] On 2 September, while fighting in Belfast still raged, Craig attended a conference of ministers in London at which he 'made a strong attack on MacMahon and a hardly less strong attack on Macready and (less strongly) on Sir John Anderson'. Bonar Law 'strongly defended Macready and Anderson against aspersions on their loyalty';[19] but Craig went on gravely to warn 'that the loyalists were losing faith in the government's determination to protect them, and were threatening an immediate recourse to arms which would precipitate civil war'. On the pretext of keeping the forces of extreme loyalism in harness Craig asked the government to approve proposals amounting to what was practically a secession of the six counties from Dublin Castle's control. An RIC commissioner should be appointed for the six counties exclusively, who should be responsible not only for the RIC in that area, but also for the control and organisation of a new reserve 'special constabulary'. This force should be armed and organised 'on military lines', and in its creation the organisation of the UVF should be used 'as was done for raising the 36th (Ulster) division when war broke out'.[20]

But Craig did not wish to hive off the six counties for purposes of the administration of public order alone. He now believed the time had come when it was necessary to create the nucleus of civil government machinery foreshadowing a separate administration for the state of Northern Ireland. The government should therefore establish a new civil authority in Belfast. The civil authority should be vested in an under-secretary responsible directly to the Chief Secretary so as to by-pass Dublin Castle completely. The authority would 'represent' the future government of Northern Ireland; its staff would work 'in conjunction with committees to be appointed locally'; and the new authority and the local committees would work together in planning arrangements 'for the transfer later of the administration of the six counties under the Government of Ireland bill'.[21] The British were sufficiently alarmed at Craig's report to take a positive decision. Balfour was in favour of 'separating Ulster administration at once from the rest of Ireland'.[22] Writing to Lloyd George on the same day (2 September) Bonar Law said that 'Belfast was as bad as possible', and he did not think Craig was 'exaggerating when he tells me there is a danger of the Orangemen getting completely out of hand and something like a genuine massacre happening'. To prevent this, Bonar Law thought 'the time has come when we ought to make special arrangements to let the loyalists in Ulster be in a position to preserve order there'. After all, the government could not 'afford to have everybody in Ireland against us'.[23]

The creation of a new administrative centre in Belfast responsible exclusively for the six counties, together with government agreement to establish a special constabulary, amounted to an impressive coup for Craig. The British were conscious of this and of the political embarrassment it could cause to themselves. Bonar Law had at first been reluctant to go along with the proposals because 'if we armed Ulster public opinion in this country would say the government was taking sides and ceasing to govern impartially'.[24] The British were therefore careful to proceed in such a way as would appear they were acting independently and on their own initiative. Craig had hoped to return to Belfast immediately with the good news, but Bonar Law refused his request for authority to make a public announcement until after the government itself publicly declared its intentions.[25] Otherwise, Bonar Law told Lloyd George, it would seem 'as if we were acting on their dictation'.[26] Also, the British did not wish their policy to be construed as a preliminary step towards the partition of Ireland (although this proved hard to avoid). Theoretically, the proposition to organise 'well-disposed persons' into a special constabulary was to apply to all Ireland, not just the six counties, and was not to involve any change in the administration of other police and military forces in Ireland.[27] But interestingly, the relevant Cabinet minutes betray the government's actual motivations: they refer to the creation of the special constabulary in 'Ireland', with 'Ireland' written in pen over the crossed out 'Ulster' in typescript.[28] Obviously the policy was in response to the demand in Ulster for a constabulary in Ulster, the only place in Ireland where 'well-disposed persons' could be found in adequate numbers. Also, the new administrator would not be an under-secretary equal in authority to, and independent of, Anderson and MacMahon, but rather an assistant under-secretary, technically subordinate to the joint under-secretaries in Dublin Castle. The appointment involved 'no delegation of authority or control of the Irish executive'.[29] This desire to avoid the appearance of presupposing the Ulster state was again reflected in the Cabinet minutes: carefully the minutes refer to the appointment of an assistant under-secretary not for 'Northern Ireland' but rather 'for the six counties of the north-east of Ireland'.[30]

The government's caution about appearances was reflected in the manner in which the news broke. The first reports on 13 September were greeted by the Loyalist public with cautious approval.[31] Suspicions returned, however, as further announcements from the Irish Office asserted the new official's subordination to Dublin Castle: he would not, as had been construed from initial reports, enjoy the full authority of an under-secretary for Ulster. The new official himself made the point when he arrived in Ireland at Dublin rather than Belfast and reported to Dublin Castle before leaving for the North. And in interviews at Dublin Castle and in Belfast the new man insisted that his appointment had no 'political significance', that it was a purely administrative position, and that he would report to and take orders from the under-secretary in Dublin, Sir John Anderson (wisely avoiding mention of the other under-secretary, the Armagh Papist, MacMahon). And furthermore, he pointed out, 'to say that his appointment was a preliminary step towards partition is . . . quite untrue'.[32]

With these statements the Unionist press became guarded, even cool to the appointment. The *Belfast Newsletter*, though non-committal in its editorials, sounded a warning through a reader's letter which it printed on the leader page on 16 September:

> In common with other Unionists I have read with much interest the announcement in your issue of today that the government have decided to appoint a new under-secretary to deal with matters relating to the six Ulster counties. This new departure may prove either a great success or one of the lamentable failures to which we are only too well accustomed. Everything will depend on the quality of the man appointed and the powers assigned him. For the last fourteen years Irish viceroys have been avowed home rulers; and with one exception Irish chief secretaries have been of the same way of thinking. The political sympathies of the permanent official staff at Dublin Castle are a matter of common knowledge. To such hands has the government of Ireland been entrusted, with the inevitable result that our unhappy country is on the very verge of irretrievable ruin. The Unionists of Ulster should make it perfectly clear that so far as their own province is concerned, this method of administration must cease, and that the man placed in charge of their interests must be one who has their full confidence. He must be none of the political charlatans who are advertising their nostrums of Devolution, Dominion Home Rule, or other Utopian scheme of 'Reconstruction'.[33]

Another Unionist organ confessed 'more than a little surprise at the terms in which his appointment is officially announced'. If it meant 'that the new official is to be in any way controlled by Mr MacMahon and Sir John Anderson – the government are simply adding a new and unnecessary wheel to an Irish system of administration already encumbered with too many useless wheels which do nothing but add to the friction of the machine and slow down its working'.[34] However, it was not long before these fears and suspicions were allayed. The new administrator for the six counties would, in practice, be given considerable scope for independent action. In political character his administration would be markedly different from the regime of MacMahon, Wylie and Cope. And despite the official's own protestations of 'strict impartiality', his appointment was clearly a concession to the Ulster Unionist Party. Sir James Craig (second in command of the party to Sir Edward Carson), Dawson Bates, Chairman of the Ulster Unionist Council and W. B. Spender, Commandant of the UVF, could not have been very worried about the new man. Indeed, they vetted him before he came, as we shall see.

British policy was now undergoing change seen by the Unionists as considerably more to their satisfaction. The government appeared to be taking a firmer line against terrorism, and criminal convictions were mounting under the Restoration of Order in Ireland Act.[35] This measure had been passed in August, conferring on the security forces the authority to arrest and imprison without trial, empowering the army to try civilians by courts martial and replacing coroners' inquests into civilian deaths with military courts of inquiry. A tougher response to violence was also seen in the increase in the number of troops and Black and Tans, in the creation of the RIC auxiliary division and in Lloyd George's insistence that by a more vigorous policy the government had 'murder by the throat'. The autumn of 1920 was also the period of police 'reprisals' against inhabitants of localities in the South where IRA attacks had taken place – actions which the Chief Secretary refused, or was at least reluctant, to condemn. It was the period of the deaths of Terence MacSwiney and Kevin Barry, the one by hunger-strike, the other by hanging, as the government refused to bow to international appeals for clemency. And it was the period of the intensification of the IRA campaign and the formation of guerrilla bands (the 'active service units' or 'flying columns'). These developments presaged Bloody Sunday and the Kilmichael ambush, which led, in turn, to the declaration of martial law in large parts of the country. Repression of the nationalists was cheered by the Ulster Unionists. The government was taking action and could no longer be accused of supineness. Creating a subadministration for the six counties and deputising special constables from among the 'well-disposed' was part of what Ulster Unionists saw as a more positive policy on the part of the government, and they expressed their approval on the occasion of the Chief Secretary's Belfast visit on 13 October. At a luncheon where the new assistant under-secretary for Ulster was one of the principal guests, Greenwood announced that the government 'were going on with the home rule bill' and 'would go forward unflinchingly to deal with the criminals, and they were breaking the terror'. He further spoke of the 'great reality . . . that Ireland is historically and in many other ways divided into two main parts'. This was a regrettable fact, but none the less a fact, 'and this is the first government that has faced this fact'.[36] Reinforcing its commitment to the Ulster Unionists was part of the government's more assertive policy and this was manifest in the creation of the special constabulary and appointment of the assistant under-secretary. It would be further manifest in the government's choice for the appointment.

Within days of the Cabinet's decision to authorise a civil authority for the North, Sir Ernest Clark accepted the offer of Sir John Anderson to fill the post of assistant under-secretary (Belfast). Clark's career had already been notable. He had served as secretary to the recent Royal Commission on Income Tax presided over by Lord Colwyn, and before taking up duties in Belfast had been deputy chief inspector of taxes in the Inland Revenue Department. His revenue background and experience in South Africa were regarded as appropriate qualifications for his present task. The official announcement by the Irish Office noted that 'his services include a period in the government of Cape Colony, where he was engaged in inaugurating a system of income taxation and acquired a good knowledge of the practical working of home rule institutions'.[37] At the Board of Inland Revenue, where Anderson had been his chief, he had offered his services in Ireland when Anderson became Irish under-secretary in May 1920.[38] Writing later at the end of his career he professed to have been ignorant of the complexities of Irish politics in September 1920. He was astonished when Anderson drolly inquired whether Clark was 'not by any chance a Roman Catholic?' However, he could learn quickly: 'but I soon discovered that Sir John's question was an essential one to ask not only from his point of view (and the government's) but from my own. Of course he realised as I subsequently did, that had I been a Roman Catholic I could never have been accepted by the northern government, or been able to carry out my duties, even had I survived to undertake them'.[39] His account of his introduction by Sir Hamar Greenwood, the Chief Secretary, to Craig, Spender and Dawson Bates portrays his initial bafflement with Ireland:

> They were full of grievances [his notes recall] and painted to Sir Hamar a picture of deathly peril which threatened all loyalists (including themselves) in the north of Ireland. At the time I failed to sympathise with them and indeed hardly understood what they were talking about, so widely did the conditions they described differ from my notions and previous experience of an 'ordered government'.[40]

Yet, the choice of Clark for the Belfast post may have been influenced to some extent by his political inclinations. In so far as these can be monitored from his unpublished autobiographical sketches, they resound with the clear ring of English Conservatism. His interview with the Ulster Unionist leaders, for example, which Greenwood had arranged to put Clark 'on show', went very well, quite possibly because of his transparent Tory outlook. He ascribes the reason for winning the Ulstermen's approval as perhaps the 'frank sincerity' of his impressions of the Irish question. But the incident he relates to illustrate his candour reveals also a politically conservative outlook that should have been agreeable to traditional Unionists:

> After Greenwood had gone, I remember vividly that Sir James Craig walked across to me and, towering above this little man, said, 'Now you are coming to Ulster you must write this one word across your heart', and he tapped out with his finger on my chest 'ULSTER'. I fear that I only saw the humour of this and not understanding its importance at the time said, 'Sir James, I can hardly do that, for the space is already occupied by two names'. 'Oh', he said, 'what are they?' I said, '"The British Empire" and "England". I am afraid "Ulster" can only be written after these'.[41]

This was good enough for Craig. In fact, in the light of subsequent events it is hard to see how it was not a strong Conservative political viewpoint that not only enamoured Clark to the Unionists but also the Unionists to Clark. 'I did not then guess', he confessed in his autobiographical notes, 'how the love of that province could grow in the heart of one becoming associated with it, nor how indelibly that name would ultimately be written across my heart in life'. In his first days in Belfast he experienced a certain degree of distrust, if not hostility, from among certain quarters of Loyalist opinion, and he believed that a certain political personage, whom he does not name, had been marked for the job, suffering 'some chagrin' when Clark was appointed.[42] But Clark knew what was expected of him and he soon dispelled Unionist apprehensions. From the start he worked consistently and uncompromisingly for the interests of the future Northern Ireland government, and in an early meeting of the Northern Ireland Parliament his name won the audible praises of the new Northern MPs.[43] At the transfer of government services to the Northern government at the end of 1921 he became permanent secretary to the Northern Ireland Ministry of Finance. Although he left this post in 1925 to pursue his career in a variety of other tasks, including governor of Tasmania, he returned to Ulster affairs in 1930–2 as member of the Joint Exchequer Board of Great Britain and Northern Ireland and kept his membership of the Unionist Club of Belfast.[44] The deposit of his papers in the Public Record Office of Northern Ireland attests to the strength of the attachment to Northern Ireland which he formed in the days when he was, in words he attributes to Basil Brooke, 'midwife to the new province of Ulster'.[45]

Within a few days of his interview with Craig, Clark had taken up residence in the Scottish Provident Buildings busily organising the Chief Secretary's Office (Belfast). Captain C. H. Petherick, 'ex-Enniskillen Fusiliers [and] the best of the young men in the inland revenue in Belfast', became Clark's private secretary; W. D. Scott, also on loan from Inland Revenue, became principal clerk in the office; J. O. Kirkpatrick, a second division clerk in the Chief Secretary's Office was transferred from Dublin Castle to become acting staff clerk; J. A. Robinson, yet another Inland Revenue official was put in charge of the registry; and finally, the office was equipped with four shorthand typists and a head messenger.[46] Clark's first months in office were largely involved with organising the special constabulary. After the Government of Ireland Bill reached the statute book at the end of 1920 he turned his attention to the practical problems of establishing an administration for the new Ulster state. Later in the book we shall be returning to Clark on several occasions and finding him championing the Northern government before and after its creation. From January to June 1921 he would work closely with the 'prospective ministry of the province'[47] in planning bureaucratic structures for the Ulster administration, and already explaining – indeed, defending – prospective Unionist policy in administration. He came to feel, in his own words, 'more like John the Baptist than any other person I can think of',[48] an apt simile, for he was indeed heralding the coming of the Northern Unionist state. As a person the Ulster Unionists found fit to organise the Ulster Special Constabulary and perform the spadework for a future government of Northern Ireland, he was the administrative expression of the Ulster dimension of Britain's Irish policy. With the creation of his post in September 1920 the policy of solving the Ulster question as a prerequisite to an overall settlement had taken a tangible form even before the Government of Ireland Act was passed. In effect the assignment to Dublin of administrators sympathetic to moderate nationalism was balanced by the assignment to Belfast of an administrator with inclinations congenial to Ulster Unionists. By the time the Government of Ireland Act reached the statute book in December 1920 the administration of Ireland was already partitioned at its centre bureaucratically and even ideologically, and the administrative machinery was installed to make both Home Rule and partition a reality.

Notes

1   *Belfast Newsletter*, 14 May 1920.
2   ibid., 21 May 1920.

3 Letter from Lynn, 'proprietor of the Belfast newspaper', to Carson, mentioned in Bonar Law to Lloyd George, 3 April 1920, HLRO Lloyd George papers, F/31/1/20.
4 ibid.
5 *Belfast Newsletter*, 23 April 1920. See also, ibid., 24 and 26 April and 1 May.
6 Hansard (Commons), 5th series, vol. 128 cols. 831–2.
7 *Belfast Newsletter*, 4 May 1920.
8 ibid., 25 May 1920.
9 ibid., 25 June 1920.
10 ibid., 17 July 1920.
11 ibid., 24 June 1920.
12 ibid., 30 June 1920.
13 Quoted in ibid.
14 Smyth was reputed to have told the RIC in Listowel on 19 June, 'The more you shoot, the better I will like you, and I assure you that no policeman will get into trouble for shooting any man'. C. Townshend, *The British Campaign in Ireland, 1919–21: The Development of Political and Military Policies* (London, 1975), p. 97.
15 *Belfast Newsletter*, 19–26 July 1920.
16 The announcement that Spender would take command of the UVF came on 23 July. In an interview the same day, he was quoted as saying that the announcement 'has no relation to the troubles existing in the city today, but the general situation requires the UVF to begin to organize, to place itself at the disposal of the government if and when it is required'. *Belfast Newsletter*, 24 July 1920.
17 Tom Jones, memorandum to Prime Minister, 24 July 1920, HLRO, Lloyd George papers, F/24/3/3; Sir A. Hezlet, *The 'B' Specials: A History of the Ulster Special Constabulary* (London, 1973), pp. 24–5.
18 *Belfast Newsletter*, 23 August–2 September 1920.
19 Tom Jones's account to Maurice Hankey, 2 September 1920, HLRO, Lloyd George papers, F/31/3/8.
20 Conclusions of a conference of ministers, 2 September 1920, PRO CAB 23/22.
21 ibid.
22 ibid.
23 Bonar Law to Lloyd George, 2 September 1920, HLRO, Lloyd George papers, F/31/1/43.
24 Jones to Hankey, as note 19.
25 Bonar Law to Lloyd George, as note 23.
26 ibid.
27 *Belfast Newsletter*, 16 September 1920.
28 Conclusions of a conference of ministers, 8 September 1920, PRO CAB 23/22.
29 *Belfast Newsletter*, 16 September 1920.
30 As note 28.
31 *Belfast Newsletter*, 14 September 1920.
32 ibid., 17 September 1920.
33 T. G. Houston, Portrush, to the editor, 13 September 1920, *Belfast Newsletter*, 16 September 1920.
34 Publication anonymous, quoted in *Irish News*, 17 September 1920.
35 Townshend, op. cit., pp. 106–9.
36 *Belfast Newsletter*, 14 October 1920.
37 ibid., 16 September 1920.
38 See typescript autobiographical notes in the Clark papers, PRONI D 1022.
39 ibid.
40 ibid.
41 ibid.
42 ibid. According to the *Newsletter* there had been speculation 'in the clubs' of London

that Sir James Craig himself would be the Northern 'under-secretary'. However, Clark may be referring to Captain Charles Craig, MP, Sir James's brother.

43   Hansard (Northern Ireland)(Commons), vol. 1, col. 126, 22 September 1921.
44   *Who's Who*, 1939.
45   Clark papers, as note 38.
46   ibid.
47   A phrase Clark uses in his autobiographical notes, as note 38.
48   Clark to Hopkins, 12 April 1921, PRONI FIN 18/1/195.

3 The Government of Ireland Bill: Blueprint for Partition

The changes in Irish administration described in the last two chapters were preliminary steps in preparation for partition and Home Rule. Legislation to bring this about had already been introduced in February 1920 as 'a Bill for the Better Government of Ireland'. For the remainder of the year the Bill slouched its way through Parliament, finally passing on 20 December 1920. The basic principle inherent in the Bill remained the same from the initial drafts written by Walter Long's Cabinet Committee on Ireland in late 1919, to the Act itself: i.e. self-government for Ireland provided that the 'Ulster majority' should not be coerced into rule from Dublin and that Ireland should not be separated from the Empire. However, important questions remained concerning what all this meant in practical terms. How much self-government was there to be? How independently from one another would two Home Rule states function? Would the new arrangements be conducive to building bridges or barriers between North and South? The provisions of the Bill affecting the machinery of government therefore must be regarded as significant, and their importance was perceived by Long's committee and by all parties in Parliament. These administrative provisions would both reflect the degree of autonomy which Britain wished to grant to native Irish governments, and be a function of permanence in Ireland's partition. As we shall see, however, the latter was something which the Ulster Unionists knew, but which the British government, at least in public, chose to ignore.

Political Parties and the Administrative Provisions of the Bill

In Parliament the Bill was not, of course, subject to the surveillance and criticism of the majority party in Ireland, Sinn Féin, who in early 1919 had refused to take its Westminster seats, constituted Dáil Eireann, and provisionally declared a republic. Parliamentary debate on the administrative provisions was dominated by several parties: the Ulster Unionists, who demanded partition for all transferred services; the Southern Unionists, who opposed partition and attempted to limit its effect by advocating the reservation of services or their transfer to the Council of Ireland; the Liberals, whose panacea for peace was granting Ireland financial autonomy; and the government parties, whose main priority was maintaining Ireland's status within the empire, if not within the United Kingdom. It must also be said that in defending their Bill, the government wished to preserve the impression that it was an inducement to Irish unity, although from an early stage they became increasingly aware of the expedience of appeasing the Ulster Unionists. The debate within Parliament, together with alternative proposals put to the Cabinet and its committee behind the scenes, and the consequent changes in official policy show that these administrative areas, in particular the transferred and reserved services, were closely scrutinised and keenly contested by the competing interests, and most successfully by, or at least to the advantage of, the Ulster Unionists.

The government parties, being dominated by the Conservatives, were able to secure the exclusion of a wide range of administrative matters from the competence of the Irish governments. Executive powers to be devolved, called 'Irish services', were those which most British parliamentarians would probably have felt well rid of from Westminster's heavy agenda. These were in the areas of agriculture, local government, public health, health insurance, local industry, home affairs, minor taxes and financing of services. But in matters of imperial concern and in matters of trade, the Conservatives were particularly anxious to see that Ireland remained subordinate to Westminster and an integral part of the United Kingdom. Thus, totally outside the definition of Home Rule under the Government of Ireland Act were matters relating to the Crown, peace or war, the defence forces, foreign affairs, dignities of title or honour, treason, citizenship, trade outside Ireland, submarine cables, wireless telegraphy, aerial navigation, lighthouses, currency and trademarks.[1] In drafting the Bill, Walter Long, himself a leading Conservative, had ignored the majority report of the Irish Convention of 1917–18 which had recommended granting Ireland power to raise and finance 'a local defence force'; 'power similar to the dominions in respect of commercial treaties as well as power to make treaties and establish relations with the dominions'; power to deal with matters of treason and treason felony; and control over external trade and the granting of bounties on exports.[2] Thus, holding Ireland firmly within the realm strategically and economically was *sine qua non* with the government and the Tories.

On the other hand, the coalition Conservatives were embarrassed by partition. They found themselves faced with the dilemma of abandoning their traditional alliance with the Ulster Loyalists and compromising the Southern Unionist wing of the party. They therefore contrived to give the Act the appearance of promoting Irish unity, reasoning that this would have the added advantage of attracting the support of Ireland's 'moderate nationalists'. First, in order to 'minimize the partition issue' and facilitate the 'future union' of the country, a Council of Ireland was enshrined in the Bill, to consist of twenty representatives from each parliament and to be equipped with certain legislative and executive powers for the whole of Ireland. In its final form the Bill provided that fisheries, railways and the Diseases of Animals Acts would be administered under the auspices of the council and that the two Irish parliaments could, by identical legislation, transfer any Irish service to the council.[3] And secondly, the government tried to appear to encourage Irish unity in terms of 'reserved services'. Certain administrative services remained reserved to imperial authority pending either unification or a request from both Irish parliaments that they be transferred to the Council of Ireland. Long's committee insisted that the powers transferred to the Council of Ireland, and the services reserved to Westminster pending North–South agreement, were incentives for North and South to unite. However, it is not clear how they arrived at the assumption that any imaginable Home Rule formula could have induced Ulster Unionists to seek unity with the South! Successful lobbying by the Ulster Unionists resulted in a measure of such complete division in the Irish executive that few could deny Asquith's charge that the Bill, far from promoting unity, permitted 'an Ulster minority for all time to veto, if it pleases, the coming into existence of [a united] Irish Parliament'.[4]

Ulster Unionist influence on the shape of the Government of Ireland Bill dates back at least to November 1919 to the early days of Walter Long's Cabinet Committee. Long's original proposals, submitted 4 November 1919, contained measures more conducive to unity than the Bill in its final form. The initial proposals consisted in holding back from the Irish governments certain services 'specially undesirable to divide' including agriculture, technical education, transportation, old age pensions, unemployment insurance, health insurance and labour exchanges. The Council of Ireland would advise the United Kingdom authorities on the administration of these services for one year, at the end of which they would be partitioned and transferred unless both Irish governments in the meantime requested their transfer to the council. Such an arrangement, the Cabinet Committee believed, was 'a powerful recognition of the objections to partition'; and the automatic transfer at the end of the year was 'a strong incentive to immediate action towards Irish unity'. The committee felt able to claim that it had 'done everything which an outside authority can do to bring about Irish unity, without in any way infringing on the freedom of Ulster to decide its own relation to the rest of Ireland'.[5] However, 'Ulster' did not agree, and within a month the Cabinet Committee had reassessed these proposals. In early November Sir James Craig asked whether the committee's report might be shown 'in the strictest confidence' to the secretary to the Ulster Unionist Council, R. Dawson Bates. Bates, said Craig, knew the 'mind of Ulster' intimately and was the best person to advise on the likely reaction to the proposals. The British were wary of Bates and at a conference of ministers on 11 November were not in favour of showing him the report, suspecting that he might be tempted to 'engineer an agitation in order to influence the government'.[6] None the less, the opinions of the Ulster Unionists henceforth began to make their mark on the proposals of the Cabinet Committee. In its second report on 2 December the committee had become 'impressed by the objection that not enough powers had been conferred from the outset upon the two parliaments', and 'by the objection that it would upset and dislocate Irish life and administration if government departments could be bandied about between various authorities one by one at different times and irrespective of taxing powers for a number of years'. Thus the proposal to reserve agriculture, technical education, transportation, old age pensions, unemployment insurance, health insurance and labour exchanges – all to be administered on the advice of the Council of Ireland pending unity – was scrapped.[7] The corollary was, of course, partition for these services.

Notwithstanding this turnabout, the Cabinet Committee still maintained that their proposals encouraged Irish unity. After all, the two Irish parliaments were still free to co-operate in transferring to the Council of Ireland any of these services they wished; 'and since the appointed day for transferring Irish services would probably be not earlier than fifteen months from the passage of the act', the two parliaments would have 'ample time to consider the disadvantages of the complete separation of all Irish services and to make arrangements with the council of Ireland before a division comes into automatic operation'.[8] Responsibility for partition in terms of administrative services, the British told themselves, would rest with the Irish parliaments.

The weakness of this argument was seen by Sir Henry Robinson, President of the Local Government Board for Ireland. Robinson was an Englishman, but had more than forty years' experience in the Irish civil service and frequently offered advice to chief secretaries and British governments on Irish matters. His political tenor may be taken as that of a Southern Unionist having accepted the inevitability of Home Rule but hoping by some means that partition might be avoided. He was under few illusions, however, about the Ulster Loyalists voluntarily co-operating in future union once institutions were partitioned. On 17 January 1920 Robinson submitted a lengthy memorandum to the Cabinet proposing the transfer of no less than twenty government services to the Council of Ireland. If this were not done, Robinson doubted whether Northern Ireland would even bother to send representatives to the council. He pointed to the recent history of the General Council of County Councils, whose 'anti-English atmosphere' was too strong for the Ulster county councils, moving five of them to withdraw from the general council. 'And if the same thing should happen in the event of the government of Ireland bill becoming law', he believed,

> it would be an end to all hopes of a Parliament of Ireland, which is the underlying principle of the whole Bill upon which all hopes of a final settlement is based. To avert this danger, it is essential to vest in the Council of Ireland full powers over all matters relating to Ireland as a whole (except those specially reserved under the Bill) where sectarian considerations do not come in, but which affect the interests of the North indirectly, to such an extent that the Northerners cannot afford to keep outside the Council and must be brought into association with the Southern delegates in order to ensure that the North participates in the services administered by the Council of Ireland.

The departments which Robinson thought could be 'administered by the central authority without inconvenience or danger of political controversies' were the Registrar-General, the National Gallery, labour exchanges, the Geological Survey, the National Museum, the National Library, the School of Art, the Congested Districts Board, the Diseases of Animals Acts, the Public Record Office, the Registry of Deeds, the Public Trustee, the Ministry of Transport, the Dublin Metropolitan Police, the Botanic Gardens, the College of Science, fisheries, prisons and lunatic asylums, the Board of Charitable Donations and Bequests and the Office of Arms.[9] If the British were really in earnest about encouraging Irish unity, this was a course they might have considered, given the grimly unyielding attitude of the Ulster Unionists on the issue.

In the next fortnight a subcommittee studied the proposals in Robinson's memorandum and dismissed them, believing that compelling North and South to co-operate in such a way 'might be regarded as an infringement of the pledge to Ulster'. Once again it was stated that the committee's own proposals sufficed in promoting the unity of Ireland because they empowered the two parliaments to transfer Irish services and certain reserved services to the Council of Ireland. The subcommittee's memorandum reiterated the principle of investing the council with none of the Irish services, again relying on 'voluntary co-operation' to bring about Irish unity.[10] Sir Francis Greer, the Irish Office parliamentary draftsman, temporarily demurred in this judgement in the case of the National Gallery, National Museum, National Library, School of Art and College of Science. He thought they might be reserved to the imperial government since they were 'obviously unitary' services.[11] Mysteriously, however, he reversed this opinion only a few days later. Holding to the curiously rigid principle that these institutions were related to science and art which in the Bill were Irish services, he concluded that they must therefore be seen as matters for domestic administration and be transferred.[12]

The Reserved Services

The 'reservation' of many services under the Government of Ireland Act (apart from the 'excluded matters') had the effect of maintaining a degree of unity in Irish administration. In principle, the Ulster Unionists did not object to reserving services to Westminster. To them it was certainly preferable to transferring services to the Council of Ireland. On the other hand, they took strong objection to services being run from headquarters in Dublin even though under the Act they would be administered under imperial auspices. In the Act there were only three instances where services were reserved specifically for the sake of administrative unity: the Post Office, the Public Record Office, and the Registry of Deeds. And even here the primary reason for reserving the services cannot be said to have been the desirability or aspiration of political unity. Indeed, in the case of the Public Record Office, an Ulster Unionist amendment, while not dividing the existing department, effectively divided the service in terms of future archival deposits.

The question of the Post Office was decided from an early stage at a meeting of the Cabinet on 22 December 1919. Some Cabinet members opposed transferring the Post Office because 'neither a state in the American union nor a state [sic.] in the Dominion of Canada had control of the post office'. They also argued that 'from the point of view of the safety of the country in time of war, it was dangerous for the post office to be in other than imperial hands'. Against this view it was argued that since the Post Office was included among the services to be transferred under the Government of Ireland Act of 1914, 'the new proposals would be greatly weakened by its ommission' from the present Bill. The Cabinet therefore agreed to the transfer of the Post Office 'in principle'; but on account of the practical difficulty involved in the working of two separate Post Office administrations in Ireland, it was decided to reserve the service until 'the northern and southern parliaments could agree on a joint scheme for its administration'.[13] Similar 'practical difficulties' might apply to many a service to be partitioned; the distinction seems to have resided in the necessity to effect a compromise with those concerned about the constitutional and strategic importance of the Post Office. At least, it was not reserved specifically as an inducement to unity.

The Public Record Office, also transferrable in 1914, was likewise reserved under the 1920 Bill pending agreement between the Irish parliaments on its joint administration.[14] Preserving the unity of the magnificent archival collection which then existed was something the Ulster Unionists could not very well object to; but they could ensure that in the future the North could enjoy a separate record office of its own – yet further emphasising the separateness of the Ulster administration. The parliamentary efforts of Captain Charles Craig, brother of Sir James, won for Northern Ireland 'the power to set up in Belfast a public record office with reference to matters arising in Northern Ireland after the passing of the act'. In drafting the Bill, Sir Francis Greer observed that since records did not come to the Public Record Office until they were twenty years old, 'what Captain Craig asked for did not necessitate any change in the present system for the next twenty years'. But although no archival material would come to a Belfast record office from the new Northern government institutions for twenty years, there were nevertheless Northern-related materials in the Four Courts Office created since 1900 which might be regarded as transferrable to a new repository in the North. It was 'probable', wrote Greer, that Captain Craig also 'wished to secure for Belfast an office to which a particular class of public records might be transferred from the beginning, e.g. northern probates and other testamentary documents of persons dying since 1900, which would otherwise be transferred to the Dublin office'.[15] Thus the Act empowered either Irish Parliament to establish its own repository for records appertaining to its own area 'which otherwise would be deposited in the Public Record Office of Ireland'. To either repository the Lord Lieutenant could order the removal 'of such probates, letters of administration, or other testamentary records granted or coming into existence not earlier than twenty years prior to the appointed day as in his opinion belong properly to the part of Ireland in which the office is situated and can conveniently be removed to that office'.[16] As in the case of the Post Office, the Public Record Office was reserved in order to maintain its unity, but not specifically as an inducement to future union. The provision, in fact, had the opposite effect for it empowered either government to set up its own record office – plainly a concession enabling the Ulster Unionists to take an important step in the consolidation of partition. The provision that Southern Ireland could also establish a separate record office was inserted for the sake of consistency following the government's policy of 'equal treatment', but like many other aspects of the Act held little relevance for the political climate in Ireland outside the north-east.

The Registry of Deeds, like the Post Office and the Public Record Office, had been designated an Irish service in 1914, but was reserved in 1920 pending joint administration by North and South. The system of chronological entries and alphabetical indexes in this very old department, which held records dating back to 1708, made its division totally unfeasible. Again its unity was preserved for purely practical reasons. Much to Ulster Unionist frustration the office was physically impossible to divide.

Other executive services, the police, inland revenue, customs and excise and land purchase, were reserved for a variety of reasons, that of future Irish union – where it existed – being secondary.

Part of the reason for the temporary reservation of police and magistracy services was theoretically partition, since they were reserved for three years or until the union of the Irish parliaments, whichever occurred first.[17] This was decided at the committee stage of the Bill on 2–3 June 1920 when a government amendment changed the terms governing the limit of the period in which police forces were reserved from 'not earlier' to 'not later than three years'.[18] The important question then arose of who would control the police in this three-year period. In June 1920 the draft Bill provided 'for the constitution of a body on which the Irish governments were represented for the administration of police during the period of reservation'.[19] Not surprisingly, the Ulster Unionist leader Sir Edward Carson strenuously objected to such an organisation suggesting 'that the control should remain with the lord-lieutenant as representing His Majesty' as was the case in the Bills of 1886, 1893 and 1914.[20] In fact, the government gave a number of promises at this stage of the debate 'to reconsider the clause with a view to radical alteration of the police proposals'. One of these was a promise to Carson that the provision for a police administration board comprising representatives of both Irish governments would be replaced by a provision for a central imperial authority over Irish police. Thus, the South would be denied influence over police administration in the North. The Cabinet Committee also contemplated the disbandment of the RIC and the Dublin Metropolitan Police as soon as a new force or forces were ready to take their place. This measure, too, was in line with Carson's thinking,[21] for it opened the door to the creation of new and separate police forces which could be organised during the reserved period. Police disbandment was not drafted into the Bill, however, for at the height of the guerrilla campaign in November 1920 Sir John Anderson persuaded the committee that the disbandment policy should be abandoned to counter the 'very adverse effect' it would have on police morale.[22] 'This force', the committee agreed on 2 November,

were now in very good condition. The men had had the clause affecting police, as originally drafted, carefully explained to them and they were quite satisfied with their treatment under the bill. Any change in the provisions for their future would be regarded by them with much suspicion. If, therefore, the committee could avoid stating that the force would be disbanded, the task of the Irish executive would be made easier.[23]

Yet, the government hardly became less committed to safeguards for the Ulster Unionists on the issue. As we have already seen, the special constabulary was at this time being organised in the six counties under imperial auspices.[24] And at the same 2 November meeting the committee adopted Carson's proposal to vest control of police in the Lord-Lieutenant rather than in a North–South committee during the period in which the police forces were reserved.[25]

The reasons for reserving inland revenue and customs and excise services were connected with the peculiar system of finance prescribed under the Government of Ireland Act. The system was based on the principle that the cost of administration in Ireland – whether imperial or domestic – should be met by revenue raised in Ireland. Ireland was to make an 'imperial contribution', supposed to be related to the benefit derived from being part of the empire. The figure, £18,000,000 annually for the first two years, was necessarily a rounded estimate and was thereafter to be recomputed annually. After the Board of Inland Revenue and the Board of Customs and Excise had collected Irish revenue the British exchequer would deduct from it the contribution, together with the cost of reserved services; the remainder would be handed over to the Irish exchequers as the 'residual share of reserved taxes' and was expected to constitute the major portion of Irish income. Both the imperial contribution and the residual share were to be apportioned between North and South by the Joint Exchequer Board, a special tribunal established under the Act to resolve inter-government financial questions. The collection of certain minor items of revenue such as death duties, stamps, excise on licences and entertainments and other miscellaneous items were transferred to the Irish governments. But the major revenue items, the imposition and collection of customs, excise duties on manufactured goods, income tax, most revenue from supertax and excess profit duties, remained the preserve of the two United Kingdom Revenue Boards.[26]

Although these matters were reserved specifically because the government wished to preserve the financial unity of the United Kingdom and not specifically to stimulate interest in the union of the Irish parliaments, section 30 of the Government of Ireland Act expressly suggested the possible transfer of customs and excise at a time subsequent to such a union. However, there was no hint in the provisions of the Act that the levying and collection of income tax would ever be transferred.[27] This had certain political significance and is perhaps a key to understanding Lloyd George's political strategy on Ireland in these years. In October 1920 the Liberals in the Cabinet, Addison, Fisher and Montague, alarmed by the extent to which British policies had alienated public opinion in Ireland, called for the liberalisation of the financial clauses in the Government of Ireland Bill. They proposed to grant 'complete financial autonomy' to both Irish parliaments by way of replacing the imperial contribution with Irish liability for 'a definite portion of the national debt'. Contribution to any other imperial expenditure should be voluntary. It was believed that 'there was too much British intervention in Irish affairs' in the Bill, and that 'the collection by English officials of customs, excise and income tax would be an irritant'. 'The government', contended the proponents of this view,

> should have the courage of its convictions and say that this new solution was put forward in the belief that it would settle the question, that no further concession could possibly be made, and that the giving of complete financial autonomy to both parliaments was the government's limit in the way of concession. Further, this plan would have the support of, and would strengthen all moderate opinion in Ireland. An additional argument put forward in support of the new scheme was that the government was in need of all the strength and backing it could obtain from public opinion in breaking up the murder gang, and doubt was expressed whether such support would be forthcoming if it was considered that the government had not gone far enough in the way of financial concession.[28]

The Prime Minister's vitriolic reply to this attack from his left is worth quoting in full in order to illustrate how strongly Lloyd George felt about the revenue question: primarily and essentially it was a bargaining counter for negotiations with Sinn Féin: [he began.]

> It would be a mistake at this stage to make any great concessions, especially when the prospects of getting anything in return were so small. Nothing would be left with which to negotiate if the Irish government adopted a conciliatory attitude. The giving of customs, excise and income tax meant a great deal, and if this were done Ireland could not remain an integral part of the United Kingdom. The scheme put forward was not compatible with her so remaining. She could either support us or not, as she chose. The test to apply was whether you could give to other parts of the United Kingdom that which you were giving to Ireland, and it was obvious that it would be impossible to do so. The retention of customs was always regarded as a sign of unity. Take the cases where there were other federal systems – Germany and the United States of America. Bavaria

was independent, had a separate king and a separate army; but they had not got customs. It was, in fact, the first thing they gave up as a symbol of unity to the German Empire. The United States did not give customs and excise to its federal states. At one time the states had had the levying of income tax, and one of the greatest political struggles in the United States had been with the object of obtaining federal control of income tax, which had been found absolutely essential in order to raise money for defence. We, who had control of income tax, were now talking of giving it up. That would be to let Ireland off financially. That was not the home rule on which he had been brought up. If customs had to be conceded in order to obtain peace, it might be considered; but he would only consider it if it was impossible to get other terms. Sinn Féin would have to come forward and bargain. But the government had already said that they were prepared to come to an agreement. By giving up customs, excise and income tax we should get nothing in return from Sinn Féin. By giving up these three things we delivered the key of the whole position to Sinn Féin; they would collect the taxes and would refuse to pay their contribution to the imperial exchequer. What should we do then? Try and get customs, excise and income tax back again? Once the machinery for collecting these taxes had been handed over it would be impossible to get it back.

Continuing, the prime minister said that he was all for justice for Ireland but at the same time it must be remembered that justice was due to England, Scotland and Wales, who had made greater sacrifices in the war than Ireland. This country would have to bear the extra burden of the financial concessions proposed, and there would be in Ireland cheap whiskey, cheap tobacco – everything cheap; and here people would be staggering under their burdens. Such a state of affairs would be intolerable and unjustifiable. Another reason was that Sinn Féin would not accept such a concession, for it was abundantly clear that they meant to have complete independence, and would not take anything less. We had got a great inheritance, and in a moment of despair must not barter it away in order to get 'Peace in our time, O Lord'! He was looking forward to using customs, excise and income tax as a means of reducing Ireland. Ulster meant to work this bill. As for the south, she would use it and the proposed concessions to extort something further. If we retained these taxes the Sinn Féiners were at our mercy. He had asked Sir Laming Worthington-Evans some time ago to work out how much of the revenue of Ireland would remain in our hands if we held only the ports, and he worked it out at something like three-quarters. He himself was in favour of holding the ports until a guarantee of some kind was forthcoming. To the counties in the south which declared a republic he would say: 'You must pay your old age pension, insurance, etc., etc.'. Such a course was not without precedent. The Roman Empire had constantly to do this kind of thing in Sicily. If we gave up customs, excise and income tax without getting anything in return, it would be the worst piece of business which this government had ever done, and he could not face the position. Such taxes ought to be imperial taxes, and it was unsound in principle to part with these things. He was still a Gladstonian home ruler, and wished to keep Ireland as an integral part of the United Kingdom, and that was why he hoped that the present bill would be proceeded with. The bill was a good and generous one, and under it, it was possible to keep the United Kingdom, which was a small country, together in some sort of unity and enable it to face the future. He would stand by the bill until someone with real authority in Ireland appeared with whom it was possible to negotiate.[29]

Clearly, Lloyd George regarded revenue control by Westminster as the important keystone of the United Kingdom constitution under the traditional idea of Home Rule. This was why its greatest significance to him – notwithstanding his claims to be a 'Gladstonian Home Ruler' – was its value for bargaining with the Irish on the crucial questions of constitutional status and Ulster.

Finally, among the reserved services the question of land purchase seems to have been the least contentious. All parties agreed that the process of land purchase should be completed. Under the Act the British were to continue to put up the credit for land-purchase schemes. However, the Cabinet Committee accepted the recommendation in the Irish Convention's report of 1918[30] to make the collection of annuities a responsibility of the Irish governments. The latter were to keep the annuities as a source of revenue, while the British deducted the correct annuities figure from reserved revenue before handing back the residuary share of Irish taxes. The advantage to the British was to relieve the imperial government 'of the difficult and invidious task of securing punctual payment of the tenants' annuities'.[31] The Irish governments would also bear the cost of collecting annuities, but this was largely offset by a 'free gift' of the annuities for 1920, about £3,600,000 to be apportioned between the Irish governments.[32] It was expected that as pending sales were disposed of, the annuities figure would rise, but would begin to diminish as holdings were paid for, finally disappearing about sixty-five years after the last sales.[33] The reservation of land purchase was unconnected with the idea of promoting Irish unity. It would remain reserved 'unless and until otherwise provided by any act of the parliament of the United Kingdom'. And the transferrable function of annuities collection was to be divided between the Irish governments.

Thus, for a variety of reasons were services retained to the authority of Westminster under the Government of Ireland Act: constitutional, strategic and commercial necessity, as in the case of the excluded matters and apparently the Post Office; the unfeasibility of administrative division, as in the case of the Post Office, Public Record Office and Registry of Deeds; the maintenance of the fiscal unity of the United Kingdom, as in the case of the revenue services (although the withholding of taxing powers was also a counter for bargaining with the South on the general political question); internal security in the first years of Home Rule, as in the case of the police forces; and imperial liability, as in the case of land purchase. It had little or nothing to do with inducing Irish unity. The one nod towards this aspiration in the Act's reserved services provisions was empowering the Irish parliaments by identical Acts to transfer the Post Office, Public Record Office and Registry of Deeds to the Council of Ireland and thus providing for automatic transfer on the date of Irish union. Otherwise we must look to the council itself to see where North and South were obliged to administer Ireland on a joint basis.

The Council of Ireland

It will be recalled that in its second report to the Cabinet on 2 December 1919 the Walter Long Committee had decided to invest the Council of Ireland with none of the Irish services at the outset. The principle of placing the onus of Irish unity on the 'voluntary co-operation' of the two Irish parliaments was confirmed in late January 1920 when the committee rejected Sir Henry Robinson's proposals to transfer several Irish services to the council, notwithstanding Robinson's more realistic assessment of what the response of the Irish parliaments to the Council of Ireland was likely to be.[34] Yet, by the time the 1920 Act was passed, three exceptions to this principle had been made. In February 1920 the government ordered the Cabinet Committee to insert a clause providing for the transfer to the council of services pertaining to railways.[35] At the committee stage of the Bill in June, Sir Edward Carson took exception to this because it prevented the Northern Parliament from 'passing any law authorising construction or improvement'.[36] Nor was either parliament allowed to pass legislation affecting railway employees. The Long Committee thought his objections 'had substance', but they were faced by the fact that 'effective railway administration was impossible unless railways were under single control'.[37] By October 1920, however, the government introduced an amendment 'enabling each parliament to authorise the construction, extension or improvement of railways within its own area'. The council would retain those 'departmental and administrative powers now vested in a department of the United Kingdom, and general legislative powers . . .'[38] Once again an administrative provision of the Bill which necessitated all-Ireland administration had been modified – as in the case of the Public Record Office – to enable either Irish government to carry on a service relating exclusively to its own area. Nevertheless, the principle of investing the council with specific executive powers had been re-established.

In June 1920 a memorandum by the Chief Inspector of Fisheries for Ireland demonstrated in persuasive terms the unfeasibility of dividing existing fisheries administration between Northern and Southern Ireland. The border would run through rivers, such as the Foyle, where the enforcement of fishery laws in different areas of a catchment basin by different authorities appeared impossible. Spawning grounds on one side of the border often led to fishing grounds on the other side. The powers of the Irish parliaments to alter fishery by-laws could result in conflict and confusion if opposite policies were adopted on the same river systems in order to satisfy the parties whose interests were in conflict, for example, flax-growers versus fishermen. It would be unlikely that either Irish government would alter by-laws respecting sea fisheries in detriment to Irish fishing 'because their chief object is to prevent the stock from being reduced by the incursion of steam trawlers from Great Britain'. But, then, policing sea fisheries would be less effectual in places like Carlingford Lough because of the difficulty of proving in which jurisdiction offences were committed and the ability of delinquents easily to evade capture by quickly leaving a jurisdiction; and more expensive on account of the cost of establishing a new administrative office with qualified staff who would have less work to do, not to mention the exhorbitant cost of building and maintaining an additional fishery protection cruiser.[39] By and large these arguments must have been convincing to the committee, for fisheries administration was now written into the Bill as a Council of Ireland service.

The third and final inclusion among the Council of Ireland services in the Bill's final form – the administration of the Diseases of Animals Acts, was not recommended by the Long Committee at all, but by the House of Lords. On 2 November 1920 the committee considered a resolution by the Veterinary Medical Association of Ireland calling for the transfer of the matter to the council, but confirmed a previous decision to reject such a proposal.[40] Nevertheless in December the Lords attached an eleventh-hour amendment to the Bill adding to the powers of the council the Diseases of Animals Acts administration. This was 'against the wishes of the government' and objectionable on practical grounds since under the Bill there would be two departments of agriculture and no central machinery sufficient for a really effective all-Ireland agricultural administration. Nevertheless, the Cabinet thought it 'inadvisable' to oppose the amendment if the Lords felt so strongly about it, and the concession was made.[41]

Out of the vast range of public administration incorporating so many government services, the transfer to an all-Ireland body of these three matters would not appear to be a serious setback for the cause of Ulster Unionism. Yet to achieve a more autonomous administration for Northern Ireland, Sir Edward Carson and other spokesmen for Ulster Unionism in Parliament launched attacks on the allocation of services to the council. They regarded the powers as too far-reaching and dangerous and were not reassured by the government's insistence that the intention was 'not primarily to increase the power of the council, but to provide in the most business-like way for the administration' of these services.[42] Later, the council would become a complicating factor in North–South relations in the aftermath of the Treaty.

Administrative Partition and Westminster Politics

In the teeth of the obvious intentions of Ulster Unionists to achieve a complete division of Irish and even, in some cases, reserved services, it would appear remarkable that the British should continue to place so much faith in the pretence that their Bill would motivate North and South to co-operate with a view to eventual union. In October, for instance, Sir Francis Greer took a second look at the Public Record Office and the Registry of Deeds and wondered whether they would be better 'vested in the Council like railways and fisheries'. The object of the two repositories in centralising legal and other records would 'be defeated if the existing collection has to be broken up and distributed between offices in Southern and Northern Ireland so far as the records can be classified as belonging exclusively to either part'. Yet, in the tone of all innocence he rationalised that, on the other hand, 'they are just the kind of services which the two parliaments might be disposed to transfer to the council by identical acts from motives of convenience and self-interest'.[43]

The British, especially the Conservatives, were reluctant to admit that partition, once in effect, would be permanent. Yet throughout 1920 Walter Long's Cabinet Committee frequently found it necessary to redraft specific provisions of the Government of Ireland Bill to meet the Ulster Unionist demands for the six counties' independence of the rest of Ireland. The paradox arises from the political dilemma which the Irish question posed for Conservatives. The traditional alliance of the previous thirty years between Ulster Unionists and British Conservatives had long begun to crack. The surging power of a more extreme nationalism after 1916 had made devolutionists of the Conservatives. Were it not for the long-standing association with the Unionists, the Tories would now gladly trade the Orange Card for a settlement. Yet, although the Ulster Unionist cause no longer carried the utility it had borne for Tories in former times, the Conservative Party remained committed to 'safeguarding Ulster' in a solution and the desire of men like Long to give Northern Unionists what they wanted was the other side of the same coin. Thus, any willingness on the part of the Conservatives to abandon their former allies in order to achieve a united Ireland under Home Rule within the United Kingdom, could not rise to meet the resolute Ulster Loyalist militancy which the Conservatives themselves had helped to foster in the past. Time would prove that when strains between the former allies reached the breaking point, as they did during British negotiations with Sinn Féin in late 1921, both Ulster Loyalist resistance and the inveteracy of the old Tory commitment to Ulster made it impossible for the Conservatives to disown the Ulster Unionists without this seriously threatening the stability and unity of the party.[44]

Thus, the British could do no more than partition the country and provide the machinery for bringing about a future union, which North and South could take up by agreement or leave alone as they chose. This is borne out in the provisions of the Bill affecting administration. In the words of a memorandum of the Cabinet Committee on Ireland, the British government's conception underlying the devolution of powers was that 'the best way to induce the north and south to begin to co-operate was to place upon them the responsibility at the very outset of deciding whether . . . obviously unitary services should be divided, or whether they should not agree to transfer them immediately to the Council of Ireland.'[45] The British, unable to reconcile the goal of a self-governing united Ireland with the particularism of Unionist Ulster, invented a political fiction which they alluded to as 'voluntary co-operation between north and south' and relied on it as evidence to the world that they had done all they could to make the Irish agree.

Notes

1   10 & 11 Geo. V, ch. 67, sect. 4.
2   Memorandum by Sir Francis Greer on the reserved services and excluded matters in the Government of Ireland Bill, CI 87, 7 October 1920, PRO CAB 27/70.
3   'First report of the Cabinet Committee on the Irish question', CP 56, 4 November 1919, PRO CAB 24/29 (also CAB 27/68). Also, the two parliaments could transform the council into an all-Ireland parliament.
4   Hansard (Commons), 5th series, vol. 127, col. 1113, 30 March 1920.
5   ibid.
6   Conclusions of a conference of ministers, 11 November 1919, PRO CAB 23/18.
7   'Committee on Ireland, fourth report', CP 247, 2 December 1919, PRO CAB 24/94 (also CAB 27/68).
8   ibid.

9 'Powers of the Council of Ireland, memorandum by the Rt. Hon. Sir Henry Robinson', CI 48, 17 January 1920, PRO CAB 27/68.

10 'Committee on Ireland, report of the sub-committee', CI 55, 30 January 1920, PRO CAB 27/69.

11 ibid.

12 'Memorandum by Sir Francis Greer', CI 57, 2 February 1920, PRO CAB 27/69.

13 Cabinet conclusion 17(19)(2), 22 December 1919, PRO CAB 23/18. The Post Office Savings Bank and Trustee Savings Banks had been reserved for a maximum of ten years under the 1914 Act. In the 1920 Bill they were reserved indefinitely or until both Irish parliaments legislated their common administration. (See memorandum by Sir Francis Greer, as note 2.)

14 Memorandum by Sir Francis Greer, as note 2.

15 'Notes on promises made in committee', memorandum by Sir Francis Greer, CI 91, 8 October, 1920, PRO CAB 27/70.

16 10 & 11 Geo. V, ch. 67, sect. 9.

17 ibid., sect. 9.

18 Memorandum by Sir Francis Greer, as note 2. See also Hansard (Commons), 5th series, vol. 129, col. 2007.

19 'Differences between the Government of Ireland Bill and the Act of 1914 with respect to powers transferred (circulated by the direction of the First Lord of the Admiralty)', CP 943, 24 March 1920, PRO CAB 24/101.

20 'Notes on promises made in committee', as note 15.

21 ibid.

22 Sir John Anderson to the Cabinet Committee on Ireland, CI 99, 1 November 1920, PRO CAB 27/70.

23 Minutes of a meeting of the Cabinet Committee on Ireland, CI 20, 2 November 1920, PRO CAB 27/68.

24 See above, pp. 26-7.

25 As note 23.

26 10 & 11 Geo. V, ch. 67, sects 23, 30.

27 ibid.

28 Minutes of a conference of ministers, 13 October 1920, PRO CAB 23/23.

29 ibid.

30 *Report of the Proceedings of the Irish Convention*, Cd 9019, 1918, *Parliamentary Papers*, vol. 10.

31 'Land purchase and home rule', memorandum by R. G. Hawtrey of the Treasury, C.I. 31, 17 November 1919, PRO CAB 27/69.

32 Cabinet conclusions 12(20)(5), 24 February 1920, PRO CAB 23/20.

33 *Government of Ireland Bill, Outline of Financial Provisions*, Cmd 645, HC 1920, *Parliamentary Papers*, vol. 11.

34 See above, pp. 38-40.

35 Cabinet conclusions 12(20)(6), 24 February 1920, PRO CAB 23/20.

36 Minutes of a meeting of the Cabinet Committee on Ireland, CI (a) 3rd, 7 June 1920, PRO CAB 27/156.

37 ibid.

38 'Notes on promises made in committee', as note 15.

39 'Memorandum by the Chief Inspector of Fisheries, Ireland', CI 76, 7 June 1920, PRO CAB 27/70.

40 Minutes of a meeting of the Cabinet Committee on Ireland, CI 20th, 2 November 1920, PRO CAB 27/68.

41 Conclusions of a conference of ministers, 15 December 1920; Cabinet conclusions 73(20)(1), 17 December 1920, PRO CAB 23/23.

42 Sir Laming Worthington Evans, 14 June 1920, Hansard (Commons), 5th series, vol.

130, cols. 975-6.
43   Memorandum by Sir Francis Greer, as note 2.
44   See D. G. Boyce, 'British conservative opinion, the Ulster question and the partition of Ireland, 1919–21', *Irish Historical Studies*, vol. 17, no. 65 (1968).
45   'Committee on Ireland, report of the sub-committee', as note 10.

4   The Transfer of Services to Northern Ireland

King George V signed the Government of Ireland Act on 23 December 1920. The next six months, until the formal opening of the Northern Ireland Parliament, was a period of political and military stalemate. Peace efforts in December 1920, initiated by Archbishop Clune of Perth and Father O'Flanagan, TD, foundered when the government insisted on the surrender of arms as the condition for a truce. The confidence of the British military that martial law could bring the IRA to heel within five months prompted the government to set the date of elections under the Act for May 1921. However, the IRA's guerrilla campaign continued to confound British military expertise, and the war persisted. Throughout the period no convincing inroads were made in the suppression of the republican forces.[1] Also, since the autumn of 1920 public opinion in Britain, aroused by reports of atrocities by the Crown forces, had been building up against the government.[2] A Labour Party commission investigating conditions in Ireland concluded that 'things are being done in the name of Britain which must make our name stink in the nostrils of the whole world'.[3] The government's standing on the Irish question did not improve when it suppressed the official army report on the Cork City burnings by the auxiliary police. Yet Lloyd George and his colleagues soldiered on under the principle that order must be restored before negotiations were possible. In fact, whether order was restored or not they gave every appearance of being determined to go ahead with the Government of Ireland Act. In March and April 1921 they resisted proposals by Southern Unionists and Liberals to take extraordinary measures which would supposedly cultivate a shift in Irish nationalist opinion to more moderate politics. Southern Unionists thought elections in the South should be postponed allowing more time for the military to gain the upper hand and for public opinion in the South to abandon the republican aspirations of Sinn Féin.[4] The Liberals disagreed with postponing elections, but thought that a settlement could be achieved sooner by declaring a 'frank and generous' truce as a preliminary to a conference with Sinn Féin. A truce, they held, was 'not a surrender' because there would be no question of conceding a republic or prejudicing Northern Ireland.[5] The government, however, encouraged by a sudden (and what proved to be temporary) upturn in military successes in April, held out against both courses.[6] Rather, they decided to proceed with the time-table for implementing the Government of Ireland Act although fully aware that Sinn Féin would sweep to victory in the elections in the twenty-six counties and refuse to work the Southern Ireland Parliament. The Act provided for this contingency in a 'Crown colony' clause, but the military implications of ruling Southern Ireland in this way were formidable. Just how formidable was realised in May and June. The Cabinet, face to face with the undoubted failure of military methods so far pursued, were advised that only substantial increments of coercive activity – vast increase in troop strength, the issue of identity cards to the public, declaring the Dáil a treasonable organisation, mass shootings, and so on – might bring the Irish around.[7] Confronted with this daunting and expensive prospect, and unsure whether it could survive British public opinion, it is not surprising that the government suddenly shifted course. The king's conciliatory speech in Belfast at the inaugural ceremonies of the Northern Ireland Parliament on 22 June was used as the pretext for the Cabinet's change of heart, and provided Lloyd George with a more palatable option than the Draconian implications of Crown Colony.[8] On 24 June he invited de Valera and Craig to negotiations without pre-conditions. This initial contact opened the way for the 'truce' between the British and republican forces on 11 July. The Lloyd George–de Valera talks in mid-July, and extended dialectical correspondence over the next two months debating the pre-conditions, resulted in the London Treaty Conference which began on 11 October.

The breakthrough of June–July 1921 was possible in large part because the government's commitment to Ulster was now practically fulfilled. The Northern state, securely in Ulster Unionist hands, was now in being. The results of the May elections in the six counties were as predictable as they were in the twenty-six. Of the fifty-two successful candidates forty were Unionists, six nationalists, six Sinn Féin. On 7 June a government was formed with Sir James Craig as Prime Minister, H. M. Pollock as Minister of Finance, R. Dawson Bates as Minister of Home Affairs, J. M. Andrews as Minister of Labour, and E. M. Archdale as both Minister of Agriculture and Minister of Commerce. On the same date the first issue of the *Belfast Gazette* (for the publication of government notices) announced the assignment of specific functions to each of the seven new departments 'without prejudice to the powers and duties of existing departments and authorities pending the transfer of services'.[9] The Unionist state had come into existence, and it remained only to be equipped with government services. But now, with the prospect of negotiations between the British and Sinn Féin at last a reality, would Ulster remain the favourite son? The manner in which services were transferred to Northern Ireland in 1921 will help to bring into relief British political attitudes and policies in the new situation.

In anticipation of the transfer of powers to the North, administrative structures were already being discussed months before the establishment of the Northern government. As early as February the Chief Secretary, displaying a telling disregard for British civil service traditions of neutrality in party politics, directed existing departments to prepare for partition by communicating with the Ulster Unionists that 'it seems desirable that communications should be opened as soon as possible with some of the persons designated to fill the offices of ministers of Northern Ireland in connection with several matters which will require immediate consideration and preliminary action on their part'.[10] The assistant under-secretary in Belfast, Sir Ernest Clark, indeed was already in continuous consultation with Sir James Craig. Clark was still involved with organising the special constabulary, but now began to interest himself in plans for setting up the Northern administration. An early piece of advice Clark offered Craig on administrative partition showed an admirable appreciation for its cultural dimension:

> The north should claim a share of the pictures and contents of museums in Dublin, and also a share of all good class furniture and books of reference in government offices. As you are aware there are in all the old offices a few pieces of furniture which are of more than intrinsic value and books of reference which are out of print. Of these things the north ought to have its fair share, and although the matter is not immediate, it might be well to prepare the way for a claim and for the cabinet, before you leave it, to settle the principle.[11]

But Clark also consulted with Craig when attending to the more mundane essentials of laying down the North's administrative foundations. Craig, for example, was directly involved in the problem of determining the appropriate number and functions of the future Northern departments.[12] In planning the structure of the civil service, Clark advised Craig about staff classification and grading, recruitment resources, conditions of employment, and so on.[13] In the matter of recruitment he warned Craig against adopting an official policy that would disadvantage Catholics in securing government employment. Perhaps not surprisingly, his advice to prohibit religious discrimination was based not specifically on any abstract principle of justice or equality; but rather on the fact that it was unconstitutional and the new government would not be able to get away with it. 'Under the Government of Ireland Act', Clark noted,

> the parliament of Northern Ireland is prohibited from making any law to give any preference etc. on account of religious belief. While it is true that a regulation by the Treasury in relation to the civil service would not be, in strictness, a law, it is submitted that such a

regulation, which might confer an advantage on candidates profess-
ing any particular religion, would be involved under this section as
being of the nature of delegated legislation.[14]

In the future Northern civil service, Clark advised, there would have to
be a 'proportion of Roman Catholics'.[15] Had someone suggested
there be none?

It may be unfair to say that Clark was utterly partisan. But in a
practical sense he was planning the administration of a single party
state. Long before the May 1921 elections, therefore, he was explaining, and at times defending, the views of the 'prospective government'
to his fellow British civil servants in London departments, and indeed
in Dublin Castle. In March, for example, Clark advised officials in
British departments that when the Unionist government came into
being it would seek a separate administration for the North of customs
and excise, income tax and the Post Office. Craig and his colleagues,
still unhappy with partition's lack of definitiveness in the Government
of Ireland Act, extended the partition crusade to the reserved services
notwithstanding that these remained under imperial authority. People
in London, wrote Clark to Harrison in Inland Revenue, 'could hardly
appreciate how intense the feeling is on such subjects here, and with
what horror communications with Dublin on the subject of income tax
would be regarded after there is a government here to manage its own
affairs'.[16] Also in March, Clark appears to have had a run-in with
Cope, his counterpart in Dublin, about rumours regarding the
allocation of civil servants between Northern and Southern Ireland.
Cope informed Clark that stories were circulating Dublin departments
to the effect that the better posts in the prospective Northern
administration were being reserved for certain officials in London and
Dublin departments with influence in the North.[17] Clark snappily
denied the rumours, suggesting that they were 'probably one of the
many things circulated to crab the start of administration here'.
Moreover, Clark retorted, a rumour was current in Belfast 'namely that
the various departments in Dublin are selecting their "duds" for
submission to the civil service committee as suitable for transfer'. If this
were the case, then the Northern government just might have to look to
civil service talent available in London.[18]

Clark's relations with Dublin Castle officials, with the possible
exception of Sir John Anderson, seem to have been rather cool. At the
start of Clark's appointment, Sturgis recorded his resentment: the
arrival of 'another little king' was surely a further obstacle to attempts
to unify police command.[19] In his early months in Belfast, on the
other hand, Clark seems to have relied on Cope's assistance in
establishing his office.[20] However, the work of both men reflected

conflicting strains in British policy: Clark's, to implement partition in line with the political control of the Ulster Unionists in their own area; Cope's to find the path of reconciliation with Sinn Féin who violently opposed Ireland's dismemberment. Direct evidence of the two men's dealings with, and attitude towards, one another is exceedingly scarce; but perhaps it is only necessary to compare Clark's popularity among the Unionists, with Cope's odium. While the Unionists had distrusted Cope since his appointment in May 1920, his reputation in the North sank to a new low in September 1921 when he attracted the hostility which moved G. C. Duggan to remark that 'in Belfast even the Pope himself is hardly as unpopular'.[21] Sectarian riots had brought Cope to Belfast where he showed the 'bad taste' to visit the Catholic Bishop of Down and Conor (Dr Macrory) in order to secure his intervention in the interests of peace, and insisted that the police should arrest a Protestant for every Catholic arrested.[22] His actions and his policy line on public order (opposing the use of the special constabulary) caused sufficient indignation in Belfast for the Northern Cabinet to write to the Viceroy 'that the Dublin officials were in a large measure responsible for the unfortunate incidents that had taken place in Belfast'.[23]

If it can be said that these conflicting expressions of British policy were held in the balance in central Irish administration, then it was in the hands of Sir John Anderson they were held. Anderson, at first glance, appears an enigmatic figure on the Ulster question. As we have already seen, he supported Dominion Home Rule in the summer of 1920, possibly without working out the full implications for the Ulster dimension of the settlement or regarding it as secondary. He opposed the scheme for a special constabulary in the North and consequently incurred the wrath of Craig. And when in the summer of 1921 the Northern Parliament and government were established, G. C. Duggan observed Anderson to be carrying out the administrative aspects of partition with something less than ardent conviction. 'Sir John', wrote Duggan in his 1922 'Periscope' article, 'began to interest himself in an academic way in the establishment of a separate government in Northern Ireland ... By tradition he had no wish to see partition'.[24] Balanced against these supposed personal feelings – and it is interesting to hear the view that Anderson actually had any! – is the fact that it was he who put Clark forward for the Northern assistant under-secretaryship, an ideal choice for the discreet appeasement of the Ulster Unionists. Clark, at least in his memoirs, clearly held Anderson in the highest regard,[25] and gave him much of the credit for laying the administrative foundations of Northern Ireland. Just as Basil Brooke regarded Clark as 'Ulster's midwife', Clark saw Anderson as 'head physician' at the birth of the Northern state.[26]

Perhaps Anderson is best described as neither pro-North nor pro-South. With the government and Parliament of Northern Ireland now in existence, and the first positive steps taken to reach a settlement with the South, Anderson was acutely aware of the delicate position in which the British government was placed. On the one hand, the establishment of the North's parliamentary institutions was a major achievement in the government's policy, and the position there would have to be consolidated. 'The ship has been launched in the North', he wrote to Sir Warren Fisher on 9 June, 'and we must hope she will prove seaworthy'.[27] On the other hand, the truce and the possibility of negotiations for a settlement with Sinn Féin gave a new conciliatory dimension to British policy towards the South which placed the interests of the North in a secondary position. In the summer of 1921 a new phase emerged in which the task of transferring full powers to the government of Northern Ireland was subordinated to the requirements of the larger Irish policy – the need to reach agreement with the South.

For example, the British would not support the idea of dividing reserved services between North and South while the outcome of political negotiations with the South was unclear. On 24 June, Clark reminded the Northern Cabinet 'that it would be desirable that in the case of reserved services such as customs, the post office, etc., Northern Ireland should be made a self-contained unit corresponding with London instead of along the present channels through Dublin'.[28] Anderson responded to Clark 'that nothing can be decided at the moment'. Yet, Anderson clearly wished to keep British options open. In early July he put Clark's proposal before department heads in the Post Office and the Boards of Inland Revenue and Customs and Excise in order to gather their confidential views on what would be involved 'from a purely administrative standpoint'.[29] The London heads in fact did not find the idea attractive. Only the Board of Customs and Excise could not object to it because the department had no central Irish administration and 'the arrangements desired were already in operation'. Inland Revenue opposed the idea 'on grounds of economy, efficiency and convenience', the Post Office 'on grounds of economy, efficiency and common sense'.[30] Anderson, however, made his own expediential calculations: 'on purely practical grounds', he believed, 'there is a great deal to be said for this suggestion so long as Southern Ireland remains in a disturbed condition. On the other hand there is a great deal to be said against it from the point of view of all-Ireland sentiment'. But in any case the present was not the time for such a measure. He foresaw the possibility that the final political settlement would make such a division a practical and constitutional necessity. If financial autonomy were conceded to the South, the principle of 'equal treatment' under the 1920 Act dictated similar concessions to the North. Sir James Craig was indeed already discussing with the British the possibility of transferring taxation powers to Northern Ireland.[31] Anderson, while he could make no promises to the North, could nevertheless comfort Clark 'that what is foreshadowed here may have to be done under an amending Act – or ultimately under the present Act if and when reserved services are taken over'.[32] Thus, Anderson, preconceived a more complete partition similar to that which would be enshrined in the Treaty five months later; for the moment, however, the British could not indulge the North while negotiations with Sinn Féin could bring forth a settlement in the South.

The British did, at least, provide the expertise for setting up the new Northern ministries. 'Experts' from London departments were attracted to the principal posts in Belfast by a 'special inducement'.[33] By September twenty-seven such officials were in Belfast on loan from United Kingdom departments.[34] Whatever the inducement was, it helped to overcome a reluctance among English officials to work in Belfast. Some of the more valuable Treasury officials were approached with offers but either entertained serious reservations or refused outright to take the interview.[35] Malcolm Ramsay, head of the establishments division, had particular difficulty finding a person for the Northern Treasury's 'finance' post and, interestingly, Maurice Headlam, the reactionary Treasury Remembrancer ejected from Dublin Castle in 1920, was for a time considered. Ramsay informed Clark that Headlam 'would be glad to return, temporarily at any rate, to Ireland'.[36] However, Headlam did not come, and C. T. Cuthbertson seems to have been loaned to the North for the job.[37] Some of the original team of officials seconded to Northern Ireland were, in fact, not English but Ulstermen: Sam Watt, the Home Affairs Secretary, who in 1920 had transferred from the Irish Office to the Admiralty when Cope moved into Dublin Castle; A. P. Magill, an assistant secretary in the Department of Finance, heretofore registrar of petty sessions clerk in Dublin Castle; and W. D. Scott, private secretary to the Minister of Finance.[38] Four others with Ulster associations took up posts with permanent status: W. B. Spender, Secretary to the Cabinet; Cecil Litchfield secretary in the Department of Commerce; C. A. C. J. Hendricks, private secretary to the Minister of Education, and James Huggett, Comptroller and Auditor-General.[39]

But in assisting the Northern ministers to fill these positions, there is some evidence to suggest that the British hoped to push certain individuals into key positions in the hope of improving the public image of partition. The position of civil service organiser, for example, was also found difficult to fill, and the attempt of the British to install H. P.

Boland provokes questions about their intentions. Ramsay sent Sir James Craig a recommendation of Boland noticeably exceptional among other officials he sent to Belfast for the interview:

> Mr Boland has had a wide and varied experience of civil service administration. He was appointed to the office of the commissioner of public works in Dublin as second division clerk in 1895 and after serving there and in the Treasury Remembrancer's office was then transferred to serve in the Ministry of Munitions during the war, after which he was appointed to a vacancy on our establishment. He is a man of about forty-five. During his service here he has been intimately concerned with the reorganization of several large departments and in this work has acquired an exceptional knowledge of the various problems of civil service organization.
>
> There is every probability that you will find a man of this type indispensable, and accordingly our proposal is that he should come to you on probation with a definite view to ultimate permanency in your service should he seem in due time to fit the bill.[40]

Ramsay seemed particularly anxious to get Boland into this position for which he was interviewed by Craig on 29 June in Belfast.[41] A few days later he again wrote (to Clark) asking 'whether you regard Boland as suitable for employment in Northern Ireland and whether as a matter of fact you think you can come to any arrangement with him'.[42] Clark's abrupt reply on the 11th is fascinating: 'I forgot whether we discussed Boland's appointment when I was with you on the 7th. I think we did, but in case we did not the decision of the northern government is "thank you very much but no". I believe you know why'.[43] Yet on the 23rd Clark was still 'hung up for someone who really understands establishment'.[44] Boland's Southern Irish Catholic background undoubtedly had much to do with it; yet there would be other Catholics at the assistant secretary level in the North. The appointment of J. V. Coyle in the Department of Agriculture came under fire from the Ulster Ex-servicemen's Association, but Coyle was strongly defended in the Cabinet by his minister, Archdale, who told colleagues 'that Coyle was a Roman Catholic, a loyalist he had known for twenty years and he proposed to appoint him as head of one of his branches – not the head of the department [as the ex-servicemen had construed]'. It was even agreed that Archdale 'should reply stating the government intended to enrol members of all creeds in their staff provided their loyalty was unquestioned and it was hoped Southern Ireland would be equally broad-minded'.[45] Was it that Boland was regarded as insufficiently 'loyal', betraying, perhaps, a tinge of nationalism? (In September 1924 he would take up the position of establishments officer in the Irish Free State Department of Finance where he served with distinction for many years.)[46] Or was it simply out of the question for the Ulster Unionists to have a man with such a questionable background in charge of civil service recruitment for the Loyalist state? Why, in any event, was he interested in working for the North? And why did the British want so much to send him there? Partition was an embarrassment to the British and would be the most difficult part of their Irish policy to defend in negotiations with Sinn Féin. Did they wish to give the Ulster policy a facelift by putting a Southern Irish Catholic in charge of recruiting the Northern civil service, and give the appearance that Catholics truly held a stake in the new state or that partition was acceptable to many in the South?

In spite of the failure to situate Boland as civil service chief in the North, the British seem to have conceived an even more spectacular plan to infiltrate the Northern administration with moderating influences. This was to install A. W. Cope as permanent secretary in the Ministry of Finance. According to G. C. Duggan it was 'a post which in point of fact by training and temperament he was not in the least competent to fill'. However, in terms of power, responsibility, precedence and salary this post was the most important position in the Northern Ireland civil service. According to G. C. Duggan the idea was Anderson's.[47] If so, it lends credit to the picture of Anderson as the cold, disinterested bureaucrat, ready to back the Unionist or the nationalist view, to ensconce a Clark or a Cope as head official in the North in accordance with the needs of British policy at the moment. Later in 1921 Clark was given the job. His notes of later years recall that 'when . . . the government of the province came into power I found that even in the civil service itself I was not without rival in the assistant under-secretary in Dublin who was, I think, favoured by the political element in the British control'. (He does not mention Anderson, presumably either unaware of, or unwilling to refer, to his involvement.) 'But Craig and Pollock and Londonderry would not have this . . .'[48] Lack of documentation makes it difficult to learn how far the idea carried; but it seems to have died by the time of the August–September rioting when Cope arrived in Belfast to pontificate about even-handed justice.

The inability of the British to place key officials in key positions in the north was but a minor setback in a new policy to impose discreet restrictions upon the Ulster Unionists' political freedom. The British might fail to find a way to make it appear that Catholics would be involved in the Northern state; nevertheless they could make it appear that the Northern state was not necessarily an absolute *fait accompli*. This they did by withholding the North's executive services. As a pretext to Craig they claimed that the Government of Ireland Act was so designed as to render it necessary for services to be transferred to both

Irish governments simultaneously. The transfer of services, they argued, presupposed the existence of two special tribunals, provided for in the Act, on which representatives from both governments must sit. The Joint Exchequer Board was responsible for determining financial questions arising between the Northern, Southern and United Kingdom governments. It was to consist of two appointees of the United Kingdom Treasury, one each from the two Irish Treasuries and a chairman appointed by the king.[49] The Civil Service Committee was responsible for 'allocating' 'existing Irish officers' (that is, those working in 'Irish' or transferrable services) as between the two Irish governments or to the Council of Ireland; and for determining compensation for officers adversely affected by the Act. This body was to consist of seven members, one appointed by each Irish government, one by a secretary of state of the British government, one by the British Treasury, two by the existing Irish officers (later to represent the Northern and Southern staffs respectively), and a chairman appointed by the Lord Chief Justice of England.[50] Long before the truce in the early months of the year, the government had been advised by their officials that the Act contemplated the simultaneous creation of both Home Rule governments, and that these tribunals could not come into being until both Irish governments themselves were in being to appoint their own representatives.[51] Now, with the truce in force and with hopes for a settlement with Sinn Féin, the British found that the withholding of services from the Northern government, pending the establishment of a Southern government, served as a convenient backdrop to negotiations.

Being left without full executive powers became a source of acute irritation to Craig and his colleagues, especially as the Lloyd George–de Valera battle over pre-conditions continued to delay the opening of talks into the early autumn.[52] They were particularly anxious to assume control over law and order forces as disorders in Belfast and elsewhere in the North proliferated. On 23 June, Craig told General Macready that he was prepared 'at three days' notice' to take over the police forces.[53] He received a consistently negative response from the British. In August, Greenwood told Spender that 'he very much wished it were possible to transfer the constabulary at once to the northern government but the legal difficulties in the way in doing so *now* were insuperable'.[54] The transfer of services generally was perhaps regarded as even more vitally important. Sam Watt, the Home Affairs Secretary, on 12 August warned the Cabinet of the embarrassing position in which the North would be placed, especially in view of the reassembling of the Northern Parliament in early September:

By delaying the formation of a government in the south, the transfer of services to the northern government can be prevented. If this view is correct and if matters are delayed sufficiently, it may mean that the whole of the northern government will prove to be a farce, and that the northern parliament will be nothing more than a debating society, as it will not have the power to legislate on or to discuss any matter arising out of the services to be transferred.[55]

Craig pressed the British to utilise the wide powers in the Act that would enable the North to take over its services. The Northern government believed that by right the British should activate section 72, the 'Crown colony' clause, which anticipated the refusal by Southern Ireland's parliamentary representatives to form the Southern Parliament. Under this provision the Lord-Lieutenant could dissolve either parliament if the majority of its members declined to take the prescribed oath to the Crown. He would then govern that section of Ireland through an executive and legislature composed of privy councillors appointed by the king.[56] But this the British could not do without prejudicing their attempts to bring Sinn Féin to a conference. An alternative pressed on the British by the Unionists was to make an order in council under section 69, an enabling clause, which conceivably could empower the Lord-Lieutenant to appoint the Southern representatives to the Civil Service Committee and Joint Exchequer Board. 'Distinguished local counsel was of opinion that that clause of the act was operative in the circumstances', so Pollock told the Northern Parliament. (Loyalist backbenchers had accused their government of 'supineness' when the Northern Parliament reopened in September.) But the British placed a different construction on this provision. Pollock explained that

the law officers of the crown decided that taking in view the whole current arrangements of the act it was impossible to issue the transfers required for the establishment of the joint bodies. We had, therefore, of course to bow to the decision of His Majesty's government in the matter. But it must not be supposed that we allowed all this subject, which has been discussed *ad nauseam*, to go by default, because we are clearly alive to the difficulties, not only in regard to finances, but in regard to the machinery of all other departments of state, which are rendered helpless in the circumstances.[57]

The violence in late August–early September caused the Northern ministers increasing unease about the Lloyd George–de Valera deadlock and the consequent continuance of the withholding of services. The importance with which the North regarded the matter is manifest in a series of letters from Craig to Greenwood appealing for the immediate handover of services and staff to enable the North to put its government and Parliament into full operation.[58] 'This is a matter of grave urgency', he wrote on 16 September,

> as I may experience difficulty in allaying public resentment and irritation in view of all that has occurred. After specially adjourning the House from the end of June in order that when we meet on Tuesday I might be in a position to announce the transfer of the various services, it will be difficult for me on the one hand to satisfy the public and on the other to prevent violent attacks on the British government for what is looked upon as a breach of faith.[59]

On the 22nd Craig reported to Greenwood that the Northern Parliament 'had two days' debate on the general position with the result that I do not believe our people will be satisfied unless a transfer of the services from Dublin is secured at an early date'. The North, he protested, were being 'left in mid-air'. Instead of waiting until '(1) negotiations with Sinn Féin break down altogether, or (2) a conference, if held, comes to some agreement', could not a government of some form be set up in Dublin so that the North could get on with its business? 'The express desire of His Majesty at the opening of Parliament is flouted', he exclaimed, 'and the difficulty of maintaining the confidence of the people is vastly increased by the patience we have exhibited when they believe that by a more bellicose attitude we may have secured the full functioning of the act within a few weeks of the state opening of our local parliament.'[60] On the 27th Craig again wrote, suggesting that if the British did not feel able to use the special powers under sections 69 or 72, why not drop the idea of the Civil Service Committee? Already, said Craig, there were sufficient numbers to fill the ranks of the new departments from local six counties applicants and from officers in Dublin who desired to go to Belfast. 'I would be wanting in candour and in my duty to the representatives of the people here', Craig again warned, 'if I were to minimise the gravity of the situation. Impatience, irritation and a want of trust is springing up owing to the consideration shown to the other side.'[61]

However, Greenwood held firm. He appreciated the Northern leader's embarrassment but could recommend no further transfer of powers to the North until some forecast of the result of the coming conference with Sinn Féin could be made. If services were conferred exclusively on the North without the benefit of the 1920 Act's tribunals, it would be impossible to deal with such practical problems as the claims of individual civil servants, finance, questions connected with the Council of Ireland, or indeed 'the general working of the act'. 'In fact nothing', said Greenwood, 'short of a detailed recasting of the main provisions of the act would be sufficient to secure workable arrangements in Northern Ireland in advance of the establishment of the government in Southern Ireland.'[62]

But almost certainly the British also hoped to use the delay to facilitate their negotiations with Sinn Féin. Throughout the efforts to reach agreement on conference pre-conditions, Cope advised the government on the importance of a united Ireland in Sinn Féin policy.[63] On 3 September he suggested to Tom Jones that it would 'make all the difference if Lloyd George would make public remarks to Ulster'. He should 'tell the north east that they must come in or lose Fermanagh and Tyrone'. If this were done publicly, said Cope, 'then the south will give up independence for the sake of the hope of Ulster's coming in'. He had been 'surprised to find how far they would go' on the question of constitutional status if concessions were made on unity. 'If he [Lloyd George] will really grapple with Ulster the thing can be done.' Of course, 'grappling with Ulster' did not necessarily mean going back on partition; rather the idea was to entice the Irish into stepping down from the republic on the sovereignty issue which was the most important to the British. The precise fate of Ulster, or rather, perhaps, how Ulster was not to be coerced, then became a matter for discussion. Something like this would actually happen during the conferences with Sinn Féin, which began on 11 October, and the issue of the transfer of services played a key part.

At the end of September, Lloyd George and de Valera at last found a formula of words acceptable to both by which the British could invite the Irish to come and negotiate in conference 'how the association of Ireland with the community of nations known as the British Empire can best be reconciled with Irish national aspirations'. At this conference both sides knew that a breakdown on the issue of partition could not be defended publicly by the British and would be seen to put the Irish in the right. 'Men will die for Throne and Empire', Lloyd George told his Cabinet. 'I do not know who will die for Tyrone and Fermanagh'.[64] Thus, if the talks were to founder, the British were determined that the break should come on the issue of sovereignty, while the Irish were intent that it should be Ulster.

The Irish proposals on the North, first discussed on 17 October, contained concessions which weakened their hand from the outset. The Unionists were offered the option of joining with the South or of maintaining local autonomy (over an area to be determined by plebiscite) subject to overriding authority from Dublin. Thus, instead of demanding complete Irish unity at the start, Sinn Féin opened negotiations giving away ground on Ulster. This approach probably prejudiced their chances of forcing the break on Ulster. Nevertheless, they temporarily disarmed the British when they made it clear that their allegiance to Crown and Empire was contingent on Ireland's 'essential unity'. The British tried to fight off the Irish charge that the six-county solution was unjust and argued from a position entrenched in the Government of Ireland Act. But the British knew they were on weak ground. Tom Jones summed up his impression of an early session on Ulster to Lloyd George in a one-line note: 'This is going to wreck the settlement.'[65]

Yet within weeks the devious and masterful tactics of Lloyd George had turned the tables. Negotiating from a position of power, the British day after day were able to whittle away at the Irish proposals. Lloyd George made full use of opposition to his government – in and out of Parliament – to pressure Griffith and Collins to a gradual surrender on both sovereignty and Ulster. On the sovereignty issues – allegiance, citizenship and defence – Lloyd George elicited sufficient assurances from Griffith to fend off with aplomb a die-hard Tory motion of censure in the House of Commons on 31 October.[66] In the process, he brought the Irish further along towards the British position. The Irish were led to believe that in his goodwill Lloyd George was asking their help to put him 'in an impregnable position on the three main issues and clearing the decks for a fight on Ulster'.[67] The Irish gave such assurances and the British found themselves in the dilemma, seemingly, of having either to coerce the Loyalists or to break faith with Sinn Féin after the latter were willing to satisfy British demands regarding sovereignty. Lloyd George thus turned to Sir James Craig to ask that Ulster might show her loyalty to the Empire by consenting to administer her Home Rule powers subordinate to a Dublin Parliament. However, 'What we have we hold' was the unanimous response of the Ulster Unionists, who were not in the least moved by the turn of British public opinion, including the Conservative press, against Northern intransigence. Even the majority of the Conservative Party joined in the plea to the Ulster Unionists to co-operate. On the other hand, the Conservative response to the idea of taking action against Ulster was another matter. Lloyd George knew that Ulster would remain intransigent. He also knew that a diehard Tory minority (possibly to be led by Bonar Law, who had come out of retirement) threatened a split in the Conservative Party that could bring down the coalition. Thirty years of the Ulster–Tory alliance could not be just cast aside. He therefore prepared well for the Conservative Party Conference at Liverpool on 17 November. As early as the 7th Tom Jones elicited an assurance from Griffith not to obstruct a tentative proposal to offer Ulster the option of remaining subordinate to Dublin or to London with the North–South boundary to be adjusted by a commission. Griffith and Collins understood the proposal to be used by Lloyd George in his attempt to draw Ulster into an Irish unity arrangement. On the 12th Lloyd George obtained another assurance from Griffith not to obstruct the proposal during the Liverpool conference. On the following day Griffith approved a memorandum by Tom Jones containing the substance of his assurances. Throughout Griffith never regarded his assurances to be more than tentative, naively believing they would help Lloyd George to secure Irish unity. For his efforts to be helpful, Griffith found himself, in the final hours of the negotiations on 5–6 December, confronted by an animated and threatening Lloyd George waving these assurances in his face and insisting that Griffith was going back on his word by his belated attempt to break off negotiations on the Ulster question. Defeated by Lloyd George's chicanery, Griffith, followed by the other Sinn Féin delegates, signed the 'Treaty'.[68]

But British guile alone was not responsible for the Irish defeat. The Irish failed to achieve the break on Ulster because of poorly planned strategy. As late as the fourth plenary session on 14 October when the Ulster question was first discussed, the Irish delegates in London had not yet received official proposals on Ulster from the Dáil Cabinet.[69] And the failure to demand at the beginning a united Ireland outright showed an unfortunate lack of tactical sense when considering that Irish unity was the issue on which they would prefer to break. Here was valuable ground ceded from the beginning.

A part of this error was the failure to realise the significance of the transfer of services as a diplomatic counter. At one point during the session of 17 October, Collins and Griffith touched on the condition of the Northern administration:

> Mr M. Collins: You will be faced with the necessity of coercing large districts into allegiance to this new North Ireland parliament. They have made no arrangements to function.
> Prime Minister: That is because of this conference. They would go ahead tomorrow.
> Mr A. Griffith: It will never function. 400,000 people when dragged in will not obey it.[70]

From this exchange can be gleaned two important points. First, that the British had succeeded in camouflaging the Northern state by means of withholding its services temporarily; this would seem to have encouraged Sinn Féin to see partition as negotiable and thus attract them to the conference. Now that the conference had opened, Lloyd George could begin to construct a defence based on the difficulty of getting anything out of Ulster. And secondly, although the Irish delegates were aware that the Northern government was not functioning, they were apparently unaware of the advantages that could be taken of this. Should it not have been part of the Irish strategy to see that while negotiations continued it *did not* function? At least, should the Irish delegates not have pressed Lloyd George for concessions from Craig before the Northern government was allowed its services? It was a valuable card the Irish did not know was in their hand, and Lloyd George did not hesitate to steal it. For in his defence against the 31 October motion of censure in the Commons, he was armed with Sinn Féin assurances not only on allegiance, citizenship and defence, but also Ulster. He gave to the House his unequivocal pledge 'that unless something happens in the course of the next few days, one way or the other, that puts the position right from the point of view of the Act of 1920, we will, either under powers we have got . . . confer the necessary powers upon the northern parliament, or we shall ask the house of Commons during the present session to pass a short act enabling us to do so'.[71] In the subsequent two weeks Lloyd George gave the appearance of being committed to try and persuade Craig to accept the overriding Dublin Parliament. He was even said to be telling his most intimate friends that if he failed, he would resign.[72] But Lloyd George was an old hand at the Irish question. As an MP he had seen 'Ulster' block Irish settlements time and time again since 1893. He was long familiar with Northern intransigence and had long learned the lesson that the most expedient policy for the British was partition and safeguarding the Ulster Unionists from political control by Southern nationalists. Rather than drive Craig to the wall and in the process force his own hand on whether to resign, he continued to elicit provisional concessions from Griffith, so much so that Sinn Féin had lost on the Ulster question long before they were aware of it. Were his overtures to Craig a real attempt to exert pressure or a demonstration for the benefit of the public and of Sinn Féin? For while he was supposed to be drawing Craig into a united Ireland he was, on the contrary, giving something very important away to him: that is, the North's services, to be transferred without a Southern government in existence. We shall allow Sir James Craig to describe what happened at his meeting with Lloyd George on 5 November 1921.

'I call it Black Saturday', Craig afterwards told the Northern Parliament, 'for it will always stand out in my memory as one of the darkest days that I have had to deal with since I have been associated with the Ulster question'. Summoned to Downing Street he arrived at 12 noon and announced that he would discuss nothing until the North's administrative powers were duly conferred. 'I do not for a moment', his speech to the Northern Parliament continued,

> desire to create the impression that either the prime minister or any member of His Majesty's government was using the holding back of the transfer of services as an engine to manoeuvre us into a different

position. Far from that being the case I can only say that the moment word was given that we were to have these services transferred, each one of His Majesty's ministers wholeheartedly and energetically set to work to see that we were met in our just demands.[73]

But the morning's cheerful and prompt readiness to transfer services to the North was apparently meant to provide sugar coating for the pill Lloyd George would ask him to swallow in the afternoon. 'Not a moment was necessary', stated Craig with proud indignation, 'to enable me to make up my mind . . . I told him it was utterly impossible'.[74] Thus, at worst, to Craig the timing of the transfer of services was a measure of cajolery. Had the Irish been stronger negotiators and tactically wiser, might it not have been a trade-off for a significant concession?

On 9 November the king made two orders in council under section 69 of the Government of Ireland Act. The one empowered the Lord-Lieutenant to appoint, on a temporary basis, Southern Ireland's representatives on the Joint Exchequer Board and Civil Service Committee.[75] The other transferred services to Northern Ireland on appointed days: 22 November, 1 December, 1 January, and 1 February.[76] Partition was now legally complete. Between 9 November and 6 December (the date of the Anglo-Irish Treaty) only one lonely voice from the ranks of Sinn Féin was raised in warning against the partition of the civil service. On 15 November 1921 the following letter was written to Dáil Eireann's Ministry of Home Affairs:

I respectfully beg to bring to your notice the fact that most of the government offices in Dublin have been notified that one-third of their staffs are to proceed under pain of dismissal to Belfast for the purpose of floating the various departments under the Partition Act. Lloyd George is apparently using the truce for the purpose of supplying Ulster with as many vested interests as possible. The transfer of these officials to Northern Ireland by orders in council in my opinion is a distinct breach of the truce and should receive the earnest and early consideration of the government of the Irish Republic. If these officials are prevented from going to Belfast it will practically make the Partition Act ineffective.[77]

So wrote one W. McKevitt, an official in the National Health Insurance Commission and volunteer in the 4th battalion, Dublin Brigade, IRA. The statement was not accurate in all its detail, but at least someone in the republican ranks realised the political value of British state apparatus in Ireland. The British certainly realised it. The administration of Ireland was both an instrument of power through which the British government exercised political control overall and a tactical weapon in Anglo-Irish negotiations consolidating at the right moment the partition of Ireland. The remark oft-repeated in many historical accounts, that during the war of independence British administration was 'brought to a standstill' or supplanted by the machinery of the Dáil, is far from accurate. It is true that there were enormous difficulties in the Chief Secretary's Office up to the 1920 reforms, that local government bodies were, in large part, operating in the name of the Dáil and that local jurisprudence was frequently in the hands of Dáil courts. Yet, most central government bodies under British auspices continued to function normally. Only in the weeks immediately prior to the truce in July 1921 did the Dáil's ministers consider direct 'action' against British central government in Ireland. Even then the prime targets were to be the instruments of law and order: Dublin Castle officials, Privy Council members, the Lord Chancellor and other judges, Four Courts officials, Crown prosecutors, sheriffs, and so on. Action against British tax collecting was also contemplated; but both Michael Collins and Austin Stack remained reluctant to interfere with public services such as the Post Office, education and other British services which the republicans 'would be unwilling to get rid of'.[78] To Sinn Féin most central government departments were significant more as symbols of authority than as instruments of power. In this chapter we have seen how little they regarded the transfer of services to the North as a matter of practical and political importance. In the next chapter it will be seen how the British were in the meantime quietly preparing the civil service for devolution and partition and how the civil service responded.

Notes

1   See C. Townshend, *The British Campaign in Ireland, 1919–21: The Development of Political and Military Policies* (London, 1975), chs 13–18.

2   See D. G. Boyce, *Englishmen and Irish Troubles: British Public Opinion and the Making of Irish Policy, 1918–22* (London, 1972).

3   T. Jones, *Whitehall Diary, Vol. 3: Ireland 1918–25* (London, 1971), p. 48.

4   Cabinet conclusions 12(21)(9), 8 March 1921, PRO CAB 23/24.

5   'The Irish elections and an offer of a truce. Memorandum by Dr Christopher Addison', CP 2829, 13 April 1921, and memorandum by the Secretary of State for India [E. S. Montagu), CP 2840, 14 April 1921, PRO CAB 24/122. Jones, op. cit., p. 53.

6   Townshend, op. cit., pp. 175, 178.

7 ibid., pp. 181–90.

8 Jones, op. cit., pp. 74–9.

9 *Belfast Gazette*, 7 June 1921.

10 'Government of Ireland Act. Memorandum by the Chief Secretary for Ireland', CP 2641, 27 February 1921, PRO CAB 24/120.

11 Clark to Craig, 21 February 1921, PRONI FIN 18/1/194.

12 P. Buckland, *The Factory of Grievances: Devolved Government in Northern Ireland, 1921–39* (Dublin and New York, 1979), p. 9.

13 'Government departments of the Northern Ireland civil service, n.d. [marked 'copy sent to Sir J. Craig, 7 April 1921'], PRONI FIN 18/1/238.

14 ibid.

15 Notes of an interview between Sir James Craig and Sir Ernest Clark, 6 April 1921, PRONI FIN 18/1/238.

16 Clark to Harrison, 25 March 1921, PRONI FIN 18/1/195. Clark added, 'I am speaking, of course, of the party which it is presumed will be in the majority (2 to 1). Great Britain is regarded with intense affection as the "Big Brother", but at present (alas!) Southern Ireland is not a relation.'

17 Cope to Clark, 15 March 1921, PRONI FIN 18/1/238.

18 Clark to Cope, 17 March 1921, PRONI FIN 18/1/238.

19 Townshend, op. cit., p. 124.

20 See Clark to Cope, 29 November 1920, PRONI FIN 44/1/1. In this letter, primarily concerned with liability for telephone expenses at Clark's residence, Clark asks Cope: 'Are you coming up to see me before Christmas – not next week-end, as I shall be away, but come as soon as you can.'

21 'Periscope' [G. C. Duggan], 'The last days of Dublin Castle', *Blackwood's Magazine*, vol. 212, no. 1,282 (August 1922), p. 182.

22 ibid.

23 Draft conclusions, meeting of the Cabinet, 4 October 1921, PRONI CAB 4/24/4. Buckland, op. cit., pp. 188–92.

24 'Periscope', op. cit., p. 184.

25 Clark recalled that Anderson had held 'the non-political point of view of an English civil servant steeped in its [sic] best traditions, including non-interference in politics'. Clark papers, PRONI D 1022.

26 ibid.

27 Anderson to Sir Warren Fisher, 9 June 1921, PRO T 162/74/E.6968.

28 Preliminary draft conclusion, 24 June 1921, PRONI CAB 4/5/2.

29 Anderson to Thompson (Inland Revenue), Hamilton (Customs and Excise) and Murray (Post Office), July 1921, PRONI FIN 18/1/294.

30 Minute sheet summarising memoranda by Thompson, Hamilton and Murray, 27 July 1921, PRONI FIN 18/1/294. Full texts of the memoranda are in the file.

31 Cabinet conclusions, 4 August 1921, PRONI CAB 4/12/2.

32 Anderson to Clark, 27 July 1921, PRONI FIN 18/1/294.

33   Hansard (Northern Ireland) (Commons), vol. I, col. 207.

34   ibid.

35   See correspondence in PRO T 162/74/E.6968 ('Northern Ireland government: arrangement for the loan of officers to'), hereafter cited as E.6968.

36   Ramsay to Clark, 23 June 1921, E.6968.

37   Cuthbertson's appointment was probably a move by the Treasury to ensure financial control during the transfer of services. While working with the Northern Minister of Finance, Cuthbertson upheld staunch Treasury orthodoxies relating to the predominance of Finance over other departments (see minute sheet, Cuthbertson to Pollock, 22 October 1921, PRONI FIN 20/EST/5045) and corresponded frequently with Treasury (Ireland) on the cost effects of departmental partition (see T 158 passim).

38   Ramsay to Craig, 15 June 1921, E.6968. Memorandum and staff lists in SPOI CSORP 1921/2602/79.

39   Hansard (Northern Ireland)(Commons), vol. I, col. 207.

40   Ramsay to Craig, 15 June 1921, E.6968.

41   Ramsay to Clark, 21 June 1921, E.6968.

42   Ramsay to Clark, 5 July 1921, E.6968.

43   Clark to Ramsay, 11 July 1921, E.6968.

44   Clark to Campbell, 23 July 1921, PRONI FIN 18/1/303.

45   Draft conclusions, meeting of Cabinet, 4 August 1921, PRONI CAB 4/12/2. Later, A. N. Bonaparte Wyse, not only Catholic but a County Dubliner, would become assistant secretary, and then secretary, in the Department of Education. He and the minister, Lord Londonderry, would put up a vain struggle against *de facto* denominational education. (See D. H. Akenson, *Education and Enmity: The Control of Schooling in Northern Ireland, 1920–50* (Newton Abbot, 1973).

46   Ronan Fanning, *The Irish Department of Finance* (Dublin, 1978), p. 72.

47   Duggan, op. cit., p. 184.

48   Clark papers, PRONI D 1022.

49   10 & 11 Geo. V, ch. 67, sect. 32.

50   ibid., sect. 59.

51   Memorandum by Sir Francis Greer, appendix to 'The Home Rule Act. Memorandum by the Chief Secretary for Ireland', CP 2444, 12 January 1921, PRO CAB 24/118. Memorandum by R. G. Hawtrey [Treasury official], 'The Government of Ireland Act. Financial procedure', March 1921, PRO T 163/4/G.256/1.

52   The Act contemplated that services would be transferred to both governments within three months of their establishment, and during this period funds were to be made available for expenses incurred in the opening of parliaments and the setting up of ministries. In July and August advances of £20,000 and £10,000 had been made to the Northern exchequer; but when the political position remained in stalemate the North requested and received an additional £130,000 financial resources calculated to keep its skeletal government functioning beyond the three-month deadline and to the end of the financial year. See PRONI FIN 18/1/293, 391; PRO T 192/63; Treasury (Ireland) letter 832/21 to [? the under-secretary], 20 June 1921, PRO T 158/3; Sir John Anderson [as secretary, Treasury (Ireland)] to the secretary, Ministry of Finance, Northern Ireland, 16 July 1921, PRO T 158/4.

53 Although he 'deprecated [Macready's suggestion of] giving up the power to enforce trial by courts martial, which he felt brought about more speedy, and therefore more effective justice'. Proceedings of a meeting [marked 'very secret'], 23 June 1921, PRONI CAB 4/4/1.

54 Report by the Secretary of the Cabinet on a visit to London, 'very secret', 10 August 1921, PRONI CAB 4/14/11.

55 Memorandum by the secretary of the Ministry of Home Affairs, 12 August 1921, PRONI CAB 4/15/1.

56 10 & 11 Geo. V, ch. 67, sect. 72.

57 Hansard (Northern Ireland)(Commons), vol. I, p. 46.

58 Craig to Greenwood, 25 August 1921, PRONI CAB 4/5/4; 1 September 1921, PRONI CAB 4/22/7; and 22 and 27 September 1921 enclosed with memorandum by the Chief Secretary to the Cabinet, CP 3369, 8 October 1921, PRO CAB 24/128.

59 ibid., 16 September 1921.

60 ibid., 22 September 1921.

61 ibid., 27 September 1921.

62 ibid., Greenwood to the British Cabinet, 8 October 1921.

63 See Jones, op. cit., pp. 99–101, 105–6.

64 ibid., p. 110.

65 ibid., p. 137.

66 ibid., pp. 151–2.

67 ibid., p. 151.

68 The classic work on the Treaty negotiations is Lord Longford, *Peace by Ordeal* (London, 1972).

69 ibid., p. 128.

70 Jones, op. cit., p. 136.

71 Hansard (Commons), 5th series, vol. 147, cols. 1414–5.

72 Jones, op. cit., p. 152, editorial note.

73 Hansard (Northern Ireland)(Commons), vol. 1, cols. 288–9, 29 November 1921.

74 ibid.

75 *Statutory Rules and Orders*, 1921.

76 22 November was appointed for the transfer of services in relation to law and order, justice, taxes and other financial services, the collection of land purchase annuities, existing public loans and the management of the church temporalities fund. 1 December was appointed for the transfer of local government, housing, public health, poor law, roads and road transport, ferries and bridges, firearms and explosives, prisons, lunatics, industrial and reformatory schools and old-age pensions. 1 January 1922 was appointed for the transfer of services relating to labour, commerce, health insurance, agriculture and all the remaining Irish services, except for education, science and art, and technical instruction, whose appointed day was 1 February.

77 McKevitt to the Ministry of Home Affairs, Dáil Eireann, 15 November 1921, SPOI DE 2/424.

78   See memorandum [by Austin Stack, Minister of Home Affairs] circulated to each
     Dáil Eireann minister, 24 June 1921, Collins to de Valera, 27 June 1921, Stack to
     O'Hegarty, 4 July 1921, SPOI DE 2/296. De Valera told Stack it was 'better to take
     no action during the present negotiations'. Stack thought, none the less that there
     was 'no reason . . . for delaying our preparations'.

5 Partition and the Civil Service

The order in council of 9 November transferring services to Northern Ireland was expedited in the midst of the Treaty negotiations in an attempt to mollify Sir James Craig and his colleagues, and to assure them that the North would enjoy local autonomy whether or not there was an overriding Dublin Parliament. In the South, by contrast, the British played down the transfer of services. They were alive to the need of a low profile for the machinery of partition before definite agreement with Sinn Féin was reached. Thus the Civil Service Committee, responsible for 'allocating' officials to the Northern government, did not meet until 8 December, two days after the Treaty was signed and after the first two appointed days – 22 November and 1 December – had passed. Yet things did not work quite according to plan under the Government of Ireland Act, when the establishment of the committee encountered resistance from Dublin civil servants. Mass action on the part of the staff was instrumental in delaying compulsory transfer until the provisional government came to power and banned the transfer of staff against their will. In the end only a handful of volunteers were allocated to Belfast. However, before dealing with these events in more detail, it is desirable to set them in context by examining British and Northern Ireland Treasury policies towards the Irish civil service in the previous two years.

British plans for the civil service in Ireland in these years were to implement the 'Whitley' reorganisation schemes and to allocate staff between North and South. 'Reorganisation' and 'allocation' became watchwords in the civil service. Both aspects of the policy were guided through by Treasury (Ireland), the Treasury division set up under Sir John Anderson replacing the Treasury Remembrancer's office in May 1920. Under the assistant secretary, A. P. Waterfield, Treasury (Ireland) personnel set themselves the task of handing over to Home Rule governments a civil service that was economical and efficient. Until the transfer of services Waterfield and his men regarded themselves as 'trustees for the interests of the Irish taxpayer, who is going to find it by no means a simple job to make home rule pay'.[1] It was not so much that a mood of benevolence towards Ireland had suddenly overwhelmed the British Treasury. Rather, the Treasury was acutely aware that civil service economy in Home Rule Ireland was financially in Britain's interest. After all, the annual 'imperial contribution' to Britain from the Irish governments would be increased or reduced depending on the rise and fall in the cost of Irish administration. Thus, as Waterfield explained to a colleague in Whitehall, 'the more money the new Irish governments spend on the civil services, the stronger will be their claim for a drastic revision of the Government of Ireland Act, and a reduction of the £18,000,000 contribution. It is therefore a matter of importance to the imperial exchequer to insist on economy as far as we can'.[2]

Achieving economy in the civil services of the United Kingdom as a whole was at this time closely bound up with the Whitley reorganisation. This was a major programme for the restructuring of grades and salaries. The 'Whitley system',[3] a product of the government's postwar reconstruction programme, was originally intended as an instrument for settling labour disputes in private industry. By establishing government-sponsored councils comprising employers and workers it was believed to be an antidote to socialism. Over 100 industries eventually set up Whitley councils, but only vigorous agitation by civil service staff associations finally persuaded the government to practice what they preached and apply the system to their own departments.[4] The machinery established under the system provided for the first time ever a medium through which staff and the higher echelons of administration could exchange views and reach compromises on several matters – of which reorganisation became the most important between 1920 and 1922. The Treasury's role in the approval of departmental reorganisation schemes in Ireland fell on the shoulders of Waterfield and his staff, whose goal was to see that all Irish departmental schemes were operating before the appointed day for the transfer of services.[5]

But, as in Britain, the working out of reorganisation schemes became a matter of contention between the Treasury and the staff side. The object of reorganisation was to reshape the general service grades of the civil service into the 'administrative', 'executive' (higher and lower) and 'clerical' classes, relating classes, grades and salaries to work performed. In theory, departmental councils formulated reorganisation schemes and submitted them to the Treasury for approval. However, as part of its 'approval' procedure the Treasury made its own detailed inquiry 'into the number, grading, degree of responsibility, hours of work, co-ordination of work and rate of remuneration' of the entire staff of the department.[6] The Whitley councils in the departments then found themselves confronted with the Treasury's counter-proposals, more often than not presuming heavy establishment reductions. In both Britain and Ireland this generated strenuous opposition from the staff side. What Treasury (Ireland) was doing, the Irish staff contended, was 'to scrap completely the schemes framed by departments and to impose without discussion unalterable schemes of its own invention'.[7] Sir Henry Robinson's memoirs leave a particularly harsh view of the Treasury's role in Ireland:

> It is an unfortunate thing that Waterfield and his staff, who had no experience of what was before them, should have been sent over to Ireland with so free a hand. All the public departments had already been cut to the bone in pursuance of Treasury circulars on war economies, and the civil servants who had hoped for some sympathy and protection from the British Treasury when matters came to be wound up, whereas, on the contrary, they now found themselves down and out, faced the new peril of being at the mercy of soulless young Englishmen bent on further retrenchments at all hazards, who seemed to think the Irish civil servants had little to complain about if they were not thrown penniless into the street.[8]

Waterfield's policies were doubtless sufficiently tough to generate resentment, but Robinson's remarks were probably somewhat hyperbolic. M. J. Gallagher, one of the most important staff representatives of the period, in later life recalled a view of Waterfield which, though possibly mellow from the passage of time, nevertheless displays a genuine respect likely to have been present in the early 1920s:

> He was thorough-going and painstaking, and he made a close inspection of the work of the various grades in each department in an effort to establish a norm. Those schemes of reorganization had been prepared in the departments and passed through the departmental Whitley Councils in accordance with the new dispensation. He was in complete agreement with staff side proposals for bringing out the best that was in a man instead of tying him down to work of measured ability. I found him easy to get on with; he appeared to speak his mind, and did not give the impression that he was merely listening as a formality. He was cooperative when we had a good case but he could be merciless if we attempted to push a lame duck through.[9]

Thus the staff's irritation with Waterfield on account of the nature of his duties was mixed with personal respect for the man and his efforts to be fair. The following contemporary profile from the *Irish Civil Servant* pawkily confirms this view:

> Sandy and slim, hook-nose on which rests a pair of spectacles . . . quick in his movements as a bird – such are the immediate noticeable characteristics of this now well-known Treasury representative. Alas! that it cannot be said he is popular as well. But in the nature of things Mr Waterfield cannot be *persona grata*, at least with the staff side, for his is the amiable occupation of tearing schemes to pieces as might

some bird of prey, until the staff side, and sometimes even the head of the department fail to recognise their own handiwork. Although he appears to revel in this sort of thing we must assume that he is merely acting zealously as a guardian of the Treasury, whose slogan, especially on the Whitley battlefield is 'economy'. Blessed word! What crimes are committed in your name, how many executive posts are slaughtered to the vote-catching music of your syllables! Zealous though he undoubtedly is, for was it not whispered when first pointed out to us that six o'clock in the morning found him at his desk? Ruthless though he be, the plea of no funds is not made until the case has been fairly well thrashed out. If the staff must be 'knocked out' it might as well be by the swift methods of a Carpentier; it is less tedious, and recovery is more rapid perhaps.[10]

Of course, Waterfield was not in the business of courting popularity with the staff. Yet with some justification he could claim that he was fighting for their interests. His objective was to guide the schemes of all Irish departments through to their completion before the transfer of services. Once the new governments were in control there was no obligation on their part to implement incomplete or outstanding schemes. The reaction of the Northern government to the Whitley programme was hinted at in August 1921. Sir James Craig, noting that reorganisation schemes 'pledged the financial resources' of the new governments, proposed to Greenwood that they 'should not be sanctioned before the transfers were made'.[11] The staff had accused Waterfield of using the race against the appointed day 'as a convenient excuse to hustle the service into the acceptance of bad schemes';[12] but in the light of the likely attitude of native government it was almost certainly in the staff's interests to have reorganisation implemented by the British Treasury before they were handed over. Also, Waterfield, although bound to act in accordance with the Treasury's policy for the United Kingdom as a whole, argued with his Whitehall colleagues for the separate treatment of Ireland in view of the special political circumstances. Throughout 1921 he urged Whitehall to allow Irish schemes to become operable by a definite date, even though this would be in advance of the date for United Kingdom schemes.[13] For a very long time Whitehall resisted this proposal. They themselves had been unable to agree with the staff in Britain on the 'effective date' from which new pay scales would be imposed; they were therefore reluctant to add to the list of English staff grievances by appointing an exclusive date for the Irish. Also, despotic Treasury officials, who had little enough sympathy for the view of English staffs had less for the Irish. In the summer of 1921 the Irish staff were seen to exploit the uncertainty surrounding the appointed day (because of political negotiations with Sinn Féin); that is, they tended to delay agreement to the brink of the transfer of services in the hope of securing better terms. The attitude of Whitehall officials was that if the appointed day passed without agreement it would be the staff's own hard luck.[14] However, Waterfield responded that although the Treasury had 'a perfectly good excuse for the failure to reorganize before the appointed day, if the staff sides refuse to accept our schemes, and we can consequently argue that the fault is theirs and not ours, yet we must admit that such a failure is a confession of weakness of administration on our part which we ought to endeavour to overcome if we can'.[15] Furthermore, he continued to insist that Ireland required separate treatment. Finally, in September he stated that Treasury (Ireland) 'cannot wait for the English departments to set the pace and decide the principle . . . We must therefore hold it to be absolutely necessary that we should proceed to get our schemes under way forthwith, so as to be as far as possible prepared for a transfer on October 1st'.[16] From 22 September schemes in Irish departments began to go into operation. By early December Waterfield felt 'very proud of the fact that almost without exception all the Irish departments proper, i.e. apart from those with headquarters in England, have their schemes formally approved and with very few exceptions have already been authorised to put them into force'.[17] Most schemes in fact appear to have been implemented in time without too great dissatisfaction on the part of the staff.

Arrangements for allocating staff, on the other hand, were met by a potentially explosive situation. With the signing of the Treaty on 6 December 1921, agitation against compulsory transfer to Belfast spread throughout the civil service in Dublin. The two staff representatives on the Civil Service Committee withdrew from its proceedings, and the Irish Civil Service Alliance, representing all staff associations, brought the committee to court. This incident was perhaps the climax of tensions that had been building since the Government of Ireland Act was passed, between civil servants in Dublin and the Ulster Unionist leaders.

It seems to have been in March 1921 that mistrust and suspicions began to mount between Dublin civil servants and their prospective Belfast employers. We have already seen in Chapter 4 how rumours were circulating Dublin departments that the better posts in the new Northern administration were being filled by English officials; and how Sir Ernest Clark quickly retorted to A. W. Cope that if reports in Belfast were true that Dublin departments were reserving their less dynamic officials for transfer to the North, then the North would be forced to look to London departments for its principal officials.[18] Mistrust intensified when the Northern Parliament and government opened in June and certain Dublin officials were seen to be paying visits to Belfast. One Dublin civil service journal could hear 'the jangling of the wires that are being pulled' and decried the 'half-furtive journeying to Belfast by more or less exalted civil civil servants'.[19] In early July a delegation of Dublin civil servants met with Hugh Pollock, the Northern Finance Minister, hoping 'to seek an understanding on the policy of initial recruitment, prospects and conditions of service in the northern departments' in order that 'applications for voluntary transfer would be forthcoming in sufficient numbers'.[20] One of the delegation, M. J. Gallagher,[21] in his memoirs recalls raising the matter of unfair access to positions in the North for certain officials:

> I took up with him the preferential selection of men from Dublin and suggested that the transfers should be carried out only as the Civil Service Committee directed, and that whatever disposition he wished to make of them should be deferred until they were at work in Belfast. The handpicking of men would be unpopular, to say the least of it, among those who had no sponsors in Belfast and who would have to go with the crowd. He did not like that but brushed it aside, saying that the government must have key men at all costs.[22]

The delegates made little impact on Pollock. They were more or less patted on the head and sent home with assurances 'that there was no intention on behalf of the northern government to interfere with the position or prospects of transferred civil servants, but that their whole object was to get an efficient service in working order as practically as possible'.[23] The delegation left Belfast without the sense of having their questions satisfactorily answered and continued to feel insecure about the Northern government's intentions. In late August they again wrote to Pollock having 'learned with grave concern that appointments have been made to higher posts, in certain of the new departments, of civil servants who are not "existing Irish officers"'. Clark attempted to reassure them that these were 'expert' officials on temporary loan from United Kingdom departments who held positions for which there were no counterparts in Dublin and whose appointments were essential to founding new ministries.[24] But the Dublin staffs remained mistrustful and incredulous.

Much of the difficulty may have been caused in large part by lack of communication between Northern and Southern authorities. This is borne out in Clark's correspondence, in which he betrayed inconsistency with his Dublin Castle colleagues on the procedure for dividing departmental staffs. In January the Chief Secretary had directed departments to draw up provisional lists of their civil servants indicating their availability for service in the North or the South.[25] Clark, believing the information was to be centralised in Dublin Castle, tried to discover from Sturgis '(a) the men who are assignable [to the Northern government], and (b) the men who are willing to come'.[26] However, he was told by Anderson that it was unlikely 'that men will be found willing to commit themselves long in advance of the actual date'; and, in any event, the North should rely on their own departmental heads, once appointed, to communicate directly with Dublin departments, to see who was willing to come to the North.[27] Clark failed to see the point. In June he wrote to Anderson that it was now essential for the North to have these lists.[28] Anderson's reply hints of exasperation:

If you look again [at the CSO circular], while heads of departments were asked to prepare a provisional distribution of staff we did not ask them to send the particulars into the Irish government. The omission was quite deliberate. The matter is rather a delicate one, and I do not think it should be the subject of official correspondence at this stage. Our object was to ensure that the ground should have been explored by the heads of departments themselves, so that they might be in a position to advise the new governments when time came. As I have said before, I think the northern departments must get into personal touch as soon as possible with the heads of United Kingdom departments administering transferrable services. I am sure that it is not possible to deal with these matters satisfactorily by correspondence, nor I think can the work be centralized in Belfast. I am sure the whole thing will prove quite simple if it is tackled on the right lines. Let the new ministers get the general hang of things by personal conference, then let them settle personnel for the principal posts, and after that there should be little difficulty in working out schemes of organization and provisional establishments. I keep on saying the same thing time after time but I am sure that in this matter I am right. We here in the chief secretary's office are really not concerned, except as regards our own branch of the work.[29]

Clark apologised for misinterpreting the circular and the Northern government undertook to appoint its departmental heads who would contact Dublin departments about available staff.[30] However, Pollock and Craig showed increasing apprehension about civil servants coming from Dublin. In August, for example, Pollock was disturbed to learn that the Civil Service Committee would be distributing officials on the basis of 'equity' rather than on what each government felt it needed.[31] Should the Northern government be landed with staff in excess of requirements they would have to be either employed or pensioned off. Also there would be scant room for the large number of local applicants from the six counties. Pollock therefore began to look for ways of reducing the number of staff eligible for allocation to the North. One of his proposals was to reserve to the Northern government final approval of the Whitley reorganisation schemes.[32] Another was to hold an inquiry among Dublin staffs to determine excess numbers, who would then be absorbed into the imperial service. This, he believed, was 'a more equitable arrangement than transferring them here, where, if they were excessive, they would have to come on our superannuation list'.[33] Both proposals proved to be unacceptable to the British. Then in September Sir James Craig, in his attempt to persuade the British to hurry the transfer of services, proposed dropping the Civil Service Committee:

> If Sir John Anderson invites to a conference the heads of departments here to consult with their opposite numbers in Dublin and arrange with them in terms of a circular to be addressed to the civil servants generally inviting them to choose under which government they will serve (quite freely and uninfluenced), we would be able to secure a sufficient nucleus to justify our taking over the services on an appointed day yet to be fixed . . . This method would, in my opinion, be much preferable to ordering the personnel here and there, possibly saddling on the north men who had no desire to come and whom the north were not particularly anxious to have. The feeling here is strong that as many places as possible should be found for the 1,600 odd applicants who have filled up forms for engagement in our local civil service.[34]

Again this was rejected by the British who were not prepared to recast the provisions of the Government of Ireland Act to suit Craig, especially at a moment when they were trying to reach agreement with Sinn Féin. Nor were they prepared to allow the North to take only volunteers from Dublin if this meant that the British were left with the liability of pensioning off those made redundant in the South. The Northern government, in short, wanted a trimmed and inexpensive, reliable and loyal – indeed one suspects mainly local – body of volunteers for their civil service. Irish officials, on the other hand, were keen to see that their rights as existing Irish officers were not prejudiced by the policies of the Northern government. Such mutual suspicions were not a promising prelude to the transfer of services. However, the Northern anxiety that their departments would be staffed by unwilling Southerners was relieved by the unwilling Southerners themselves, as we shall see.

When the Transfer of Services Order suddenly appeared on 9 November Anderson had to act quickly to prepare *ad hoc* arrangements to enable the North to administer services from the appointed day. On

10 November he directed departments 'to allot for temporary service to the north the officers who are in their opinion suitable for such duty, notwithstanding that they may intend to recommend them to the civil service committee for ultimate retention in the south'.[35] He noted that 'the existing staff, when divided, will not be fully sufficient for the separate administration of the services in question in both areas. In such cases it should be borne in mind that greater weight must be given to the needs of the newly created departments in the northern area . . .'[36] But what now of Northern Ireland's permanent staff? Would there be sufficient volunteers to fill the ranks of Northern departments? In fact it had become apparent that few officials in Dublin wished to work in Belfast. Waterfield thought it was 'practically certain that the balance will have to be made up by compulsory allocation'.[37] But this was not to be.

The Civil Service Committee first met on 8 December.[38] The committee was fortunate in its make-up in that four of its seven members had all been actively involved in the Whitley negotiations and thus had a 'working understanding of each other'.[39] Two were from the 'official side', Waterfield representing the Treasury and James MacMahon (Anderson's co-under-secretary) representing the 'Southern Ireland government'; and two from the 'staff side', Michael Gallagher and Sam Sloan representing 'existing Irish officers'.[40] The Northern government was represented by Sir Ernest Clark, who by this time had become permanent secretary in the Department of Finance, the North's most senior civil service position.[41] The 1920 Act provided that a further member be appointed by a British secretary of state, and in order to strengthen its hand on the committee the Treasury saw that the Home Secretary's appointment was a Treasury official – R. A. Johnson agreeing to the task. Finally the chairman, appointed by the king, was Sir Courtauld Thompson.

The career of the committee thus constituted was, however, short and stormy. The signing of the Treaty caused some considerable confusion in the Irish civil service, especially in so far as it seemed to place a question mark on the future of Northern Ireland. Was the North not theoretically a part of the Irish Free State? In time would it not become, at best, a regional administration, possibly with a restricted area under an all-Ireland parliament? Should not the Free State government be involved in the allocation of officers? And since the Government of Ireland Act appeared to have been superseded, was the Civil Service Committee the proper body to allocate staff? It seems that Gallagher and Sloan were personally not opposed to the continuation of the committee as were many of their colleagues; they were more concerned with achieving a fair deal for all individual civil servants than they were with the political question.[42] On the other hand, their constituency was composed of the existing Irish officers, many of whom, emboldened by the Treaty, now affected a militant stance against the committee. Thus at the first meeting Gallagher and Sloan submitted a letter of protest on behalf of the Irish Civil Service Alliance. The statement challenged the validity of the constitution of the civil service committee inasmuch as the member to be appointed by the government of Southern Ireland has not been properly appointed in a manner laid down by the act'.[43] To emphasise their views a mass meeting was staged on 12 December. It was attended by 'about 1500 men and women representing all existing Irish officers of the permanent and temporary staffs', and including representatives of all staff associations. The meeting 'unanimously' passed a resolution

> that even if the civil service committee were legally constituted, in view of the situation created by recent political developments, and in view of the fact that the vast majority of existing Irish Officers look forward with pleasure to serving under the government which will emanate from the Anglo-Irish Treaty, this meeting desires to protest against the eleventh-hour attempt to deprive them of this privilege by the institution of a body nominally intended to safeguard their interests, but whose real function is to facilitate a political manoeuvre.[44]

The staff were limited in the extent to which they could oppose the committee. In the Dáil, Sinn Féin had not yet agreed whether to accept the Treaty, and were therefore in no position to deal with such details as the position of the civil service. But after taking legal advice, the Civil Service Alliance saw that the committee's proceedings could be brought to a halt if the High Court would grant an injunction on the basis that MacMahon's appointment was *ultra vires*. The alliance chairman, Dr Con Murphy, wished to go even further and tried to persuade Sloan and Gallagher to dissociate themselves completely from the committee. The two officials refused to close the staff's options by such action; but they agreed not to sit on the committee until the High Court decision was handed down. On the 15th they consequently withdrew rather than 'expose themselves to legal proceedings and the consequences thereof'.[45]

British interpretation of the Treaty naturally differed from that of the Dublin civil service staffs. As far as the British were concerned the Government of Ireland Act's provisions for the method of staff distribution still held. Sir John Anderson assured the committee that should a High Court decision invalidate the order in council under which MacMahon had been appointed, 'steps would be taken to place the matter beyond doubt by appropriate legislation'.[46] Anderson also favoured a firm line against the staff in their other militant action. In view of their boycott of the committee's questionnaire, he thought they might be approached with a 'friendly warning' that 'the government here will take a very serious view of refusal on the part of individuals to give information required to enable transfers to be carried out'.[47] As Gallagher and Sloan were aware, the British still held the purse strings. However, neither MacMahon nor Waterfield thought the hard line appropriate. It was 'premature, if not useless', MacMahon replied to Anderson,

> to approach the staff side at this moment. We shall have enough work for the committee for the next couple of meetings in allocating establishments and in transferring volunteers to Belfast. We know that there are volunteers and we have their names and at the last committee meeting we were all agreed that volunteers might be transferred at once. If and when the Treaty is ratified we can much more easily persuade the staff to accept what will then be an agreed constitution as between Dublin and Belfast.[48]

However, within the committee itself, North–South tensions were brewing. Gallagher found Clark particularly offensive with his bluster about 'setting up' the South African government in 1906; his being 'not at all disposed to see a more delicate position here'; and 'his "hill tribes" outlook . . . scarcely veiled'. 'He had a list of men he wanted transferred from Dublin and at once'. It was as though 'we were so many chattels to be divided up'. By contrast, Gallagher found MacMahon 'very amiable and willing', with 'a surpassing knowledge of the service and its aspirations'. MacMahon was, of course, no friend of the Ulster Unionists, and Gallagher found himself 'more and more drawn to him; we began mutually to support each other in what became more a north–south controversy rather than an official–staffside contest'.[49] For his part, Clark found the atmosphere of the committee to be uncongenial to Northern interests. He had brought with him 'letters from all the ministries of Northern Ireland containing lists of Irish officers who were stated by the ministry to be (a) persons whom the ministry were willing to have allocated; (b) who were willing to be so allocated; (c) to whose allocation the transferring departments had no objection'. Yet, the committee insisted 'that the information furnished by these letters should be supplemented by the signature to the questionnaire recently issued of all officers on those lists . . . and that then the lists should be sent to the transferring departments for any remarks'.[50] This irritated Clark. Although the aim of the committee was 'to make the position perfectly secure' – that is, that due reference would be given to the 1920 Act's provision to take the personal wishes of officers into account – Clark believed that the other members of the committee were deliberately perpetrating a delay in allocating officers to the North. 'It will be observed', he wrote years afterwards on his copy of the minutes of 15 December,

> how even in the absence of Messrs Sloan and Gallagher delay was immediately started. Any ordinary business body would have made the transfers on the statement of a government department that these conditions were fulfilled, running the risk of having to rectify errors afterwards, but the business of delay in order to hamper the northern government had already commenced. (It must be remembered that several of the departments in the north had started to function as early as 22 November 1921.)[51]

Even when the staff's litigation against the committee foundered in the High Court,[52] the committee continued to pursue the policy of exhausting the supply of volunteers for the North before resorting to compulsory allocation. Clark did not oppose this course in principle; by 17 January, 200 volunteers had been allocated to Belfast. However, the British officials in Dublin were concerned that the committee's work should get the approval of the provisional government now being formed in accordance with the Treaty. Were MacMahon and Waterfield therefore intent on delaying compulsory transfers until the provisional government came to power? If they hoped the new regime, in turn, would acquiesce in their work, they were soon disappointed. On 17 January the provisional government issued a proclamation which seemed to ban any further transfer of staff to Belfast.[53] In deference to the provisional government and to its political difficulties the committee decided to discontinue its meetings and to 'lay the question before the head of the Irish committee of the British cabinet'.[54] Clark was incensed. 'Were the British government', he remarked in his notes, 'really anxious for the northern government to succeed?'[55]

The ban was lifted some weeks later, but the committee's meeting was the last to be held in Dublin. In the words of a Treasury official, the civil service question had become 'removed to the whirl of Irish politics'.[56] The Civil Service Committee would eventually re-form in May 1922, but only to allocate officially the remaining 100 volunteers (who were in fact already in Belfast) and to begin the review of compensation cases for Northern officials.[57] Thus, although 'Irish services' were partitioned, the Irish civil service was not, except to the extent of the 300 volunteers. Compulsory allocation was avoided, in part, because of resistance from the civil service itself but also because, with the Treaty, the British saw the need to strengthen the ground of the Irish pro-Treaty party. In the South the Civil Service Committee thus became a symbol of the Government of Ireland Act and, as such, it was found expedient to jettison it.

Notes

1　Waterfield to Upcott, 15 June 1921, PRO T 158/3.
2　ibid.
3　After J. H. Whitley, subsequently Speaker of the House of Commons, who presided over the Reconstruction Ministry's Committee on relations between Employers and the Employed. See L. D. White, *Whitley Councils in the British Civil Service: A Study in Conciliation and Arbitration,* (Chicago, 1933).
4　In Great Britain the system functioned through the machinery of a central National Joint Council. This consisted of an equal number of representatives from the 'official' and 'staff' sides. Departmental joint councils were similarly constituted. While the National Joint Council came to decisions on general service questions, the departmental councils discussed departmental problems. Departmental councils referred to the national council for matters requiring decisions affecting overall policy. (See White, op. cit., ch. 1.)
5　In July 1919 an Irish Civil Service Joint Council was established with James MacMahon, the Dublin Castle under-secretary, as chairman. The Irish Joint Council held powers to discuss whatever it might judge to come under the headings '(a) exclusively Irish questions, or (b) exclusively Irish aspects of general questions'. However, much to the disappointment of the Irish civil service, the Treasury insisted that final approval for the Irish council's decisions should remain with the national council in London. After the Ramsay–Bunning Report of 17 February 1920, proposing a general scheme for civil service reorganisation, departmental joint councils were organised among Irish departments. Dublin departments frequently being rather small, several working in close proximity sometimes joined together to form single councils. For example, the Whitley council for the 'associated departments of Dublin Castle' represented the staffs of the Chief Secretary's Office, the RIC office, the general prisons board, etc. In all, fourteen departmental councils and ten working committees were organised among departments with headquarters in Ireland. Sources are: the papers of M. J. Gallagher, including his unpublished memoirs and a printed memorandum, marked 'private and confidential – not to be issued to the press', entitled 'Application of the Whitley Report to the administrative and legal departments of the civil service in Ireland. Report of a provisional joint committee appointed on 17 July 1919 by a conference of heads of government departments in Ireland and representatives of civil service associations'; MacMahon to the secretaries, National Whitley Council, 2777, 18 February 1920 and MacMahon to the Treasury, 4288, 18 February 1920, SPOI CSO government letter books, VIII B/8/13, pp. 184–5; *Irish Civil Servant,* vol. 1 no. 8. (June 1921), p. 52.
6　Anderson to the Lord Chancellor, 23 August 1921, PRO T 158/1.
7　*Irish Civil Servant,* vol. 1, no. 9 (July–August 1921), p. 59.
8　Sir H. A. Robinson, *Memories: Wise and Otherwise* (London 1923), pp. 293–4. On the other side of the coin, when Robinson retired in early 1922, Waterfield complained to Anderson that 'evidence is accumulating of the lamentable extravagance with which Sir Henry Robinson administered public funds as accounting officer of the local government board during his last two years of office'. (Waterfield to Anderson, TI 688/22, 727/22, 4 April 1922, PRO T 158/8).

9   M. J. Gallagher, 'Memories of a civil servant', unpublished memoirs.
10 *Irish Civil Servant*, vol. 1, no. 4 (February 1921) p. 22.
11 See correspondence in PRONI FIN 18/1/356.
12 As note 10.
13 Waterfield to R. A. Johnson, 21 December 1920 and 10 March 1921, PRO T 158/1,2; to R. R. Scott, 16 May 1921, PRO T 158/3; to J. H. Craig, 6 July 1921, PRO T 162/66/E.5703/1, 7 July 1921, PRO T 158/4, 19 August and 14 September 1921, PRO T 162/95/E.11302.
14 J. H. Craig [Treasury official] to Waterfield, 11 July 1921, PRO T 162/95/E.11302.
15 Waterfield to J. H. Craig, 7 July 1921, PRO T 158/4.
16 Waterfield to J. H. Craig, 14 September 1921, PRO T 162/95/E.11302.
17 Waterfield to Rowe-Dutton, 2 December 1921, PRO T 158/6.
18 See Chapter 4.
19 *Irish Civil Servant*, vol. 1, no. 9 (July–August 1921), p. 58.
20 Robson to Pollock, 14 June 1921; Robson to Petherick, 29 June 1921, PRONI FIN 18/1/283.
21 The others were W. G. Mulvin, W. Robson and Sam Sloan, all prominent in various staff associations and in the Irish Civil Service Alliance. Sloan and Gallagher were to become the staff representatives on the Civil Service Committee.
22 Gallagher, unpublished memoirs, op. cit.
23 Notes taken by Sir Ernest Clark of the interview between Pollock and civil service delegation, 2 July 1921, PRONI FIN 18/1/283.
24 Mulvin to Pollock, 29 August 1921, Petherick to Mulvin, 6 September 1921, PRONI FIN 18/1/283.
25 CSO circular 2429, 20 January 1921, copy in PRO T 163/4/G.251/1.
26 Clark to Sturgis, 29 March 1921, PRONI FIN 18/1/238.
27 Anderson to Clark, 26 April 1921, PRONI FIN 18/1/238, 303.
28 Clark to Anderson, 29 June 1921, PRONI FIN 18/1/303.
29 Anderson to Clark, 1 July 1921, PRONI FIN 18/1/303.
30 Clark to Anderson, 2 July 1921, PRONI FIN 18/1/303.
31 Pollock to Craig, 26 August 1921, PRONI FIN 18/1/356.
32 ibid.
33 ibid.
34 Craig to Greenwood, 27 September 1921, enclosed with memoranda from the Chief Secretary sent to the [British] Cabinet, CP 3369, 8 October 1921, PRO CAB 24/228.
35 Anderson to the secretary [of the several departments], circular 24111/20, 10 November 1921, PRO T 160/220/F.8126.
36. ibid.
37 Waterfield to J. H. Craig, 16 November 1921, PRO T 162/95/E.11302. This was the general rule for most departments, but a notable exception was the transferrable section of the Board of Inland Revenue, where volunteers for the North were 'so many that there is little doubt that the civil service committee will not have to allocate any additional staff for compulsory transfer'.
38 The minutes of meetings of the original Civil Service Committee, 8 December 1921–17 January 1922 are in PRONI FIN 30. A copy of the minutes of the first meeting on 8 December are in SPOI CSORP 1921/3866/3.
39 Gallagher, unpublished memoirs, op. cit. Also, the committee's secretary, W. Maguire, was official-side secretary on the central Irish Whitley Council. Gallagher was staff-side secretary.
40 'Existing Irish officers', that is, those who would be transferred to the Northern or Southern Irish government or to the Council of Ireland, were not organised as such. Sloan and Gallagher were elected by the staff side of the central Irish Whitley Council from among candidates put forward by the various staff organisations. This

was in accordance with regulations drawn up by the Treasury. See PRO T 164/31/P.27147A.

41 R. D. Megaw, the Northern Parliamentary Secretary for Home Affairs, represented the North at the first meeting, but was replaced by Clark afterwards.

42 Gallagher, unpublished memoirs, op. cit. Documentation on these events is in SPOI CSORP 1921/3866/3 and CSORP 1921/2429/221. Also, in his unpublished memoirs, Gallagher devotes a most interesting and informative chapter to 'The strange case of the Civil Service Committee'.

43 Statement submitted by existing Irish officers at the first meeting of the Civil Service Committee, 8 December 1921, SPOI CSORP 1921/2429/197 annexed to CSORP 1921/3866/3.

44 *Freeman's Journal*, 13 December 1921, newscutting in SPOI CSORP 1921/2429/221.

45 Gallagher, unpublished memoirs, op. cit.; Civil Service Committee minutes, second meeting 15 December 1921.

46 Anderson to the secretary, Civil Service Committee, 14 December 1921, SPOI CSORP 1921/3866/3.

47 Anderson to MacMahon, telegram, 14 December 1921, SPOI CSORP 1921/3866/3.

48 MacMahon to Anderson, telegram, 14 December 1921, ibid.

49 Gallagher, unpublished memoirs, op. cit.

50 Civil Service Committee minutes, second meeting, 15 December 1921.

51 ibid.

52 'Murphy & others vs. H. M. Attorney-General & others', hand-written account of the judgement by the Master of the Rolls, 21 December 1921, SPOI CSORP 1921/3864/2.

53 'Transfer of services hitherto administered by the British government in Ireland', provisional government proclamation, 16 January 1922, SPOI CSORP 1921/3864/2.

54 Civil Service Committee minutes, fifteenth meeting, 17 January 1922, PRONI FIN 30.

55 From notes filed with Civil Service Committee minutes, PRONI FIN 30.

56 Gilbert to Niemeyer, 27 May 1922, PRO T 158/9.

57 PRONI FIN 30.

6   British Withdrawal

After nearly two months of hard-fought negotiation, agreement for an Irish settlement was reached in London. The Treaty, signed 6 December 1921, provided that Ireland would become a Dominion, styled the Irish Free State. The Free State would enjoy sovereignty subject to inclusion within the British Commonwealth of Nations and to other imperial trappings. (The position under the Treaty was to be based generally on constitutional relations between the Empire and Canada.) Northern Ireland would remain outside the Free State until one month after the Treaty was ratified by the British Parliament; during this month Northern Ireland could elect to contract 'out' of the Free State, but a boundary commission would then delimit the border according to 'economic and geographical' circumstances and to 'the wishes of the inhabitants'. For good or ill, the Treaty marks a watershed in Irish history. For the British government the Treaty was an outstanding success. The agreement was so overwhelmingly accepted in Britain that the Irish question could now be regarded as closed. In Ireland the Treaty was a mixed blessing. In the long term it proved to be that 'stepping stone' to fuller independence which Michael Collins had predicted; that is, sufficient political freedom had been achieved for successive Dublin governments to whittle away at the British link until there was a republic in fact and in name. Yet, a large minority condemned the Treaty as falling far short of the national aspiration, and it proved to be the bone of contention in a tragic and bitter civil war having lasting repercussions in Irish political life. The Ulster dimension of the agreement at the time seemed to favour unity rather than partition: in the North this view was reflected in the angry reaction of the Ulster Unionists who felt betrayed by the agreement's provision for a boundary commission; in the South it was reflected in a complacency and lack of discussion about the North on the part of both sides of the Dáil's Treaty debate. Yet, the South's obsession with the constitutional question was such that partition was allowed to go by default. In the next quarter century, while the republic in the South was being secured, Dublin governments might be justly accused of comparative neglect of partition, disinterest in Northern Ireland's community relations, and an inability to come to terms with the viewpoint or the tenacity of Ulster Unionists. From 1922 the border was left intact and the six-counties Parliament decidedly under the overriding authority of Westminster.

Thus, 1922 was a formative year in Anglo-Irish relations. If cataclysmic for the Irish, for Britain it was one of guarded relief.

However, though the main political issue was resolved, the administrative implementation of the settlement emerged as a matter of tremendous size and complexity. On the agenda for the first Anglo-Irish ministers' conference in January were such matters as amnesty, indemnity and compensation, the termination of martial law, military evacuation, the transfer of government property, the transfer of departments, financial arrangements, the position of the judiciary, and not least important or contentious the procedure for regularising the provisional government and ratifying the Treaty.[1] No systematic analysis can be offered here of the labyrinth of administrative activity which brought about the transfer of power. However, it is possible to take some measure of the interplay between political policies and administrative procedure and so to throw light on the process of Britain's disengagement from Ireland. In essence, for the British, this involved striking a balance between three priorities: the constitutional position of Ireland within the empire, the credibility of the Free State provisional government and the rights of Northern Ireland under the Government of Ireland Act.

Implementing the Treaty: (1) The Constitutional Position

No sooner was the Treaty signed than the British began to worry about constitutional procedures for bringing the Treaty into effect. In the time before the Irish Free State could be constituted, a provisional government, nominated by the 'members of the Southern Ireland Parliament', would take over the administration of the twenty-six counties. The British were intent that the steps for establishing the provisional government and for constituting the Free State should be constitutional and should afford no opportunity for the Irish to bypass imperial authority over the Free State. By 11 December Cabinet conferences were discussing these procedures. At a meeting of the Cabinet's Irish Finance Committee, Sir Robert Horne, the Chancellor of the Exchequer, expressed alarm at the apparent 'remarkable misunderstanding' with the Irish delegates regarding the provisional government's powers. Griffith and Collins, stated Horne, were apparently under the impression that the provisional government from the beginning would be free from financial restriction and be able to spend money 'on other things than those for which the British parliament had given authority'. They did not appreciate the legal position regarding finance, that is, that 'the British government was collecting duties and taxes in Ireland, but depended for authority on the votes'. They did not realise, it seemed, that without legislation it was beyond the competence of the British government to grant financial powers to the provisional government; the Comptroller and Auditor-General could not allow funds from the exchequer for any other purpose than those provided for in the votes.[2] The difficulty could be resolved by bringing the 'Crown colony' clause of the 1920 Act into force. However, the British knew that Griffith and Collins could never agree to the provisional government being set up under the despised Government of Ireland Act, representing the policy they had fought against for the previous two years.[3] No legislation was possible before the end of the parliamentary recess in February. On what legal basis, therefore, could the provisional government exercise its functions?

The answer was provided by Sir Francis Greer, the Irish Office draftsman. The only alternative, stated Greer, was 'to set up an administration on an admittedly irregular basis'. Yet, the arrangement he proposed was not so irregular in terms of British constitutionality because the authority of the Irish government remained vested in the Lord-Lieutenant. The Lord-Lieutenant would form a committee – which would be the provisional government – who would advise him on the administration of government services. The old Dublin Castle 'Irish government' – the Viceroy, Chief Secretary and law officers – remained the lawful executive authority in Ireland, but the orders of the Chief Secretary to the departments would be framed in accordance with the advice said to be given to the Lord-Lieutenant by the executive 'committee'. In this way a *de facto* government could come into being under existing imperial authority and without the benefit of new legislation.[4] The discussion was taken up on 21 December by a new Cabinet Committee (the Provisional Government of Ireland or PGI Committee) under the Colonial Secretary, Winston Churchill.[5] Churchill's committee decided that the Irish Free State could be legally established in three stages. There would first be created a 'makeshift' – the term was soon changed to 'temporary' – provisional government, in law an *ad hoc* executive committee to advise the Viceroy. Legislation would then be passed initiating the second stage, a 'regularised' provisional government with its own exchequer, responsible for administering Southern Ireland and drafting a constitution. At the third and final stage further legislation would give legal effect to the constitution and so bring into being the new Dominion.[6] Here again, British advisers saw difficulties: the last step was yet another necessary procedure which had not been discussed with the Irish plenipotentiaries. The Cabinet were warned that the Irish signatories had 'not faced the fact that the Treaty does nothing to create any organ in Ireland capable of giving a legal sanction to the Irish constitution when framed'.[7]

In Ireland on 7 January, after extended and acrimonious debate since

14 December, Dáil Eireann finally voted by a slim majority to accept the Treaty. On 14 January the pro-Treaty majority, plus the four Trinity College MPs convened as 'members elected to sit in the House of Commons of Southern Ireland'. This was the body designated by the Treaty to approve the agreement and nominate the provisional government.[8] The new ministry took office on Monday, 16 January, with Michael Collins as chairman. On the 18th Collins dispatched to London two of his ministers, Duggan and O'Higgins, to begin conferences with the PGI Committee on the Treaty's implementation.[9] In a short time, heads of working arrangements were drafted covering the wide range of matters relating to the transfer of power.[10] However, it was obvious that the Irish were unhappy with British proposals for bringing the Free State into existence. Could the British not ratify the Treaty by a 'one clause bill', with both the Treaty and the constitution appearing as schedules? On the 23rd Churchill reported to the Cabinet:

> It was clear that the Irish wished, if possible, to avoid the necessity for the setting up of a Provisional Government and Parliament for Southern Ireland by an Act of the Imperial Parliament and would like to obtain a Free State Government and an approved constitution within the shortest time possible, and that an Irish Parliament should be elected as soon as the fresh registers could be prepared.

Churchill appeared willing to work out an arrangement agreeable to both sides:

> It was worthy of consideration whether without infringing on the Treaty it was possible to ratify the Treaty and approve the constitution of the Free State by means of a one clause Bill. There were great advantages from the point of view of the Irish ministers in getting their draft constitution approved by the Parliament for Southern Ireland not only because the followers of de Valera abstained from attending that body, but because they could contend that their constitution derived its authority from the Treaty and not from a British Act of Parliament.[11]

Back in Ireland on the 24th Collins addressed the committee appointed by the provisional government to draft the constitution. Informing them of the proposed Bill, he stated that 'the British government promised, if both sides were in agreement, to put it through their two houses without the alteration of a single word'.[12] The constitutional committee were therefore 'instructed to have their work completed by the end of February',[13] presumably so that the constitution could be included as a schedule to the Bill.[14] The

Irish notes of the 21 January London conference state that Lloyd
George had 'practically committed himself' to the proposal, though he
had first to get the opinion of his legal advisers.[15] On the 23rd the
British Cabinet concurred that 'if an agreed bill and constitution was in
draft by 8th March, no technical objection need be raised to the
attendance of Free State representatives at the Genoa
conference'.[16] However, the idea foundered, it seems, because
there was no way the Irish constitutional committee would finish its
work by the end of February.[17] The Irish seem to have had some
illusions about this, but British officials had none.[18] On the 24th
an *ad hoc* committee of British advisers concluded that the Act ratifying
the Treaty might also empower an Irish parliament to enact its own
constitution; but the Act must also specify the terms of the
constitution's most vital provisions in order to ensure conformity with
the Treaty.[19]

Very soon the provisional government themselves appear to have
realised the impracticability of drafting a constitution in so short a time
as a few weeks. At least the Irish ministers no longer spoke in terms of
the constitution itself being a schedule to the Treaty Bill. Rather
naïvely they now hoped the British would simply ignore the anomaly of
ratifying the Treaty without ratifying the constitution. On 31 January
the Colonial Office official, Lionel Curtis, arrived in Dublin to discuss
the ratification procedure with provisional government
representatives.[20] Duggan and O'Higgins were assigned to meet
him on the following day and were 'directed to make no statement
which might compromise the ratification of the constitution being
subsequently allowed to go by default'.[12] These words, from the
minutes of the provisional government meeting on 31 January, would
seem to indicate that Collins hoped the British would ratify the Treaty
in such a way as to allow the provisional government to assume not only
the administrative powers of the Free State, but the Dominion
authority of the Free State – *before* the constitution was drafted. The
terms of the constitution would then be finalised by the Free State
exclusively, while the British would have already ratified it 'by default'
in ratifying the Treaty. Here was an early attempt by Collins to secure
the vital ground that could give him the widest manoeuvreability on the
Irish political scene: that is, by achieving the freedom to formulate a
constitution that would square with republican ideals more than did the
Treaty, he would be in a position to resolve his differences with, or
indeed undermine the position of, de Valera and the anti-Treaty forces.

However, with Curtis on the job, this was not to be. In the course of
two meetings with Curtis on 1 and 2 February Duggan and O'Higgins
insisted on dropping the second schedule to the Bill (outlining matters
to be covered in the constitution) because otherwise it 'would jeopardise

the political situation'.[22] This was acceptable to Curtis, but he would not hear of any proposal to consider the constitution ratified before a final draft was passed into law by the United Kingdom Parliament; and so far as he was concerned the provisional government's 'assurances that the constitution will be shown to the British authorities before publication and that it will not be objectionable in any of the points raised'[23] were not good enough. Moreover, the Treaty could not be regarded as having been 'ratified' until the constitution was also 'ratified' because the Northern Ireland Parliament would have to be in a position to view the finalised Irish Free State constitution in order to judge whether it was in its own interests to 'remain' with the Free State or to 'opt out'. The controversy now became focused on the question of the date from which the 'Ulster month' would run, the Irish arguing that it ran from the date of the Treaty Bill, the British that it ran from the date of the Constitution Bill. On 5 and 6 February the discussion was taken back to London, but meetings between Churchill and Collins, and between the Irish law adviser, Hugh Kennedy, and the British Attorney-General, Sir Gordon Hewart, also reached stalemate.[24]

The pro-Treaty Irish must have regarded the outcome of this matter as important in their dispute with their republican opponents in Ireland. Darrell Figgis, the vice-chairman of the constitutional committee, accused Curtis of being not a believer in 'liberty and confederation', but

> an autocratic imperialist in disguise. I feel that you will protest against this designation, but I am sure that if your views are right, then the Treaty is wrong . . . When we hear that it is the intention of your side to ratify what you pick and choose of the Treaty, and leave the rest hanging in the air for the future, it is not difficult to foresee what the instant effect will be throughout the country.[25]

However, after the Sinn Féin ard-fheis of 22 February the issue lost its urgency for the Irish ministers. In an attempt to smooth over their differences the pro- and anti-Treaty factions of the party agreed that elections should be postponed until June and that the constitution should be published before the elections in order to enable the electorate to judge the constitution and the Treaty together. The party 'truce' bought time for the provisional government *vis-à-vis* their position in Ireland, and the dispute over the date of the Ulster month no longer held its propaganda value.[26] On 20 March Hugh Kennedy communicated the new position to the British government:

> While it is held by the Irish plenipotentiaries and the minister of the

provisional government that in the strict reading and interpretation of the Treaty the month in which north-east Ulster must exercise its option should run as from the date of the passing of the bill, they recognise that a strong argument might be made for the advisability of allowing north-east Ulster to consider the constitution of the Irish Free State before exercising this option and they are willing, therefore, to waive their interpretation and to agree that the month shall run from the date of the passing of the act adopting the constitution.[27]

The Irish Free State (Agreement) Act was passed on 31 March giving the Treaty the force of law, regularising the provisional government and enabling the British to transfer government functions by orders in council.[28] In the light of both British and Irish interpretations the Free State came into existence on 6 December 1922. In the Irish interpretation the provisional Parliament gave the constitution the force of law on this date with the passage of the Irish Free State (Saorstát Eireann) Act;[29] they regarded the British Act on the same day as 'adopting' the constitution as part of the overall agreement rather than as granting Ireland a constitution. In the British view, the Irish Free State (Constitution) Act, passed at Westminster, not only adopted the 'constituent act' of the Irish Parliament, but became the law which granted the Irish Parliament the authority to enact their constitution. But the question remains whether the ambiguity of article 17 of the Treaty was merely a case of careless drafting or a deliberate attempt to bury constitutional procedure in order to make the Treaty more palatable to the Irish.

Implementing the Treaty: (2) The 'Temporary Provisional Government'

In a well-publicised ceremony on Monday, 16 January 1922, the newly formed provisional government 'took over' Dublin Castle as the British army marched out, its band playing 'Let Erin Remember'. On the same day the new government drafted a proclamation for publication in Tuesday's press: that

> all law courts, corporations, councils, departments of state, boards, judges, civil servants, officers of the peace and all public servants and functionaries hitherto acting under the authority of the British government shall continue to carry out the functions unless and until otherwise ordered by us pending the constitution of the parliament and government of Saorstát na hEireann and without prejudice to the full and free exercise by that parliament and government when

constituted of all and every its powers and authorities in regard to them or any of them.

Moreover, the new ministers prohibited

> the appointing or the altering of the status, rights, perquisites or stipend, or the transfer, or dismissal of any officer, servant, employee, or functionary of the state without the specific authority in that behalf of this provisional government or the minister thereof having authority from us in the particular case.

> And we do further prohibit the removal, tampering with or destruction of any records, documents, correspondence, accounts, books, writings, or papers of a public nature or relating to, or which came into existence for the purpose of any matter or thing connected with such government or administration or any branch thereof.[30]

On the 18th, Collins allocated portfolios. He himself insisted on controlling the all-important business of finance. E. J. Duggan was given home affairs, Kevin O'Higgins economic affairs, P. J. Hogan agriculture, Fionan Lynch education, W. T. Cosgrave local government and Joseph McGrath labour. Eoin MacNeill, though a member of the government, was given no portfolio. J. J. Walsh was appointed Postmaster-General but was not a member of the government.[31] Collins distributed lists of existing departments, categorised by ministry, and instructed his colleagues each 'to have a copy of this list before him and to study it carefully so that the various inquiries may be dealt with properly and promptly'.[32] However, it is difficult to say whether the new ministers involved themselves very deeply in the administration of all those departments over which their ministries were supposed to be responsible. Rather, central organisation in the new ministries developed slowly, and control over the old departments remained loose. Day-to-day administration appears for the most part to have been left very much in the hands of civil servants. This explains why during the 'temporary' provisional government period, 16 January to 31 March, departmental expenditure for the most part remained within reasonable range of the parliamentary votes. But there was one exception. Postmaster-General J. J. Walsh, as has been stated, was not a member of the provisional government; he was therefore not preoccupied with political questions to the same degree as other ministers and possibly had more opportunity to become actively involved in the administration of his department. His permanent secretary (or 'acting administrator') was P. S. O'Hegarty, the only departmental head not previously a civil servant.[33] Also, the Post

Office was the only department whose minister was pulled up by the British for unauthorised expenditure. In its initial reports, the Churchill Committee had seemed unequivocal about the authority over departments which the provisional government should exercise: 'If statutory authority to give direction of any kind is required and such authority cannot yet be obtained, the British authority who now has power to give such directions should be told to act upon such instructions received without responsibility except for execution.'[34] Walsh, however, seems to have overstepped the mark. On 4 February Sir Evelyn Murray, Postmaster-General for the United Kingdom, wrote to Masterton-Smith, chairman of the Churchill Committee's technical subcommittee, concerning a 'good many difficulties cropping up' in the GPO, Dublin. One was that a person of inferior rank had come into a position of authority solely on the basis of his knowledge of Irish. (O'Hegarty?). The problems 'seem to arise from the fact that the provisional government or their representatives are apparently in control of the post office at the present time'.[35] In his short period in office Walsh appears to have undertaken several costly projects not covered in the parliamentary votes. These included long-distance motor services to deliver post to places affected by the railway strike at a cost of £600 per week, and also the repair of telegraph poles destroyed in the recent conflict, on which he had already spent £14,000. His proposals for the future included supplying the Irish government with £50,000 worth of over-printed stamps at cost for sale to stamp collectors, provision of free telephone services for Irish ministers, and a scheme, at an estimated cost of £113,000, for the installation of telephone wires, which he hoped would relieve unemployment.[36] At a meeting in London with Murray, Kellaway (Post Office Secretary in Dublin) and Lionel Curtis on 21 February, Walsh impressed the British as having overestimated the scope of his authority over the Post Office, as the minutes of the meeting show:

> Mr Walsh was naturally anxious to have full ministerial authority at once, but Mr Curtis explained to him that this would not be possible until the treaty had been ratified . . . Mr Curtis pointed out that if the British Post Office acted as the agents of the Irish Free State, Mr Kellaway must retain responsibility for his department and he suggested that the best thing might be for Mr Walsh to act in the capacity of liaison officer with the British Post Office. Mr Walsh agreed to this and Mr Kellaway said that he would give instructions to his staff to deal with Mr Walsh's proposals sympathetically. Any proposals which involved large questions of principle [were] to be

referred to Mr Kellaway at the same time . . . Mr Walsh agreed this was satisfactory . . .[37]

Walsh also desired the authority to appoint staff, notifying Kellaway only after appointments were made. But again Walsh was guided gently but firmly to the British view 'that the arrangement should be that appointments should be made by Mr Walsh in agreement with the Irish postal authorities'. Any differences of opinion were to be 'referred to Mr Kellaway and the appointment held over'. It may have been some consolation to Walsh when the British officials assured him that 'the signing of names in Irish could be dealt with by Walsh without reference to the British authority'.[38]

The Post Office incident illustrates the limitations of the Irish ministers' *de facto* powers during the 'temporary provisional government' period. The British were particularly concerned with the amounts involved. They were happy to hear from Walsh that he understood that extraordinary expenditure in his department would be met ultimately from Irish Free State funds.[39] Yet from Treasury (Ireland) Waterfield observed this affair with not a little apprehension. He was not certain whether Walsh even had the sanction of the provisional government Ministry of Finance for his operations. If not, it would be a difficult matter to recover funds from the Free State.[40] He hoped that, in any case, British protests in this instance would make it clear to all the Irish ministers 'that they must seek financial authority before they indulge in any abnormal expenditure expecting that we shall foot the bill'.[41] However, he recognised that if the provisional government were to be seen as the *de facto* government, there would be instances in which the Treasury would simply have to 'look the other way'.[42]

Implementing the Treaty: (3) The Transfer of Functions

Even when the provisional government was regularised under an Act of the British Parliament, its Dominion powers were limited. Under the Irish Free State (Agreement) Act, the very order in council handing over administrative powers transferred not 'services', as had been the case with Northern Ireland, but rather the 'functions' of existing departments.[43] This terminology underscored the temporary nature of the provisional government. Even 'departments' technically remained organizations of the imperial government, but their 'functions' for the time being were carried on by the provisional government and paid for by its exchequer.

Perhaps the best contemporary elucidation of the arrangement was made by Hugh Kennedy, the provisional government's law adviser:

> The provisional government was a body set up for the administration of the twenty-six counties during the period between the Treaty and the time when a full omni-competent government would be created by means of a constitution under the Treaty to function permanently and in complete authority in all departments of government. That period was limited not to exceed one year and if the government proper were not duly constituted before the expiry of the year the provisional government was to die of efflux of the prescribed time, whereupon the administration of the twenty-six counties would (in default of the new agreement) revert to the British government.
>
> The provisional government then was (a) temporary only, merely a transitory machine: and (b) partial, concerned only with one aspect of government, namely, the administrative. The transfer of functions order must be interpreted in the light of these essential considerations which are perhaps kept in view by referring to the provisional government as the 'temporary administration'.
>
> For the purposes of such a temporary administration it was necessary to transfer temporarily some of the functions of government, and that is what the transfer of functions order did. It was not a complete transfer of government or even of any department of government. It was a temporary transfer of the administration of certain functions of government for a period not to exceed a year.[44]

Indeed, several functions of future Free State administrative machinery were withheld from provisional government control by express agreement between Churchill and Collins. On 4 April they agreed that the 'transfer of functions' of most departments should take effect, but with six significant exceptions.[45] Two of these departments remained under British control for essentially administrative reasons; a third in deference to the interests of the Northern Ireland government; and the remainder as constitutional or strategic safeguards for Britain.

The Land Commission was retained by the British for an administrative reason, viz. 'the great complication of land purchase finance'.[46] Initially, provisional government ministers had hoped to deal with land purchase themselves 'without even the assistance of British credit'.[47] Civil servants in the Irish Department of Finance, whose conservative influence on financial policies was rapidly growing, may have been responsible for the change in the Irish position on land purchase. By 6 March the PGI financial subcommittee believed 'it was almost certain that the British government would be asked by the provisional government, to undertake as agents . . . the functions of the land commission', at least for a part of the 1922–3 financial year.[48] By the 21st the Irish in fact agreed to British control for the time being.[49]

Administrative difficulties also prevented the transfer of functions of the Board of Trade mercantile marine branch, relating to the work of the Irish lights commissioners.[50] As in the case of the Land Commission, the Irish ministers initially believed that the administration of this service should be transferred to themselves – 'preferably', said Kevin O'Higgins, 'for the whole of the Irish coast, or in the alternative for that portion of the coast which . . . comes under the jurisdiction of the Irish Free State'. However, what may not have been fully appreciated was that the main beneficiary of the Irish lights service was British shipping for which navigational aids around the Irish coast were essential. Ninety-five per cent of the cost of maintaining these aids in Irish waters came from 'light dues' collected at British ports. Understandably, the Board of Trade regarded the transfer of this expenditure to the provisional government as a possible risk to the quality of lighthouse administration. It was consequently reserved during the provisional government period. Later, various proposals for new arrangements were put forward. The Board of Trade wished to maintain the unity of the service and suggested the formation of a 'financial advisory committee of the general lighthouse fund', composed of representatives of the Board of Trade, shipping interests and lighthouse authorities. An alternative scheme, but one the British found undesirable, was British subsidisation of a new Irish authority to administer lights in the Free State. Northern Ireland, as might be expected, also had ideas on the subject and pressed for a separate Ulster authority, or alternatively for bringing Northern Irish coastal lights under the authority of the Scottish commissioners. In the end, existing arrangements were left intact and to this day the Irish lights commissioners maintain the lighthouse network for the whole of Ireland under the supervision of the United Kingdom Board of Trade.

The Registry of Deeds remained reserved in 1922 as a safeguard to the Northern government. Deeds registers were impossible to partition, and in order to protect Northern Ireland interests, Northern ministers warned the British against allowing the department to pass to the provisional government's physical control; they, in fact, wished to set up their own registry, even though this would entail Northern solicitors in the next twenty years having to make two separate searches for their clients in the six counties.[51] From the Free State standpoint the department was temporarily reserved in the South in deference to the Ulster option: in fact in November, on the eve of the Free State, the Treasury persuaded the Irish ministers to leave under imperial control most of the departmental functions excepted from the 1 April order until 1 April 1923 'on political grounds'. The continued reservation of the departments during the Ulster month would 'avoid the appearance of forcing Ulster to pre-judge her decision on the question of separation'.[52]

Two further areas of administration were reserved to the British as safeguards to the Crown: the functions of the Clerk of Crown and Hanaper, and the collection of quit rents.

The British regarded control of the Clerk of Crown and Hanaper as vital to the constitutional position during the provisional government period. In February the provisional government had approached the Clerk of Crown and Hanaper, Gerald Horan, with the request 'that the proclamation [of elections] should be in the name of the provisional government and that writs of election should not be in the usual form – in the king's name and under the great seal – but in the form of summons to the under-sheriffs'. Horan 'presume[d] no difficulty will arise if such forms are so altered pending the setting up of the constitution, and I am very willing to assist in any way I can'. However, it occurred to him that 'as I am, I suppose, an imperial official, I should be officially sanctioned to undertake this work . . .'[53] Anderson was horrified. Horan's letter, he claimed, raised 'important constitutional questions' directly involving the 'position and function of the representative of the crown during the provisional period':

> The forms customarily used in these proclamations and writs are adorned by a wealth of expression handed down from the middle ages, and there can be no doubt that a good deal of the verbiage is surplusage and so far as it would be distasteful to those now in authority in Ireland can properly be discarded. The fundamental issue, however, remains as to whether the authority to be involved in the action necessary to bring the new parliament into being is to be that of the king's representative or that of an executive authority purporting to act independently of the king's representative.[54]

The Cabinet's technical subcommittee on Ireland agreed with Anderson 'that if writs were issued which departed in substance from the statutory form it would be open to anyone to challenge the validity of the election, and this might very well be done by the de Valera party'. It was also feared 'that if reference to the crown and lord lieutenant were omitted . . . it would be far more difficult to insist on the inclusion of such references when the Free State had been constituted'.[55] Thus was foiled yet a further Irish plot to assume a degree of unilateral sovereignty by means of eliminating procedures involving the Crown.

The Quit Rent Office, the British reasoned, was another department whose functions would have to be withheld from the provisional government for constitutional reasons.[56] This small department was responsible for collecting Crown revenue from certain foreshores. The property involved was 'not a valuable asset', merely 'some sloblands in Dublin Bay, something near Kinsale and something in County Clare on the Shannon estuary'. However, the importance of the matter to the British was not so much the financial position of the king, but rather the potential danger to the recognised principles of the Crown–Dominion relationship if the property was transferred as part of the machinery of Dominion government. The question was argued to a deadlock in February 1923, the British claiming the right to be paid the capitalised value of the property 'in order to prevent the interest of future sovereigns from being affected by the transfer'; the Free State claiming that the lands should pass to them as an ordinary departmental asset under the Transfer of Functions Order.[57]

Finally, in its restrictions on the transfer of power to the provisional government the British showed themselves to be concerned not only with administrative and constitutional necessity, but also strategic precaution in the event of the provisional government foundering or breaching the Treaty. With such considerations in mind they resisted the transfer of the Post Office Savings Bank. The Post Office Savings Bank held about £9·6 million in assets in Southern Ireland. The Treasury official, O. E. Niemeyer, proposed that the government withhold control over the bank as a way of freezing the assets in view of the 'uncertain' political position and as collateral against £5 million in various British claims on Irish funds. The PGI Committee felt that it could not absolutely insist on retaining control. They had agreed with Collins 'that provision be made for division of the assets and liabilities of the Post Office Savings Bank' as between the British and Irish Post Office Banks. But, as Niemeyer craftily observed, 'we didn't say when the division was to take effect' (though admitting 'I think it was assumed that it would be forthwith'). The PGI Committee took Niemeyer's point and agreed 'that if the provisional government press us very strongly the British government would have to acquiesce in the transfer of the Post Office Savings Bank by April 1st, but that every endeavour should be used to procure a postponement for the present of cash transfer'.[58] These endeavours were successful and not only the Post Office Savings Bank, but also the Trustee Savings Banks remained reserved until 1 April 1923, when the political position had become more stable and the first Anglo-Irish financial agreement had been reached.

Notwithstanding such exceptions, however, Collins and his colleagues must have welcomed the transfer of state apparatus to their effective control, bolstering their confidence in the face of the deteriorating political situation. In April and May 1922 peace efforts grew increasingly desperate as the anti-Treaty section of the IRA became more entrenched and shooting incidents more frequent. Collins never ceased in his attempts at compromise and conciliation with the republican side. Had the zenith of his efforts, the Collins–de Valera pact of 24 May, been carried out, the British would have regarded the Treaty as breached. The pact, an attempt to remove the Treaty as an election issue, involved an agreed panel of candidates representing the existing strength of both sides in the Dáil. It also involved a draft constitution in which there was found no place for the Crown. The British deplored the pact and could accept neither republican membership of the provisional government nor the draft constitution which Collins and Griffith brought to London in early June. Capitulation to Lloyd George and Churchill led to the events which slid rapidly to civil war by the end of the month. Collins's apparent last-minute repudiation of the pact before the 16 June elections, the publication of the draft constitution only the morning of the election with the king re-enthroned, the success of a majority of candidates holding pro-Treaty views, British pressure on Collins to drive Rory O'Connor from the Four Courts after the assassination of Sir Henry Wilson in London, the republican kidnappings and commandeerings which at last wore Collins's and Mulcahy's patience thin – all finally led to the outbreak on 28 June. Decisive action on the part of the provisional government made the British rest easier. They rested easier still after Collins's death on 22 August, knowing his successors to be of a more conservative mind, anxious to implement the Treaty and willing to fight the republicans.

However, for a long time before all this took place, the British, especially their officials dealing with Ireland, maintained a kid-glove attitude towards the provisional government. With tact and caution they dealt with the revolutionaries-turned-constitutionalists, doing everything possible to make the way politically easier for them to carry out their part in implementing the Treaty. An important example of this was the role played by Treasury (Ireland).

Treasury (Ireland) and the Provisional Government

Waterfield and his staff played an important part in reinforcing the provisional government's stability. In their twenty-nine months in Ireland, they sought to achieve a thorough overhaul of government apparatus in Ireland before its transfer to indigenous governments. Actuated by a desire to hold an equitable balance between the interests of the Irish taxpayers and the interests of government employees, they sought to hand over a bureaucratic apparatus that was economical, efficient and reorganised on the basis of the most up-to-date structures.

In enforcing restrictions on departmental expenditure in accordance with Treasury policy in the United Kingdom as a whole, in overseeing the Whitley reforms and bringing reorganisation schemes into effect before the appointed day, and in co-ordinating special civil service exchanges between Great Britain and Ireland, the Treasury in Ireland was instrumental in enabling their successors in the ministries of Northern Ireland and the Irish Free State to set their administrative institutions on a firm footing. Waterfield's achievements in the previous two years had made continuity in administration possible during the transition period. Ironically, however, the completion of his work, the purpose of which was to stabilize Irish government administratively, was now to be delayed in the interests of stabilizing the provisional government politically. The immediate result of the provisional government proclamation, quoted earlier, was to bring to a halt all the machinery at the heart of administrative transition under the Government of Ireland Act. The Civil Service Committee, the Joint Exchequer Board, exchange of staff between Great Britain and Ireland, Treasury (Ireland)'s unfinished staff reorganisation schemes as well as normal staff adjustments, and the operations of the Irish Civil Service Joint Council (the Whitley Council), all came to a full stop. Initially, Waterfield was not unduly concerned believing the restrictions would be temporary. He assured colleagues in Whitehall that

the new government do not intend to apply the prohibitions contained in the proclamation as rigidly as might appear at first sight. Their main object is publicity. They want to make a display of having taken over control as completely and effectively as possible as soon as they were installed. Their second object is to prevent themselves from being compelled by an enemy treasury to accept liability for salaries at rates which they had not approved and thirdly they want to prevent the northern government from having the pick of the best men in the south before they get into the saddle and see that both sides have a fair dip into a common pool.[59]

On 23 January he communicated a long memorandum to the provisional government detailing the Treasury operations affected by the proclamation and suggesting arrangements under which these operations might resume.[60] He assured the new ministers that pains had been taken all along to maintain normal austere Treasury policies, and that reorganisation schemes were being implemented in Ireland on the same principles as they were in Great Britain and with the same measures of economy that would have been applied if the United Kingdom Treasury were to remain indefinitely responsible for the cost. Apart from an economical reorganisation of the civil service, wrote

Waterfield, measures of economy had been taken in other ways. Certain high-ranking posts – the most important being the resident commissioner of the National Education Board[61] and the vice-president of the Local Government Board[62] – had been intentionally allowed to go unfilled; and other important administrative questions were left undecided for the consideration of a native government in Southern Ireland. In the light of this record, Waterfield hoped the provisional government would allow Treasury (Ireland) general authority to complete outstanding points of reorganisation; to sanction the appointment of staff on a temporary basis; to complete the steps necessary to appoint eligible temporary staff to vacant permanent posts; and finally to continue to sanction exchanges of volunteers between departments in Great Britain and Ireland,[63] 'as it seems clearly in the interest of the provisional government to obtain the services of willing employees'.[64]

The provisional government were slow to respond. For some weeks Waterfield found it 'impossible to get answers out of them on any subject'.[65] Only when Michael Collins appointed a civil servant (William O'Brien) as secretary in his ministry was Waterfield able to establish communication with the provisional government. Eventually he was allowed to proceed with certain matters. By 14 February O'Brien had secured for Waterfield 'a general agreement that outstanding questions of reorganization . . . may now go forward in the ordinary way'.[66] Gradually Irish suspicions of the Treasury subsided and Collins began to consider seriously Waterfield's offer to act as agent to the Department of Finance for purposes of transferred work after 1 April. For the remainder of his time in Ireland, that is, until 31 October, Waterfield's duties winding up imperial finances gradually gave way to duties connected with transferred services.[67]

Provisional government policies were not always what Waterfield would have liked. He was particularly unhappy about the way their Ulster policies affected his own programme for carrying out procedures under the Government of Ireland Act. In spite of many attempts he and Niemeyer could not persuade the Irish ministers to co-operate in reconstituting the Joint Exchequer Board and Civil Service Committee. In April Niemeyer's plan was 'to have a vitual joint exchequer board under another name, though without statutory powers. Assuming that the conclusions of this body were accepted by both governments, as I think we might assume, what would then happen would be that by a curious coincidence the joint exchequer board would make an order for Northern Ireland arriving at identical conclusions.'[68] Niemeyer believed that North and South had to come together to make such decisions in order that the Joint Exchequer could legally split Irish funds.[69]

However, it will be recalled that political tension was mounting seriously in April and May. In May, Collins came nearest to compromising with the republicans. Relations with the North became dangerously embittered. Political tremors were felt in the activities of government departments. Collins even placed an embargo on departmental communications with Treasury (Ireland) on financial questions, unless they first went through the Ministry of Finance. On 20 May, the day of the pact, Waterfield's assistant (B. W. Gilbert) informed Niemeyer that 'most departments had already ceased to correspond with us on these subjects, and this embargo has now closed the door in other cases. Until, therefore, they agree to the committee, there is nothing to be done but wait'. He understood that O'Brien was agreeable to the suggestion but was unable to get Collins to decide on the matter which by this time was entangled in the webs of Irish politics.[70]

Waterfield was experiencing similar frustrations in his attempts to reconstitute the Civil Service Committee. He believed there to be a need for a tripartite board to allocate pension costs for the surplus of civil servants in Dublin departments. The surplus had resulted from the shortage of volunteers for Belfast and the provisional government's ban on compulsory transfers. In March, O'Brien had persuaded Collins to lift the prohibition on the transfer of the remaining 100 or so volunteers, not so much as a goodwill gesture to the North, but rather to avoid financial responsibility for them from 1 April.[71] ('By hook or by crook', said Waterfield, most of these had already made their way to positions in Belfast under quiet arrangements with the Northern government.)[72] Collins remained adamant that there should be no compulsory allocation. As no more Dublin officials would be transferring to Belfast, 'allocation' now became a question of how pension liability for excess staff should be allocated among the three governments.[73] Waterfield was angered to find that the provisional government would recognise no Northern representative on any tribunal for dealing with this matter. He believed that the effect of this was to release the North from any liability. It was the provisional government's position, he complained on 30 June (incidentally, with the civil war now in two days' full swing), that if the British were 'able to recover the cost of concessions from the north, that is our affair and nothing to do with them; all that they care about is that we shall foot the bill in the first place'. He favoured placing 'all the pressure we can on the south to meet the north for this purpose', and felt it was 'really ridiculous that they should expect us to play the whipping boy for their gratification'.[74]

Doubtless, it was indicative of the confusion of these days in Ireland, on the eve of civil war, that the central British policy had, in effect, changed imperceptibly over the Treasury's heads. Waterfield and Niemeyer, it seems, had missed the point about the constitutional position. In Hugh Kennedy's interpretation, the Northern Parliament was a subordinate parliament. It might choose to be subordinate to the United Kingdom Parliament or to the Free State Parliament.[75] Thus financial questions arising between the Free State and United Kingdom were matters for resolution exclusively between the two superior parliaments. Being a subordinate polity, Northern Ireland had no official place in the discussions, notwithstanding that decisions would affect her position. British Cabinet advisers seem gradually to have accepted Kennedy's view. The provisional government, Anderson advised Niemeyer, had 'very strong ground for saying in the case of most departments that the allocation of staff is a matter between the two governments only'.[76]

The tone of Waterfield's letter quoted above was remarkably excited. This was possibly because Waterfield had further reasons to be indignant with the provisional government. As he sat in Dublin Castle writing his impeachment of their bad faith (within easy earshot of Free State cannon, and on that very day, the Four Courts explosion – distressing enough!), he almost certainly still had in mind a very angry letter from Sir Ernest Clark in Belfast. The Civil Service Committee had, in fact, reconstituted itself without Southern Ireland representatives and met in London on 16 May. Not only did the provisional government refuse to allow either itself or Southern staffs to be represented; it also seems to have been involved in a rather high-handed attempt to sabotage the committee. A group of Dublin civil servants claiming to speak for the staff side of the Irish Civil Service Joint Council purported to 'revoke' the appointment of Sam Sloan. (Sloan was a member of the original committee, had gone to the North and was now representing existing Irish officers in the six counties.) The fact that Collins had already proclaimed the end of the Whitley system in the Free State did not seem to have any bearing! Waterfield, still having difficulty communicating with the provisional government and treading on eggs in the tense political atmosphere of May–June 1922, decided to play it safe and honour the revocation. Recalling the committee's experience in December he decided not to risk potential legal proceedings by the provisional government or opportunities for them to lodge protests with the British Cabinet. Waterfield knew the Northern government would not be intolerably inconvenienced: the committee still had a quorum and continued to meet, with Sloan attending as unofficial 'observer' for Northern officers.[77] Yet it was embarrassing for the North, and Sir Ernest Clark, piqued at the campaign of administrative obstruction against the Northern government and the tendency of the British to look the other way, unleashed his exasperation on Waterfield on 16 June:

> To be perfectly frank, this government had very little gratitude to spare to anybody with regard to the provision of staff, neither to the provisional government nor to the civil service committee. The sudden exodus of the last named on the day that the provisional government came into existence annoyed me more than enough. Just think how you would have considered it if you had been in my place at that time starting a government and pressed for a staff which we could not get transferred![78]

(Possibly, Waterfield was still smarting from this assault when he set down his own tirade against the provisional government on 30 June.) Waterfield answered: he could fully appreciate Clark's difficulties 'and sympathize in your *cri de coeur*. All that can be said is that we had our troubles also, and that we were honestly trying to hold the balance between the divergent interests as best we could. Let us hope that henceforth things will run on smoother lines.'[79]

North versus South

Yet, how evenly did the British hold the balance of the divergent interests of North and South? Let us first trace the development of North–South tensions in their administrative relations.

In January Michael Collins declared his 'north-east Ulster policy' to be one of 'peace'. At the discussions which led to the Craig–Collins agreement of 24 January, Collins promised to lift the Southern economic boycott of Belfast goods, while Craig promised to do what he could to end the persecution of Catholics. The two also agreed that the British representative on the Boundary Commission might be dropped. Collins 'suggested strongly' to Craig 'the impossibility of two govern-ments in Ireland' and proposed that representatives for the whole of Ireland should come together to draft an all-Ireland constitution. In the interest of agreement Craig did not refuse unequivocally, but replied 'that the time was not ripe for this'.[80] At a provisional government meeting on 30 January, at which the Catholic Bishop of Down and Conor (Joseph MacRory) was present, Collins again stated that he favoured peace. He 'would either have to fight the North or make peace with it. A peace policy had been started and should get a fair chance'.[81] To Collins, however, 'peace' did not mean an end to his determined opposition to partition or his intentions eventually to bring down the Northern state. Nor, apparently, did Collins feel that a 'peace' policy necessarily contradicted a policy of 'non-recognition' of the Northern government. He seems rather to have envisaged a boycott of Northern government authority on the part of individuals and organisations among nationalists in the North. Such a boycott was to receive the moral and financial support of the provisional government. At the 30 January meeting Dr MacRory prophetically expressed fears 'that if the policy of non-recognition was adopted, the people in the North would have to fight alone'. Collins countered that 'non-recognition of the Northern Parliament was essential – otherwise they would have nothing to bargain on with Sir James Craig'. He promised MacRory to 'finance schools in the six counties where the teachers and managers do not recognise the Northern government. He would also support local bodies taking a similar course of action'.[82]

In the following weeks the provisional government tried to create a supporting base for the non-recognition campaign by formulating policies of obstruction and non-cooperation in various administrative areas. On 1 February Collins stated that Northern local government councils refusing to recognise the Belfast regime were 'to be supported in every way. If the Northern parliament refuses grants, the provisional government must provide the necessary funds . . .' On the following day the provisional government considered 'the question of the Land Commission and the collection of annuities for the Northern Parliament' and declared that 'the Belfast Parliament is to be hampered in every possible way' in this matter. At the same meeting the Minister of Agriculture, P. J. Hogan, 'read a letter from Mr Archdale of the Belfast Agriculture Department asking for an interview to arrange certain matters in connection with the transfer of services. It was decided that no facilities for the Belfast departments should be given'.[83] In February, a Southern Ministry of Education official visited schools in Belfast and its environs, Derry, Omagh, Castlecaulfield, Dungannon, Lisburn, Hollywood, Strabane, Fintona and Armagh, and interviewed 'persons of influence and teachers strongly nationalist in their outlook'.[84] His message was simple: any school manager or teacher who refused to accept school grants or paycheques from the Northern Ireland government would be paid from Dublin. Dozens of Catholic schools immediately joined ranks behind this campaign and on 24 February the provisional government made its first payment of £5,000 for the purpose.[85] These developments may have been the beginning of what Collins is said to have promised to the Northern divisions of the IRA: that although the Treaty seemed to be an expression of partition, 'the government has plans whereby they would make it impossible, and that partition would never be recognised even though it might mean the smashing of the treaty'.[86]

However, neither Collins nor Craig could control the livelier spirits among their followers; there would be no such 'peace' as they had hoped. The uncertain position of Northern Ireland under the Treaty and IRA activity along the border left Loyalists feeling insecure. Arson and assassination multiplied in February and March. Pogrom flared and thousands of Catholic refugees fled south from Belfast. A further, more elaborate agreement – the Collins–Craig pact of 30 March – was Collins's final attempt to ease tensions in the six counties through concordat with Craig. His major concerns were to consolidate the provisional government in the South and heal the rift in the IRA. If the Northern Catholics could hold on while the South sorted itself out, Collins might then turn greater efforts towards undermining the Northern government. In May there were signs that precisely this might happen.

Collins blamed Craig for the collapse of the 30 March pact, although more culpable figures in the Northern government were Dawson Bates, Minister of Home Affairs, and his officials. (According to a recent authority, 'there was, indeed, a sad contrast between the prime minister's good intentions and the hostile spirit in which the ministry of home affairs acted' in carrying out the pact.)[87] There was no evidence that Catholics expelled from jobs were being reinstated, that Catholics would be welcomed in the special constabulary, that more than a tiny handful of political prisoners would be released, or that the pogrom was abating. The level of violence grew, Catholics coming off the worst, those killed between 6 December 1921 and 31 May 1922 being double the number of Protestants (147 to 73).[88] North–South relations continued to plummet lower and lower. The Collins–de Valera pact of 20 May was seen by Ulster Loyalists as an ominous threat, in fact 'as a prelude to a concerted attack'.[89] Indeed, the Northern divisions of the IRA were reorganised and supplied with arms by Collins. And not least significant, Collins turned the administrative screws against the North even tighter.

In May Collins was still hardly in a position to launch a military campaign against Northern Ireland. However, he knew the North was weak. Administratively it had still not been consolidated. In view of the increasing chances of *rapprochement* with anti-Treaty factions, it was important for Collins to keep the North weak if he could. He would make it his business to see that the North's powers would be strictly confined to the limitations of the 1920 Act. To his fellow ministers in the provisional government he sent this directive: 'It is most desirable for general administrative purposes that you should get the advice of good experts on the exact powers and limitations of the Northern

Parliament in the British act of 1920. These should be studied very carefully and your experts should prepare for you whatever statements are necessary explaining and simplifying these powers and limitations.' He instructed his colleagues 'to watch carefully to prevent any extensions of these powers'. In fact they would have to do more than that: 'You will also need to have a scheme prepared for non-cooperation in every possible way with the Northern Parliament, and in addition, a scheme towards making it impossible to carry on'.[90]

It is difficult to determine from available government archives in Dublin how resolutely each minister carried out these directives. On 15 May Collins felt compelled to remind ministers of his instructions and 'emphasized the importance of not losing sight of this matter'.[91] However, in at least two areas there is evidence that provisional government ministries conscientiously pursued obstructive policies. In education the policy of paying Catholic teachers continued to thrive. In mid-May, when the original funds for this purpose (almost £70,000) were exhausted,[92] Collins helped education officials break through red tape in order to tap the new Irish exchequer. Paying Northern teachers was politically a risky business. As education services were transferred to the Northern government on 1 February, the policy blatantly violated the Treaty. The provisional government's involvement had been kept secret and teachers were not told precisely who was paying them. Thus Collins was assured that 'the necessary steps [were being taken] to prevent the bank officials from knowing the source from which the money is being paid the teachers'.[93]

The Ministry of Agriculture also took the obstruction policy quite seriously. Collins's minister, P. J. Hogan, hoped to take advantage of the situation where few government officials, involved with the country's major industry, transferred to Northen Ireland.[94] In May Hogan circulated a memorandum regarding 'possibilities of cooperation and non-cooperation' with the Northern government. The memorandum displayed a decided bias towards the latter. Through non-cooperation Hogan believed that

> much greater loss can be inflicted and greater difficulties placed upon [the Northern Ireland] government than upon the government of the Irish Free State. The latter have at their disposal a complete organization with a trained staff in the veterinary branch of the department, whereas in the six counties there is no such organization and it will be exceedingly difficult to establish one, especially if they are forbidden access to office records or if they are unable to obtain the services of a member of the existing staff of the veterinary branch who would be capable of forming such an organization.[95]

Hogan believed the Treaty legitimised this policy because the executive functions of the Council of Ireland (fisheries, railways and the Diseases of Animals Acts) in Southern Ireland had passed to the provisional government, while in Northern Ireland they had not passed to the Northern government. He argued that pending the establishment of the council the provisional government should act as agents of the British in the North.[96] While he could not persuade the British of the wisdom of this course, he nevertheless succeeded in getting them directly involved in the administration of the Diseases of Animals Act so as to minimise *de facto* control by the Northern ministry. He also succeeded in maintaining Southern control over government veterinary inspectors stationed at certain of the fourteen local cattle depots. 'A number' of these were refusing paycheques from the imperial authorities and continued to accept salary from Dublin.[97] Among them the key appointment was at Derry, the North's second port, where not only did a Mr McCloskey grant export certificates on behalf of the provisional government, but he was staunchly supported by the local cattle dealers who would not recognise the Northern government's appointee, Mr Robinson. The Northern government attempted a clampdown but were beaten by a boycott of the cattle dealers, a threat to Robinson's life, and the English Ministry of Agriculture. The latter – apparently as a result of misinformation from the Irish Office – accepted the certificates of either inspector notwithstanding that the Northern ministry ordered McCloskey's to be refused![98]

Other instances of the obstruction policy can be seen through the eyes of Northern officials. They had seen evidence of a concerted campaign even before Collins's circular of 4 May. On the 5th the Northern Cabinet Secretary, W. B. Spender, intimated to all the Northern ministries that Craig wished to send a comprehensive report of their complaints to the Colonial Office. They were to submit to Spender by 10 May, a statement giving the following particulars:

(a) Particulars of all officials due for transfer to Northern Ireland from Southern Ireland whose transfer has been in any way obstructed.
(b) A similar list in regard to documents and records.
(c) Any acts of obstruction on the part of the provisional government or on the part of imperial representatives in Dublin in carrying out the proper transfer of duties.
(d) Any appointments made by the provisional government or imperial government with consultation of the ministries of Northern Ireland, or matters with which the latter are concerned.
(e) Any other complaints.[99]

The results disclosed that obstruction was hardly being applied in any comprehensive way. In the Ministries of Commerce and Home Affairs there was scant complaint against the provisional government. The Ministry of Labour had felt 'great embarrassment'[100] when important files had not been transferred initially; yet since then 'the provisional government abandoned its attitude, and it is now possible for us to obtain any document we require'.[101] Most complaints centred on the failure to transfer records, the ministries most inconvenienced being Finance, Agriculture and Education. In Finance Clark was particularly irritated with the Dublin Registry of Births, Deaths and Marriages, which he regarded as 'the worst offender' of all in connection with the transfer of departmental records.[102] However, the departments hit the worst by non-cooperation from the South were Agriculture and Education. From Agriculture, the Dublin authorities were withholding records whose subgroup titles filled a long list of seven foolscap pages. They dealt with a great variety of agricultural matters including the activities of agricultural schools, competitions, Acts of Parliament regulating the sale of fertilisers and feeding stuffs, seed, food and drugs, the marketing of eggs, crop diseases, horse-breeding, flax schemes, as well as financial and establishment files relating to transferred staff.[103] Education's complaints were the most extensive, filling twenty-four pages. Under several categories complaints were registered. It is perhaps sufficient to quote one short paragraph pointing out the provisional government's 'acts of obstruction' in 'general administration': 'In regard to matters of general administration there is no disposition on the part of the provisional government to cooperate with the ministry. On the contrary, there appears to be a policy deliberately directed to making it as difficult as possible for the ministry to carry out its functions.'[104]

Pollock and Clark took the Ulster case on administrative issues to London in late July.[105] A discussion paper submitted by Pollock complained that the administration of transferred services was being 'rendered very difficult by the failure and in some cases the refusal to transmit from Dublin official documents relating to Northern Ireland and necessary for the proper continuance of the services. The same difficulty had been experienced in securing the loan or transfer of personnel'. There were instances in border areas where customs and excise taxes were being demanded of 'Northern taxpayers by officers resident in the Free State, to all appearances in the name and for the benefit of the provisional government'. In the marine branch of the Board of Trade it appeared 'that the provisional government or its officials are claiming to exercise powers in Northern Ireland. A protest has been addressed to the Board of Trade by this ministry'. Not only did Pollock wish to bring to an end provisional government interference in the transferred services, he also demanded that reserved services administered in the six counties should not be carried out from Dublin. He ignored the provisions of the Treaty which contemplated that reserved services would pass finally to the United Kingdom or the Free State only when Ulster took the option to remain in or leave the Free State. He insisted, for example, that it was 'very desirable that the transit of northern mails through the Free State, which is now in a state of civil war, may be avoided' and that in border areas 'post offices should be so placed that a Northern Ireland post office may be always available for residents in Northern Ireland'. Also, Pollock claimed, the Northern government might be appointed as Crown agents in matters relating to quit rents and foreshores. (This would necessitate a transfer of Northern-related records from the Quit Rent Office in Dublin, but according to Pollock 'the northern government is advised that such segregation can be easily effected'.) Lighthouses might 'be administered by a mixed commission, containing representatives of the chief northern harbour authorities and making use of the equipment of the Belfast Harbour Commission which already has some experience of lighthouse supervision'. And strong objection was taken against the action of the British in allowing the provisional government to take physical control' of the Registry of Title (the land registry) and the Public Record Office before Northern-related records were sent to Belfast. 'The results of this policy', stated Pollock alluding bitterly to the archival catastrophe of 30 June,

> are manifest in the ruins of the Four Courts which contain the remains of many documents which could and should have been transferred to Northern Ireland months ago. We can have no guarantee that at any moment the records relating to Northern Ireland in other government departments may not suffer the fate of the documents in the Four Courts . . .
>
> In view of the complete destruction of the Public Record Office, Dublin, the creation of a northern record office becomes imperative, as it is not to be expected that Northern Ireland will send its records to a city whose inhabitants have shown so little respect for record repositories.[106]

Having read Pollock's proposals, an Irish Office official (G. G. Whiskard) observed that they 'all . . . tend in the same direction, namely the more complete severance of the government of the six counties from the rest of Ireland; and they all presuppose that the right of Northern Ireland to opt out of the Free State under article 12 of the Treaty will be exercised'. He did not doubt that this was precisely what would happen. However, to take any action at this time which assumed 'that the six counties are already permanently severed from the rest of Ireland' would be contrary to the spirit of the Treaty and provoke justifiable resentment and protest on the part of the provisional government. Any division between North and South of the Registry of Deeds, quit rents, foreshores and lighthouses at present 'would be unnecessary, inconvenient and impolitic'. The destruction of the Public Record Office was complete but if there were records in existing departments ripe for deposit, their division might be effected by agreement between North and South, 'but it should in any case await the expiration of the Ulster month'. And 'inasmuch as it cannot be assumed that the six counties will not be included in the Free State, or that if they are so included, the Free State will desire to retain a separate central [land] registry in Belfast, it is submitted that for the present only temporary accommodation is necessary' for Northern Ireland title documents.[107] Many Northern departmental records did remain in the 'physical custody' of the provisional government, and a schedule of such records produced by Clark a few days later impressed Irish Office officials as 'rather formidable'. Sturgis wrote to Cope in Dublin that he might 'please do what you can to get the provisional government people to hand them over, even though you can only get a few at a time. It will help keep Clark and Pollock quiet!'[108]

The Irish Office and North–South Relations

This comment from Sturgis reflected increasingly chilly relations between British officials in the Irish Office and the Belfast government. Indeed, Lloyd George and his closest advisers thought that the British government should at least be seen to be taking a sterner line with Northern Ireland. In this way they hoped to shore up the provisional government against Irish opponents of the Treaty. A recent commentator has observed that 'a position somewhat similar to the late 1960s, early 1970s was developing, particularly in Belfast, and the forces of law and order in the six counties were even less well accepted then'.[109] Obsessed and preoccupied with the Treaty conflict in the South, perhaps the provisional government missed the opportunity for a fuller measure of Irish unity in 1922.

On the other hand, a vital Northern Ireland ally in the British Cabinet was Winston Churchill, the Colonial Secretary, who believed the British should continue to support fully the Ulster government. North and South, he maintained, ought to be able to develop closer ties if the provisional government showed itself genuinely conservative and repudiated de Valera and the republicans once and for all.[110] Indeed, part of Churchill's vision was borne out. With the outbreak of civil war and following Collins's death, the political divide in what had been the Sinn Féin party became unbridgeable. Also, the Dublin regime came to find conservative policies essential to its stability. However, it could never afford the unpopularity that would attach to the development of close ties with the North. In a much more direct way than Churchill, British officials in the Irish Office had to deal with the two seemingly irreconcilable Irish communities. If they expected the Southern government (*a*) to survive and (*b*) to co-operate in the partition of government institutions, they would have to treat the South sympathetically while presiding over North–South contentions.

As might be expected, the Northern regime began to hold the British almost as much to blame for their grievances as the provisional government. On 11 May, W. B. Spender, the Northern Cabinet Secretary, complained to the Colonial Office 'how greatly [Northern departments] are being handicapped in their administration by the authorities – whoever they may be – in Dublin'; but also he enclosed one of the departmental reports in order to show how 'it throws a responsibility upon the British government . . .'[111] On the 17th he again wrote, enclosing all the departmental reports on provisional government 'obstruction' and made a comment highly revealing of the Northern government's view of Irish Office officials:

> I know that you will be told by the Irish Office that the most important records – namely those of the Land Commission – have been transferred to us, but if you knew the action we had to take to get these records, I am afraid that you will be convinced that the Irish Office cannot claim very much credit for helping us in this respect. Speaking quite frankly, I think that Mr Cope is so afraid of hurting the susceptibilities of the provisional government that he is quite prepared to overlook the obligations of the imperial authorities in seeing that Northern Ireland is not handicapped by the establishment of the Irish Free State.[112]

Since February the Irish Office at 38 Old Queen Street, London, had replaced the Chief Secretary's Office, Dublin Castle, as the central machinery for British administration in Ireland. The nerve centre of the old regime – shorn of most of the Irish bureaucratic apparatus now in the hands of indigenous executives – thus retreated to London after centuries in Dublin Castle. Here it telescoped and consolidated the remaining scattered elements still under its aegis. The Treasury prepared a centralised Irish vote for the 1922–3 financial year covering the remnants of imperial liabilities: the 'rag bag vote', as it was termed, would finance the operations not only of the Irish Office (including what was left of its 'branch' at Dublin Castle), but also the reserved services in Northern Ireland and those departments whose functions were not transferred to the provisional government on 1

April.[113] Sir John Anderson was now styled 'secretary to the Irish Office', but on 21 March was succeeded by Mark Sturgis. Anderson was promoted to the post of permanent under-secretary to the Home Office, although, as such, he remained generally responsible for the administration of Irish policy. James MacMahon remained the official under-secretary in Dublin; but A. W. Cope, still assistant under-secretary, was Britain's key official in Ireland performing the work of a liaison officer between Collins and Churchill and carrying on a continuous battle for political reconciliation between the British and Irish governments. Cope thus remained a sort of political trouble-shooter while Sturgis and his deputy, G. G. Whiskard, handled administrative affairs from London. Yet also, because Britain's relations with the Free State were supposed to be carried on through the Colonial Office, a further special department was established in that ministry with Lionel Curtis as head. This office was originally intended to absorb gradually all Irish Office functions in relation to the Free State.[114] In practice, however, overlap and confusion developed between it and the Irish Office. By June, Sturgis and Whiskard were warning the Colonial Office that the absence of any real liaison had made the position dangerous: 'We have a very complete Irish registry, you have another and for all I know the cabinet secretariat may have a third. . . . Letters come to Churchill on all sorts of subjects, go to Curtis who gives them to Freeston who sends a reply, while often we may have registered papers on the subject.'[115] Whiskard estimated that 60 per cent 'of the daily work of the Irish Office is work for which Churchill and not Greenwood is responsible . . .' The amount and character of the work was such that 'it would be out of the question for the work to be done by Curtis's department, as, apart from the fact that the staff at his disposal is too small to cope with it, I do not think that they themselves would suggest that they had the experience of Irish administration and affairs necessary to enable them to deal with these matters in detail'.[116] Soon, an arrangement was worked out whereby the Colonial Office was responsible for 'the formulation of general policy, including all negotiations and correspondence between the British and provisional governments'. The Irish Office, in addition to carrying out work relating to the Chief Secretary's functions, also became responsible 'for the carrying into effect of the policy laid down by the colonial office'. Document-swapping liaison arrangements were established on a daily basis between the Irish Office and Curtis's department to prevent future overlap;[117] and the Irish Office in effect became a Colonial Office branch for the execution of policy.

With regard to the government's Ulster policy, most or all of these officials took the Lloyd George view: the Northern position under the 1920 Act must be safeguarded, but the provisional government's consolidation was more of a priority. Sturgis and Whiskard, as we have seen, were particularly concerned that the Northern decision to opt out of the Free State should not be presupposed. The position of the Council of Ireland services under the Treaty had made the situation particularly awkward for them, since whatever the administrative arrangements, the political sensibilities of North or South were offended. The North wanted an agency agreement between the Irish Office and their own Department of Agriculture, and it seems that the Chief Secretary was on the verge of signing such an agreement in May, but backed off in deference to Hogan's protests.[118] In late July a branch of the Irish Office was set up in Belfast with the limited purpose of carrying out the Diseases of Animals Acts administration. This 'branch' consisted of a Mr Kenny, an official of the Northern Department of Agriculture, in so far as he performed executive work in relation to the Diseases of Animals Acts. Also, a Captain Brand, from the English Board of Agriculture, arrived in Northern Ireland to carry out the technical duties of the superintending veterinary surgeon. Only with reluctance did the Northern government accept this arrangement, claiming there would be 'inevitable delays entailed by constant reference to London', and such delays were dangerous, especially in the event of an outbreak of disease. Hogan none the less continued to protest claiming that the essence of an agreement between Churchill and Collins was 'that the work in Northern Ireland shall be administered by the chief secretary in consultation with the southern ministry; and that the northern government had no legal right to be consulted'.[119] Thus, in September Whiskard suggested yet another compromise. He proposed an arrangement devolving all the executive work on Captain Brand and, except for regular consultation, divorcing diseases of animals work completely from the Northern Department of Agriculture. If this were done, Whiskard promised, the McCloskey situation in Derry could be rectified.[120] The Northern department was incensed. 'First of all', responded the permanent secretary, J. C. Gordon,

we must protest strongly against the lack of consideration shown to this ministry throughout these negotiations. At the outset we were asked to take on the agency arrangements and when everything had been running for some time that arrangement was set aside and superseded by the agreement of 27 July, which we reluctantly accepted. It is now proposed that this ministry should have no official association whatever with the diseases of animals work in Northern Ireland.

We do not understand the suggestion that efficiency is being considered. So long as Northern Ireland has a separate ministry of agriculture and until some committee for securing coordination in the administration of the Council services in both the North and the South has been set up it appears obvious that no real efficiency or economy can be secured if diseases of animals work is completely divorced from the appropriate ministry in Northern Ireland.

Had the 1920 act been put into operation in the north and in the south, a Council of Ireland would have been established, on which the north would have had representation, which would have ensured that the agricultural interests of Northern Ireland would be fully considered. If the present proposal goes through, Northern Ireland, whose money is being spent on the service and whose livestock industry is involved, would have no say whatever.[121]

Only under certain conditions would the North agree to a new arrangement. First, a formal agreement would have to be made ensuring full consultation with the Northern department. And secondly Captain Brand – though his 'good intentions' and 'friendliness to our government' were not in doubt – would have to be replaced by someone with 'a direct interest in the success of the northern government'. Loyalty in this person was 'essential', said Gordon, 'because neither diseases of animals nor fisheries could be worked without frank and intimate cooperation with the police force, Northern Ireland'.[122]

Northern pressure bore fruit in a matter of weeks. In October an Imperial Secretary's Office was set up to administer the Council of Ireland services and certain other reserved services, that is, the Registry of Deeds, land purchase, supreme court matters and parliamentary registration and elections. The holder of the office for the three and a half years it existed was S. G. Tallents. Tallents was an Irish Office official and not a Northern officer as Gordon had pressed for. None the less he had in fact already proven his acceptability among Northern Unionists for his role in the inquiry into the operation of the Northern government in June. Lloyd George had ordered this inquiry as a substitute for the commission of inquiry demanded by Collins to investigate the failure of the North to keep the Collins–Craig pact of 30 March. Although Tallents had been critical of the performance of certain ministers and ministries, his inquiry posed no threat to the Northern state, but rather offered helpful advice on how the Northern government might function more smoothly.[123] As Imperial Secretary he was 'attached to the governor of Northern Ireland' and under personal authority from the Minister of Transport for the administration of railways and from the Home Secretary for other matters. Tallents's instructions for most purposes therefore came directly from Sir John Anderson, Home Office permanent under-secretary, rather than through the locally unpopular Irish Office who were also responsible to the Colonial Secretary for Free State affairs.[124] The office continued to function until after the boundary agreement of December 1925.

The Consolidation of Partition

In August 1922 an opportunity arose for the provisional government to foster a constructive relationship with the government of Northern Ireland. At the beginning of the month Free State leaders believed that it was time to reassess policy towards the six counties. Heretofore, the attitude of hostility and non-recognition had been influenced to a considerable degree by pressure from anti-Treaty factions. But now, having defeated the anti-Treaty candidates in the 16 June elections (notwithstanding the Collins–de Valera pact for an agreed election) and scored significant military advances against the 'irregular' forces in the early weeks of the civil war, the provisional government had a freer hand to determine what relations with the North should be. On 1 August a five-member committee was appointed to consider the question.[125] The committee included Patrick Hogan who, as we have seen, took a strong line against Northern control of diseases of animals work, and Michael Hayes, who as Dáil Minister of Education worked closely with Fionán Lynch in the policy of paying Northern Catholic teachers. But it also included Ernest Blythe who, though a Gaelic enthusiast and activist in the forefront of the separatist movement since 1906, was also an Ulster Protestant and probably the only member of the provisional government who had a realistic insight into how the Ulster Protestant mind worked. Blythe produced a memorandum for the committee stressing the futility of both military operations and attempts at economic sanctions against the North, and insisting that 'peaceful and orderly conditions' would first have to prevail before Northern Protestants could be persuaded to join with the Free State. But not only must 'all thought of force' be abandoned; as a corollary the Free State must also cease 'any relations with or any encouragement of any section in the north who refuse to acknowledge the right and authority of the northern government'. He argued that immediate steps could be taken to 'prepare the way for a state of feeling which may lead now or in the long run to the unity of Ireland'. These included urging Catholic members of the Northern Parliament to take their seats, measures to prevent border incidents, urging Catholics to disarm under a guarantee of protection from the British, and requesting prisoners in the North 'to give bail and to recognise the courts'. He was emphatic that the provisional government should stop the payment of Catholic teachers in the six counties. 'From the point of view of finance, educational efficiency and public morality it is indefensible. In the case of the primary schools, we should take the step of approaching Lord Londonderry through a suitable intermediary and arranging that the teachers who remained with us shall not be penalised.' The provisional government, wrote Blythe, should also 'stop all relations with local bodies in the six counties and should try to arrange that those which have been suppressed should be restored on condition of recognising the Northern government'. The provisional government, Blythe realised, would be accused of abandoning the Northern Catholics. Yet the answer to this was

> obvious. The belligerent policy had been shown to be useless for protecting the Catholics or stopping the pogrom. There is of course the risk that the peaceful policy will not succeed. But it has a chance where the other has no chance. The unity of Ireland is of sufficient importance for us to take a chance in the hope of gaining it. The first move lies with us. There is no urgent desire for unity in the north-east and it would be stupid obstinacy for us to wait till the Belfast attitude improved.[126]

Collins was shot on 22 August. Cope wrote to Churchill, who in turn wrote to Craig, that North–South relations should now improve. On the 29th Craig tried to encourage his Minister of Agriculture, Archdale, writing that 'Cosgrave and his entourage' might be 'more reasonable to deal with than Collins'. Churchill had told him that 'they have expressed the earnest desire to cooperate with us in the most friendly manner – I give this for what it is worth and trust it may prove accurate'.[127] Craig also wrote hopefully to his Minister of Education, Lord Londonderry that the new Dublin government seemed to have 'reversed the decision of [their] predecessors regarding the payment by Southern Ireland of the salaries of teachers in Roman Catholic schools in Northern Ireland'. Both he and Londonderry agreed that the Northern government should now be willing to 'smooth over the matter', 'waive the need of apology' from the South, and enter into negotiation with the provisional government as to what the North's financial liability might be.[128] However, Blythe was unsuccessful in convincing his colleagues of the utility of the overtures he proposed. Archdale saw no sign of co-operation from Hogan who continued to pay McCloskey's salary in Derry[129] and who in October urged his fellow ministers to protest to the British against the creation of the Imperial Secretary's Office.[130] Also, the provisional government, having failed to get the Northern Catholic clergy and teachers to approach the Northern government themselves, continued to pay teachers until the end of October.[131] In the meantime, not hearing from the provisional government, Craig's conciliatory mood wore thin. The short-lived period of Northern goodwill was probably worn away by 6 October when the Northern Cabinet took a decision to postpone the question of teachers' fees to be repaid to the South.[132]

Thus the Free State remained essentially antipathetic to Northern Ireland. True, they abandoned their blatantly obstructive tactics, but this was primarily due to considerations of practicality and cost. They remained adamant that the Treaty be adhered to in regard to the North, and were watchful of actions which might presuppose that Ulster would opt out of the Free State. For example, in November Cosgrave rebuked Chief Justice Molony for attempting to order the transfer to Northern Ireland of land registry documents. Molony believed this to be his duty under the Government of Ireland Act; but Cosgrave maintained that, as a judge, Molony was 'trespassing on the domain of politics, for such an order has implications in relation to the future decision of the north-eastern counties on the question of remaining within the Free State and to the findings of the boundary commission'.[133] Nor were the provisional government interested in initiating any significant measure of North–South co-operation. What overtures were made were inadequate and tardy. For example, in September 1922 the provisional government authorised the Minister of Education, Eoin MacNeill, to discuss with Lord Londonderry reciprocal arrangements for teacher training. However, they let the matter drift, apparently because of the embarrassment of the continued payment of Catholic teachers.[135] MacNeill brought the matter up again in February and March 1923, and finally in April wrote to Lord Londonderry. Londonderry replied that he would be happy to meet MacNeill in London or Belfast at any time, but he thought it fair to inform MacNeill that the Northern government was bringing to an end its arrangement with the Church of Ireland training college in Kildare Place 'as it appears that we are able to train as many teachers as we require under training arrangements which we have instituted in Belfast'.[136]

The provisional government's difficulty about normalising relations with the Northern government may have stemmed from the Southern ministers' own physical and psychological isolation from the situation in the North and the strange inability of the Southerner to come to grips with the reality of Ulster Loyalism and its power in the north-east; and having failed to come to terms with it, they chose to ignore it.

In 1922 and into 1923 and after, there was, in fact, no policy on the procedure for treating with the North. In February 1923 MacNeill pressed Cosgrave for a decision:

There are other questions that require arrangements between the two governments. Such arrangements can only be effected in one or other of two ways: 1st. Regarding the Belfast government as subordinate to the British government – to open discussion through the British government. 2nd. To have direct relations with the Belfast government. A third course is to drift on doing nothing and this promises no advantage. I therefore propose that the question of direct or indirect official relations with the Belfast government . . . should be treated as a question of general policy requiring to be decided without delay.[137]

Cosgrave said he favoured direct communication but, as we have seen, MacNeill received from Lord Londonderry a polite rebuff.[138] Without any statement of policy, North–South communications were passed through the British – sometimes having to circumnavigate an incredibly circuitous passage from the Northern department to the Northern Cabinet Secretary, to the Imperial Secretary, to the Home Office, to the Colonial Office, to the Free State Governor-General, to the Free State Cabinet Secretary, and so on.[139] Only after the boundary agreement of December 1925 did the respective Cabinet Secretaries, C. H. Blackmore for the North and Dermot O'Hegarty for the Free State, open direct communications on certain matters, such as government records, and in the process they made some attempt to create goodwill.[140] However, for the remainder of the Cosgrave era their cordial relationship remained an oasis in a desert of mutual estrangement and isolation.

Thus in 1922 provisional government policies were in the main propagandist, at their crudest formulated without any clearly defined objective other than preventing Northern administration from operating, at their most diplomatic formulated with a view to safeguarding the constitutional integrity of the Irish Free State. There was no attempt to breach the political/administrative barriers rapidly being built between North and South. But neither should the Northern government be seen as blameless in the legacy of mutual suspicion. Since the Government of Ireland Bill was introduced in the House of Commons in early 1920, Ulster Unionists had consistently demanded partitioned government services in Ireland including (at least since March 1921) separate administration for reserved services. While the provisional government ignored them, the Northern Unionists felt that they could afford to blame the South for the lack of co-operation between them; but the only sort of co-operation with the South they had any real use for was co-operation for a more complete division of Irish administration. Both governments by their attitude and actions collaborated in consolidating partition for the succeeding generations. The British trod a wary line between them, being extra careful to protect the forms of the metaphysical 'essential unity of Ireland' while it lasted; at the same time they were satisfied that their own aims – the withdrawal of direct British rule, partition and Ireland's status within the empire – had been achieved through the administrative apparatus.

Notes

1 'Report of a cabinet committee appointed to consider what steps should be taken on approval of the Treaty between Great Britain and Ireland, for giving effect to its provisions, and more especially for the establishment of a provisional government for Southern Ireland in terms of article 17', PGI 18, PRO CAB 27/155 (also CP 3601, CAB 24/132).

2 Minutes of a meeting of the Cabinet Committee on Irish Finance, 12 December 1921, PRO CAB 21/248. For a further examination of the British legal interpretation of the Treaty, see J. McColgan, 'Implementing the 1921 Treaty: Lionel Curtis and constitutional procedure', *Irish Historical Studies*, vol. 20, no. 79 (March 1977).

3 According to Lionel Curtis, the Colonial Office adviser on Irish affairs, reference to the 1920 Act in the Treaty 'was struck out because the mere mention of it was found to be a bugbear to the Irish delegates'. See 'Memorandum on the provisional government as contemplated by article 17 of the Treaty, by Lionel Curtis', SF(B)40, 10 December 1921, PRO CAB 21/243, cited henceforth as Curtis memorandum, 10 December 1921.

4 'Note by Sir Francis Greer', appendix 1 to Curtis memorandum, 10 December 1921.

5 Cabinet Committee memorandum PGI 1, 21 December 1921, PRO CAB 27/154. At the time of its establishment members consisted of Sir Laming Worthington-Evans (Secretary of State for War), Sir Gordon Hewart (Attorney-General), Sir Hamar Greenwood (Chief Secretary for Ireland) and Lord Fitzalan (the Viceroy), with Tom Jones and Lionel Curtis as secretaries.

6 Summary of conclusions of the first three meetings of the PGI Committee, 21 December 1921, PGI 14, 23 December 1921, PRO CAB 27/154. Part of the conclusions reads: 'In the event of a favourable vote by the present Southern House of Commons, Mr Griffith and his colleagues should be invited to discuss immediately with the British government the establishment of a "makeshift" government preceding the creation of a provisional government.' Memorandum PGI 16, a revision of PGI 14 and of the same date, changed 'makeshift', to 'temporary provisional'.

7 Curtis memorandum, 10 December 1921.

8 A copy of the minutes of this meeting is in the archives of the Taoiseach's Office, SPOI S.1. Nowhere in the agenda or the minutes of the meeting or in Griffith's letter summoning the members can be found the expression 'Parliament of Southern Ireland'.

9 Conference minutes 22/N/60(1), 18 January 1922; 22/N/60(2), 19 January 1922, PRO CAB 21/249 (also CAB 43/6).

10 See *Heads of Working Arrangements for Implementing the Treaty*, Vol. 1, Cmd 1911, HC 1923, *Parliamentary Papers*, vol. 18, p. 123.

11 Churchill's account of recent meetings with Irish ministers in Cabinet conclusions 3(22)4, 23 January 1922, PRO CAB 21/252.

12 'Extract from Mr Collins's statement at a constitutional committee meeting', 24 January 1922, SPOI S.3124.

13   Provisional government minutes, 26 January 1922, SPOI G.1/1.
14   See Irish memorandum of conference in London between Collins, Duggan and O'Higgins, and Lloyd George and Churchill, 21 January 1922, SPOI S.11: 'There was discussion as to the means of giving effect to the treaty, and as to the best form the legislation in the imperial parliament might take. The suggestion was favoured that a one-clause bill should be passed to ratify the Treaty with the articles of agreement as schedule (1) and the constitution as schedule (2)'.
15   ibid.
16   Cabinet conclusions 3(33), 23 January 1922, PRO CAB 23/29.
17   Curtis had considered 'the all important question as to how much time is likely to elapse before an Irish constitution has been framed, passed into law and given effect to by the holding of elections', in his 10 December memorandum. 'The assumption seems to have been that two or three months might cover these processes . . . [However,] the settled determination of the Irish leaders is a fact to be held in mind. If Ireland is to initiate the first draft of her own constitution it is not rash to predict that months will elapse before the draft is ready for submission to the British government . . . The process of agreement on this point between the two governments is not likely to be easy or short. To those who have witnessed the evolution of a dominion constitution it is difficult to conceive that a regular government of the Irish Free State will be constituted within six months. Nor would it be surprising if the twelve months contemplated in article 17 had elapsed before this point had been reached. The officials whose views are reflected in this memorandum agreed that it was wise to consider the provisional government as an arrangement more likely to extend to twelve months than to three.'
18   This was another development that was no surprise to Curtis. Again his 10 December memorandum: 'If, on the other hand, the government desires to gratify Irish wishes to the full extreme, and to face all the risks involved, the procedure suggested in this memorandum can be adapted for the purpose. That procedure involves the passage of a bill early next year. A clause might be added to that bill providing that the new parliament of the provisional government should have power to enact the Irish constitution. In this event, however, it would have to be specifically stated in the British Act that the constitution so enacted would be valid only in so far as the courts and privy council on appeal might decide that its terms were in harmony with those of the treaty. Unless this were laid down by statute the safeguards of the treaty would be robbed of their effect.'
19   'Report of the Attorney-General's committee on legislation required to establish the Free State', 24 January 1922, PRO CAB 21/252. Members of the committee were Greenwood, Anderson, Hewart, Greer and Liddell, with Curtis as secretary.
20   Provisional government minutes, 31 January 1922, SPOI G.1/1.
21   ibid.
22   ibid., 1 February 1922.
23   ibid., 2 February 1922.
24   Conference minutes, 22/N/60(3), 5 February 1922; 22/N/60(4), 6 February 1922, PRO CAB 21/249 (also CAB 43/6).
25   Figgis to Curtis, 9 February 1922, PRO CAB 27/154.
26   Newscuttings in the Kennedy papers, UCDAD P4.
27   Read by Viscount Peel to the House of Lords, 21 March 1922, Hansard (Lords), 5th series, vol. 49, col. 663. Ironically, by the time the dispute was resolved between the British and the provisional government, Northern Ireland herself was showing she was hardly interested in surveying the terms of the constitution before deciding to join or to remain out of the Free State. In March a series of amendments to the Irish Free State (Agreement) Bill proposed in the House of Lords were gauged to reinforce the security of Northern Ireland's position under the Treaty

and included a proposal that the Ulster month should start from the date the Treaty Bill was passed. While the provisional government had wished to secure immediate legal recognition for the Free State, the North was now equally anxious to opt out of it. However, the government side easily defeated the motion, and a clause was included in the Bill expressly providing that it would not be the same statute which ratified the Treaty for purposes of the 'Ulster month'. See also, Cabinet conclusions 22(22)3, 29 March 1922, PRO CAB 23/29; and Churchill's speech on 30 March 1922 in Hansard (Commons), 5th series, vol. 155, col. 1691.

28 12 Geo. V, ch. 4.
29 13 Geo. V, ch. 1; Irish Free State (Saorstát Eireann) Act (no. 1 of 1922).
30 'Transfer of services hitherto administered by the British government in Ireland', proclamation by the provisonal government, 16 January 1922, SPOI CSORP 1921/3864/2.
31 See SPOI S.1 and CSORP 1921/3864/2.
32 Collins to each member of the provisional government, 19 January 1922, SPOI S.1.
33 Provisional government minutes, 1 February 1922, SPOI G.1/1. See also R. Fanning, *The Irish Department of Finance* (Dublin, 1978), pp. 38, 78–9.
34 Memorandum by Winston Churchill, PGI 2, 21 December 1921, PRO CAB 27/154.
35 Murray to Masterton-Smith, 4 February 1922, PRO CO 739/5/20146.
36 Post Office memorandum, 21 February 1922, PRO CAB 21/248.
37 IF Committee, 1st minutes, 21 February 1922, PRO CO 739/5/20146.
38 ibid.
39 ibid.
40 Treasury memorandum [attached to Post Office memorandum] on 'Post Office in Southern Ireland', submitted to PGI finance subcommittee, IF 4, 21 February 1922, PRO CAB 21/248.
41 Waterfield to Sir Henry Bunbury, 4 March 1922, PRO T 158/7.
42 ibid.
43 *Irish Oifigiuil*, 14 April 1922. See also ITC 7th conclusions, 28 March 1922, PRO CO 739/4/15083.
44 Kennedy to Hogan, 19 January 1923, Kennedy papers, UCDAD P4.
45 Supplemental agreement to the Provisional Government (Transfer of Functions) Order as to the date of the transfer of the Clerk of Crown and Hanaper, 5 December 1922, PRO CO 739/8/58790.
46 ITC 6th conclusions, 21 March 1922, PRO CAB 21/252.
47 Treasury memorandum [by O. E. Niemeyer] to PGI finance subcommittee, 17 March 1922, PRO CAB 21/248.
48 IF subcommittee conclusions, 6 March 1922, PRO CAB 21/248.
49 As note 45.
50 Sources for this paragraph are found in the correspondence and memoranda of PRO CO 739/10/16790, 21206, 63882; CO 739/22/14374, 28809, 40057.
51 The Minister of Finance for Northern Ireland to the Prime Minister of Northern Ireland, 12 June 1922, subsequently annotated and submitted to the British Cabinet's Irish technical subcommittee, 21 July 1921 [as a discussion document for meeting held 26 July 1922], PRO CO 739/13/35785 (also PRO CAB 27/158 and 160).
52 Waterfield to Niemeyer, 16 October 1922, PRO T 158/9.
53 Horan to Anderson, 20 February 1922, PRO CAB 21/250.
54 Note by Sir John Anderson, 21 February 1922, ibid.
55 Minutes of a meeting of the ITC subcommittee, 21 February 1922, ibid.
56 Sources on this matter are in the correspondence and memoranda in PRO CO 739/10/17873; CO 739/22/22753, 34706, 39284; CO 739/23/48225.

57 In September 1923, however, Waterfield began to have doubts about the substance of the British claim and by January 1924 he had heard that Crown lands in Canada had been transferred to that Dominion in 1867. 'If that were the case it would give the Free State an almost unanswerable argument against our claim, provided that crown lands were on the same [*jure coronae*] footing.'

58 Treasury memorandum [by O. E. Niemeyer] to PGI finance subcommittee, IF 7, 4 March 1922 [considered by the subcommittee on 6 March], PRO CAB 21/248. Report of committee appointed by the Treasury, IF 4, 2 March 1922 and IF subcommittee conclusions, 6 March 1922, PRO 21/248.

59 Waterfield to J. H. Craig, 19 January 1922, PRO T 158/7.

60 Memorandum by Waterfield to provisional government, 23 January 1922, PRO T 158/7.

61 As a result of the death of William Starkie.

62 As a result of the retirement of Sir Henry Robinson.

63 '. . . on the principle of "head for head" exchange of officers in the same rank, and as a rule of approximately the same age and pay . . .'

64 Waterfield sent copies to James MacMahon requesting him to forward the memo to the provisional government. (See Waterfield to the Under-Secretary, 190/22, 21 January 1922, ibid.) He also hoped to meet with the new government: 'The matter is so complicated that I should be glad if it could be arranged for me to have an interview with the provisional government at a very early date, at which I could explain the whole position more fully and give details of any cases on which the ministers might desire to have further information.' Although he apparently received no interview right away, he 'had a very interesting talk' with Cosgrave on 6 March on the replacement of Sir Henry Robinson, the position of ex-servicemen and the transfer of volunteers to the North, and other matters in which he found Cosgrave generally co-operative on all points. (See Waterfield to Anderson, 7 March 1922, PRO T 158/7.)

65 Waterfield to Percy Thompson, 8 February 1922, PRO T 158/7.

66 Waterfield to H. C. Eyles (Office of Woods), 14 February 1922, PRO T 158/7.

67 By August the work of his assistant, B. W. Gilbert, was wholly integrated in the Irish Department of Finance.

68 Niemeyer to Masterton-Smith, 3 April 1922, PRO CO 739/10/17365.

69 ibid.

70 Gilbert to Niemeyer, 20 May 1922, PRO T 158/9.

71 Waterfield to O'Brien, 9 March 1922, PRO T 158/8.

72 Waterfield to Clark, 28 February 1922, PRO T 158/7.

73 See files concerning 'staff arrangements on notification of constitution of Irish Free State, 1922–7', PRO T 162/85 (and 86)/E.9478 (and subseries); also 'Ireland: schemes for transfer of staff to provisional government under article 7(i)(b); financial agreement, 24 November 1922–13 August 1924', PRO T 162/95/E.9764.

74 Waterfield to Niemeyer, 30 June 1922, PRO T 164/31/P.27147A (also T 160/108/F.4159/1).

75 See, for example, Kennedy to the chairman [of the provisional government, Michael Collins], 20 May 1920, Kennedy papers, UCDAD P 4.

76 Anderson to Niemeyer, 8 July 1922, PRO T 164/31/P.27147A.

77 See PRO T 164/31/P.27147A and T 160/108/F.4159/1.

78 Clark to Waterfield, 16 June 1922, PRO T 164/31/P.27147A.

79 Waterfield to Clark, 24 June 1922, ibid.

80 Provisional government minutes, 23 January, 2 February 1922, SPOI G.1/1.

81 ibid., 30 January 1922.

82 ibid.

83 ibid., 1 and 2 February 1922.

84 Memorandum from the Department of Education, marked 'not circulated', November 1932, SPOI S.1973B.
85 See SPOI S.1973 A and B and several files in PRONI ED 13.
86 Michael Hopkinson, 'Collins, de Valera, Mulcahy, Liam Lynch: attitudes to the Irish civil war', unpublished paper delivered to a meeting of the Irish Historical Society, 9 September 1980. I am grateful to Dr Hopkinson for supplying me with a copy of his very original and interesting paper.
87 P. Buckland, *The Factory of Grievances: Devolved Government in Northern Ireland, 1921–39* (Barnes & Noble: Dublin and New York, 1979), p. 205.
88 ibid., p. 196.
89 ibid., p. 195.
90 Minute sheet, Collins to E. J. Duggan [Minister of Home Affairs], 4 May 1922, Kennedy papers, UCDAD, P 4.
91 Provisional government minutes, PG 17, 15 May 1922, UCDAD P7/B/243.
92 Secretary, provisional government to the Minister of Education, 18 May 1922, SPOI S.1973A.
93 [?O Dubhtaigh] to Collins, n.d. [? late May–early June 1922], SPOI S.1973A.
94 Waterfield to Clark, 25 March 1922, PRO T 158/8.
95 'The administration of the Diseases of Animals Acts in Ireland by two separate authorities', unsigned, n.d. [? May 1922], Mulcahy papers, UCDAD P 7/B/243.
96 PGI committee, 16th conclusions, 10 March 1922, PRO CO 739/5/20147.
97 Provisional government minutes, PG 52, 6 July 1922, copy in Mulcahy papers, UCDAD P 7/B/244.
98 For the Northern government's correspondence and memoranda on this matter see PRONI CAB 9E/3.
99 PRONI CAB 9A/1/1.
100 Magill (Home Affairs) to Spender, 10 May 1922, Litchfield (Commerce) to the Secretary of the Cabinet, 9 May 1922, ibid. Commerce perceived 'a certain passive obstruction'.
101 Dale to the Secretary of the Cabinet, 11 May 1922, ibid.
102 Clark to Spender, 9 May 1922, ibid.
103 Coyle to Spender, 9 May 1922, ibid.
104 Memorandum enclosed with McQuibban to the Secretary of the Cabinet, 10 May 1922, ibid.
105 ITC committee, 12 conclusions, 26 July 1922, PRO CO 739/13/35785.
106 The Minister of Finance to the Prime Minister [of Northern Ireland], 12 June 1922, annotated and submitted to the British Cabinet's Irish technical subcommittee on 21 July 1922 as a discussion paper for meeting [held 26 July], PRO CO 739/13/35785 (also PRO CAB 27/158 and 160).
107 'Irish Office observations on [Pollock's] proposals', memorandum by G. G. Whiskard, ITC 58, 25 July 1922, PRO CO 739/13/35785 (also CAB 27/160).
108 Clark to secretary ITC committee, 29 July 1922, Sturgis to Cope, 8 August 1922, PRO CO 739/13/37398.
109 Hopkinson, as note 86 above.
110 P. Bew, P. Gibbon and H. Patterson, *The State in Northern Ireland, 1921–72: Political Forces and Social Classes* (Manchester, 1979), p. 51.
111 Spender to Masterton-Smith, 11 May 1922, Clark to Spender, 9 May 1922, PRONI CAB 9A/1/1 (also PRO CO 739/13/35785).
112 Spender to Masterton-Smith, 17 May 1922, PRONI CAB 9A/1/1.
113 Whiskard to Waterfield, 4 February 1922, Whiskard to Treasury (Ireland), 9 February 1922, PRO T 162/79/E.8003.
114 T. Jones, *Whitehall Diary, Vol. 3: Ireland 1918–25*, ed. K. Middlemas, (London, 1971), p. 194.

115   Sturgis to Masterton-Smith, 28 June 1922, PRO CO 739/12/35095.
116   Whiskard to Sturgis, 28 June 1922, ibid.
117   ibid.
118   Gordon to Archdale, 14 July 1922, PRONI CAB 9E/3.
119   Hogan to Waterfield, 4 August 1922, PRO T 158/9.
120   Whiskard to J. V. Coyle [assistant secretary Northern Ireland Department of Agriculture], 20 September 1922, CAB 9E/3.
121   Gordon to Whiskard, 26 September 1922, PRONI CAB 9E/3.
122   ibid.
123   Bew, Gibbon and Patterson, op. cit.
124   Home Office memorandum 440 210/20 [by Sir John Anderson], 8 January 1923, PRO T 162/88/E.9905. At the end of the provisional government period when the Free State was set up and the office of Chief Secretary was abolished, the Colonial Office staff, Freeston and Antrobus, were absorbed into the Irish Office; from 6 December 1922 Old Queen Street dealt with all Irish business and became responsible to the Colonial Office for matters relating to the Free State and to the Home Office for matters relating to Northern Ireland.
125   Extract from provisional government minutes, 1 August 1922, Blythe papers, UCDAD P 24/62.
126   'Policy in regard to the northeast', memorandum [by Ernest Blythe], 9 August 1922, Blythe papers, UCDAD P 24/70.
127   Craig to Archdale, 29 August 1922, PRONI CAB 9E/3. Interestingly, in a letter to Craig complaining about the McCloskey affair on 23 August, Archdale made the following comment: 'Bad job Collins being killed if true.'
128   Craig to Londonderry, 19 September 1922, Pollock to Craig, 21 September 1922, Craig to Pollock, 23 September 1922, PRONI FIN 18/1/314. Pollock, however, thought the provisional government should 'stew in its own juice'.
129   Until, it seems, in October when the British government made new arrangements in Derry port for diseases of animals administration. (Provisional government minutes, PG 33(a) [copy], 10 October 1922, Mulcahy papers, UCDAD P 7/B/245). In January 1923 the Free State Executive Council expressed little interest in a report that cattle drovers in Derry refused to recognise McCloskey's successor, appointed by the Northern government. (Executive Council minutes C.1/36, 27 January 1923, copy in Mulcahy papers, UCDAD P 7/B/245).
130   Provisional government minutes PG 41(a), 19 October 1922, copy in Mulcahy papers, UCDAD P 7/B/245.
131   SPOI S.1973 A & B. Months later, when financial matters were to the fore in Anglo-Irish relations, Cosgrave began to think about trying to get the money back, but was reluctant to initiate the proceedings directly with the Northern government. A British official described the meeting in July 1923 at which Cosgrave broached the subject: 'Mr Cosgrave was visibly suffering under a strong feeling that the action of the south in the matter had been quite unjustified, and that they could not really put up a claim to the north for a refund of this money; and he did not actually ask Ormsby-Gore to put up a claim for him. His position was, as it were, that it would be very jolly if the north were to offer of their own accord to refund the money so paid.' A meeting between Cosgrave and Craig only drew from the latter a counter-claim of £1,000,000 'due to traders and others in Northern Ireland on account of goods seized and destroyed on the railways in Southern Ireland'. (Whiskard to Sturgis, 12 July 1923, Curtis to Whiskard, 21 July 1923, PRO CO 739/20/38464.)
132   Northern Ireland Cabinet draft conclusions, 6 October 1922, PRONI CAB 4/54/5.
133   See SPOI S.1864.

135 See 'Payment of Catholic teachers in the northeast', provisional government [? Department of Education] memorandum, n.d. [? September–October 1922], SPOI 1973 A.

136 MacNeill to the President, 27 February 1923; extract from Executive Council minutes, C.1/60, 26 April 1923, SPOI S. 1973.

137 MacNeill to 'Acting Secretary' [of the Free State Executive Council], 27 February 1923, SPOI S.1730.

138 Rúnaídh aire to each minister, 1 March 1923, SPOI S.1730; Lord Londonderry to MacNeill, 26 April 1923, SPOI S.1973.

139 See PRONI CAB 9A/1/1.

140 See ibid. and SPOI S.3111 A and B.

Conclusion

Britain's political policy in Ireland in 1920–2 was a success. It was a success because the government's basic principles were upheld in the settlement: Ireland remained part of the empire and the new Irish state was established constitutionally notwithstanding the 'war of independence'. Also the Ulster question was solved, without 'coercing' the Ulster Unionists, by means of partition. Thus, the British left Ireland on their own terms: the non-separation of Ireland from the empire, and the non-coercion of 'Ulster'. Why and how was the problem resolved so favourably for the British? The answer, at least in part, lies in the administrative history of British disengagement. In no small way political success was achieved through the adroit exploitation of administrative apparatus and with the help and advice of the civil servants who managed that apparatus.

The administrative steps for a constitutional withdrawal began with the reform of Dublin Castle in the spring of 1920. The appointment there of a large team of dynamic and politically liberal officials not only facilitated the start of Anglo-Irish negotiations (albeit that these were more than a year in coming), it also ensured a successful, smooth transfer of powers. For, at the Treaty of December 1921, there were on hand, in charge of government machinery to be transferred, officials with whom the provisional government could freely liaise, people untainted with the Unionist ascendancy background and viewpoint of their predecessors, and openly favourable to the Dominion settlement and to representative democracy in Ireland.

In the intervening months between administrative reform in Dublin Castle and the signing of the Treaty, the other British priority, resolving the 'Ulster problem', was attended to, again to a significant degree in terms of bureaucratic machinery. The installation at Belfast of Sir Ernest Clark not only presaged partition four months before the 1920 Act became law, but initiated it in a practical way by the establishment of central administrative apparatus working in the interests of the prospective Northern Ireland government. The British thus gave the Ulster Unionists their official blessing and active assistance in the process of building the wall of administrative partition. From an early stage Sir James Craig and his colleagues realised the importance of control over the components of administrative apparatus. Ever since the first proposals for a new Home Rule Bill in the reports of Walter Long's committee in 1919 they had attempted to influence the shape of various provisions in the Bill with a view to the complete separation of the two Irish administrations. Later, on the eve of their election to power in the new Northern government, they contemplated that once in office they would press for even greater administrative isolation from the South than the 1920 Act had provided, in the division of reserved services. This particularism in administrative control also came into conflict with the 1920 Act's civil service provisions: from its beginning in the summer of 1921 the Northern government became partial to recruits with local and 'loyal' origins, and regarded with suspicion the majority of existing Irish officers who could have been compulsorily allocated to Belfast under the 1920 Act.

On the other hand, British policy interests placed constraints on Northern Unionist freedom of action where it affected British efforts to settle with the South. The establishment of a Parliament and government in Belfast in June 1921 – implementing a major plank in British policy – gave the British the freedom they needed to negotiate with Sinn Féin, and this meant a temporary halt in the process of vesting the Northern government with powers. During the delicate negotiations with Sinn Féin which followed in the second half of 1921, the British would at least have to exercise considerable discretion in the timing of the transfer of services to Northern Ireland. Northern services were at first withheld in order to give Sinn Féin the impression that Ulster autonomy might be bargainable; but once Sinn Féin conceded Ulster autonomy, services were transferred as part of a (feigned?) ploy by Lloyd George to attract Craig to a compromise in some sort of all-Ireland arrangement. Craig, of course, remained immovable. Lloyd George resorted to the boundary commission idea and to eliciting from Griffith the letter of assurance not to 'queer the pitch' of the government's struggle with the diehard Tories. This was the letter used against Griffith at the eleventh hour of the negotiations to defeat the Irish on the Ulster question. In any case, the significant result of the transfer of services was that partition was now achieved in the practical sense: the establishment in June 1921 of the state, Parliament and government of Northern Ireland was now consolidated in November by vesting that government with administrative powers. In 1921 the Northern state was given the full go-ahead and partition was a fact.

In 1922 the Southern state would be established and given a fuller measure of autonomy than the 1920 Government of Ireland Act. The settlement was nevertheless still consistent with imperial supremacy, and in this administration and administrators played a major role. For example, on account of the advice of constitutional experts such as Lionel Curtis, the method by which executive power was transferred to the Irish Free State ensured consistency with Dominion precedent: the Free State must be an imperial creation, must in its establishment follow procedures which could not be interpreted as bringing the Free

State into existence on the authority of the Irish through 'default' by the British; nor could the provisional government, without legislation, be regarded legally as a 'government' but a transient executive committee in whom were temporaiily vested the 'functions' of certain departments in so far as they related to 'Southern Ireland'. Michael Collins and his provisional government had hoped to usher revolution in through the back door; or at least they hoped to undermine their republican opponents' position by being able to claim that the Free State was set up on the Dáil's authority and not by an Act of Parliament. However, Lionel Curtis and Sir John Anderson were diligent sentries. In order to ward off Irish attempts to skirt around constitutional procedures they insisted that the Treaty had to be ratified by Parliament not once, but twice. It is small wonder that the 'Collins–de Valera pact' constitution could not get through the net: indeed, from the British, viewpoint the pact, and the constitution it produced, would appear to have vindicated Curtis and his punctiliousness about constitutional procedures.

Yet, at the same time, the British were keenly aware of republican opposition to the Treaty and to the provisional government which upheld it. If they would not permit the immediate establishment of the Free State for constitutional reasons, they were none the less fully cognisant of the need for an interim executive that was stable and strong and able to weather formidable opposition to the Treaty within Ireland. Steps were taken to see that the provisional government, in both its 'temporary' and 'regularised' stages, would be regarded publicly as the *de facto* authority in Southern Ireland. Most departmental machinery was placed in the hands of the new ministers, and existing departmental heads were directed to be responsible to them and to comply with their instructions. Officials in the Irish Office and in Treasury (Ireland), notwithstanding unanswered queries, delays and perhaps a certain amount of hostility from the provisional government, none the less played a full role in bolstering its stability. With patience, caution and restraint they co-operated with the provisional government in finding its financial feet and supported it politically as far as they could against Northern Ireland, if not in policies of obstruction, then in preventing the North from being able to presuppose its option to contract out of the Free State before 6 December 1922.

With the two Irish governments finally off the ground, both set about consolidating control over their administrative apparatus. But in exploiting this apparatus for political ends, the provisional government's efforts, at least in so far as its Northern policy was concerned, must be deemed a failure. Ultimately they also served to hinder, rather than improve, any remote chance there might have been for some measure of Irish unity. During the Treaty conferences, Sinn Féin negotiators had failed to appreciate the significance of the transfer of services to the North. Now, as head of the government in Dublin, Michael Collins came to believe that partition might be undermined by non-cooperation with Northern ministries; by encouraging and financially supporting sections of people in the six counties refusing to recognise the Northern government; and generally by obstructing the process, begun under the British, of dividing the administration. Arguably, there was a chance that these measures and other action Collins was taking against the North could have had some effect. In the interest of the provisional government's stability, British advisers in the spring of 1922 were urging sanctions against the North for failure to implement the Collins–Craig pact. However, the Southern factions, in their splendid isolation from the conflicts within the North, did not take advantage of the weakest side of British policy, could not distract themselves sufficiently from the constitutional quarrel to rally to the rescue of Irish unity. The obstruction campaign, as it was, probably suffered from lack of comprehensive strategy and a clear definition of objectives. Also, since November 1921 it had become a duty of Dublin departments under the British to co-operate with Northern ministries in setting up departmental machinery by means of the loan of officials and the transfer of office records. To interfere with this process, which had already begun in their departments, provisional government ministers had to be particularly active; and only in education and agriculture was the obstruction policy very seriously pursued for a time. Ministers were, at any rate, preoccupied mainly with the chief public issue in the South, that is, the Treaty controversy and the development of civil war. The outbreak of civil war at the end of June tended to reduce the significance of the Northern issue in Southern politics and soon the provisional government entertained the idea of discontinuing active anti-Northern policies. Yet, the easing of North–South tension in August–September 1922 was not followed up by the pursuance of friendly relations with the North. Rather, the provisional government ignored the government in Belfast and took up the Northern question only where it threatened to compromise the provisional government's authority under the Treaty as caretaker for the Free State. Questions of unity were subordinated to questions of constitutional status, and the result was to reinforce regional isolation and political partition.

However, in terms of consolidating sovereignty, the Irish administration served the Free State well. In fact, a major reason why the new Irish state enjoyed relative political stability in its first decade was the inheritance of a working body of administration from the British. This experience differed from that of many other ex-colonies whose political stability, such as it was, had to be underwritten by military and dictatorial regimes. Despite economic backwardness, civil war at its birth, and the boycott of its Parliament for five years by one of the major political parties, the Free State nevertheless achieved, by 1927, the general acceptance of party alternation in government. This political stability was made possible by sound administrative foundations. The civil service was handed over reorganised and intact. Of 21,000 civil servants who transferred to the Free State civil service, less than 1,000 resigned in its first few years; there were a few hundred cases of exchanges between departments in Great Britain and Ireland; and only about 300 officials working in the South before 1922 now joined the Northern Ireland service. Although the multitude of semi-autonomous boards were soon swept away, the bureaucratic entities remained. Buildings, office equipment, records, organisation, functions and procedure remained, as did personnel, who merely transferred allegiance from the Chief Secretary or Boards of Commissioners to the Free State ministers. The Ministers and Secretaries Act of 1924 consolidated groups of services under ministerial departments and defined, in law, ministerial responsibility for departmental action. Thus the basic continuity enjoyed by the Irish administration in terms of staff and bureaucratic machinery ensured the Free State's survival and stability. The Free State worked because it adapted and utilised administration inherited from the British.

In contrast with the South's failure to sabotage partition in administration, Northern Ireland's desire to break all administrative connection with the South, where this was at all feasible, was fulfilled. Ironically, however, this was as a result of the Treaty more than as a consequence of their own diplomatic efforts. In the summer of 1922 Pollock and Clark worried lest the provisional government should control departments in Dublin administering reserved services in Northern Ireland. Yet the inevitable result of the Treaty's 'Ulster option' was that Northern Ireland would remain subordinate to Westminster rather than to Dublin, and that this would necessitate the removal from Dublin to Belfast of the reserved services' central offices. And when the British acquiesced in the provisional government's prohibition of compulsory civil service transfer to Belfast, Northern Ireland was free to employ the vast majority of its civil service from local recruitment resources. Thus, though it would not be politic for them to admit it, the Treaty inadvertantly achieved for the Northern Unionists that more complete administrative partition they had hoped for, but could not find in the Government of Ireland Act 1920.

Thus, the disengagement of Britain from direct rule over Ireland was a success. In 1920-22 British administrators prepared to end their role as decision-makers in the Irish administration. As their final act they presided over the transfer of powers to central governments in the Irish Free State and in Northern Ireland. In this way they afforded the new Irish ministries the facilities to lay stable foundations for the new states.

The task was a difficult one, for it entailed the formulation of procedures constitutionally consistent with both the Treaty and the Government of Ireland Act, documents which frequently contradicted one another in their interpretation. Yet, as arbiters in North-South contentions over disputed administrative spheres, British officials enjoyed reasonable success: while preventing the Northern government from prejudicing the Treaty by premature administrational partition, they also prevented the provisional government from perpetrating any really effective or lasting administrative incursions in the six counties. In the end each side got what it most wanted in administrative transition: the South, sovereignty; the North, partition; the British, a settlement to the Ulster question, a constitutional withdrawal from the South and, for the moment, the preservation of the empire.

Source Analysis

Most of this book is based on primary sources, the archives of government departments and the 'semi-official' material among the private papers of individuals. The following analysis is set out first by the location of materials (London, Dublin, Belfast), then by repository, record group or collection and, where useful, the item used or examined. Following the primary source analysis is a list of secondary and printed sources.

PRIMARY SOURCES

London – Public Record Office (PRO)

CABINET

By 1919 the British Cabinet's secretariat, or Cabinet Office, was confirmed as a permanent part of the machinery of government. The office was responsible for arranging Cabinet meetings, circulating memoranda, recording the minutes, or 'conclusions', of meetings, keeping files and providing the secretariat for Cabinet committees. The minutes of Cabinet meetings and ministers' conferences (CAB 23) might be said to form the core of Cabinet archives. Other Cabinet records researched for this book were created in the execution of policy or the administration of the Cabinet Office, that is, registered files (CAB 21), memoranda (CAB 24), the reports, proceedings and memoranda of Cabinet committees (CAB 27), and a group of records compiled relating to conferences on Ireland (CAB 43).

CAB 23 – conclusions
The Cabinet held eighty-two meetings in 1920, ninety-three in 1921 and fifty-nine in 1922. Ireland was discussed at a large number of these meetings, taking its place among the other vital issues of the era, for example, peace treaties, domestic reconstruction, industrial strikes and unrest, and the economic situation and unemployment. Volumes 18–32 cover the period late 1919–22. This is a vital source in following the trends of the government's Irish policy. The minutes usually follow the course of discussion at length, but were written with the deliberate intent to obfuscate disagreement. It is therefore usually impossible to ascertain how individuals at meetings and conferences differed in their views. On the other hand, statements (sometimes lengthy soliloquys) by Lloyd George and others are frequently recorded and provide an important insight to their respective approaches to the Irish question. It is important to use CAB 23 in conjuction with Tom Jones, *Whitehall Diary, Vol. 3* because the account of meetings Jones kept in his private papers frequently supplements what is in the official record.

CAB 21 – registered files
Subject files consisting of correspondence and memoranda. The following were the most useful to this work.

/207 Position of English civil servants in Ireland, August 1920.
/243 Irish settlement: negotiations between His Majesty's government and Irish leaders, 1921.
/248 Irish settlement: Southern Ireland: financial arrangements, 1922.
/249 Conference on Ireland with Irish ministers, 1922.
/250 Ireland: provisional government of, 1922.
/252 Irish Free State (Agreement) Act, a Bill to give effect to article 17 of the Treaty, 1922.

CAB 24 – memoranda
This group consists of reports and memoranda circulated to members of the Cabinet to provide the basis of discussion or to give information. Volumes 92–139 cover the late 1919–22 period. Documents are individually numbered. The 'CP' series began with no. 1 on 4 November 1919 and reached no. 4379 by the end of 1922. Several were of direct use for this work. CP 1693 (which, like Cabinet minutes, should be read with Tom Jones *Whitehall Diary*) reveals the die-hard opposition in the Cabinet to the conciliatory proposals of Dublin Castle officers. Also, several memoranda in early 1921 show how political influences had a bearing on determining the time-table for implementing the Government of Ireland Act, 1920.

/109 Notes of a conference with officers of the Irish government. CP 1693, 23 July 1920.
/118 The Home Rule Act. Memorandum by the Chief Secretary for Ireland ['prepared by the parliamentary draftsman to the Irish Office on the practicability of holding elections for the parliament of Northern Ireland in advance of those of the parliament of Southern Ireland . . .']. CP 2444, 12 January 1921.
/120 The Government of Ireland Act. Memorandum by the Chief Secretary for Ireland ['on the progress of the arrangements made for bringing the Government of Ireland Act into operation and on certain points requiring early decision by the cabinet']. CP 2641, 27 February 1921.
/121 Government of Ireland Act. Memorandum by the Chief Secretary for Ireland [submitting a 'timetable of proceedings for the first elections and first meetings of the parliaments of Southern and Northern Ireland . . . based on the assumption that Tuesday, the 3rd May, will be fixed as the appointed day for the establishment of the two parliaments and the provisions immediately consequential thereon']. CP 2723, 16 March 1921.
/122 The Irish elections and an offer of a truce. Memorandum by Dr Addison. CP 2829, 13 April 1921. [Memorandum] circulated by the Secretary of State for India [E. S. Montagu, relating to the offer of a truce]. CP 2840, 14 April 1921.
/123 Elections in Ireland. Proposed offer of a truce. Memorandum by Dr Addison. CP 2906, 4 May 1921.

A memorandum by the Chief Secretary on 6 October 1921 (CP 3369 in CAB 24/128) throws light on the tensions between the Northern and British governments over the withholding of services from Northern Ireland. It comments on attached letters from Sir James Craig who 'urges that full executive powers should be conferred forthwith on the government of Northern Ireland by the transfer to that government of the functions now exercised by various departments in Ireland in so far as they relate to Northern Ireland'. Other documents were used from CAB 24, but these were produced by the various Cabinet committees and are thus duplicates of reports and memoranda found of the records of these committees in CAB 27.

CAB 27 – Reports, proceedings and memoranda of Cabinet committees
The records of the following Cabinet committees were essential sources:

/68–70   Committee on Ireland, CI series, 1919–20. Vol. I, reports and proceedings; Vols II and III, memoranda CI 1–104. Also,

/156   Government of Ireland Bill amendments subcommittee, CI(A) series, minutes of meetings, 1920. Chaired by Walter Long, First Lord of the Admiralty. These records are vital evidence for tracing the formulation of government policy in regard to those provisions of the Government of Ireland Bill relating to administrative services, particularly the reserved services and the Council of Ireland services. Running through the reports to the Cabinet, and memoranda frequently written by the parliamentary draftsman Sir Francis Greer, is the rationale that the initial partition of all transferred services will encourage North and South to re-unite, and that failure to re-unite places the responsibility of partition not on the British but on the Irish.

/151   Committee on the Government of Ireland Act, GIA series, proceedings and memoranda, 1921. Chaired by H. A. L. Fisher, Minister of Education. Useful for determining the mechanics of implementing the Government of Ireland Act and establishing the 'appointed days'. A memorandum by Sir Francis Greer (GIA 3, [?] March 1921) points out the technical reasons for not appointing days for the transfer of executive services and financial powers before parliaments and governments come into existence.

/153–4   Committee on the Provisional Government of Ireland, PGI series, 1921–2. Vol. I, reports and proceedings; Vol. II memoranda. Also,

/161   PGI(A) series, memoranda, 1922. Chaired by Winston Churchill, Secretary of State for the colonies. Especially useful for its reports on the steps to be taken to transfer responsibility for affairs in Southern Ireland to the provisional government. Its early memoranda reflect the development of the British concept of the provisional government. The committee drafted the heads of working arrangements agreed on with Irish ministers, 24 January 1922. The material overlaps considerably with registered files CAB 21/243, 248–50, 252.

/158–60   Committee on the Provisional Government of Ireland, technical departmental subcommittee, ITC series, 1922. Vol. I, proceedings; Vol. II, memoranda ITC 1–92. Chaired by Sir James Masterton-

Smith, under-secretary in the Colonial Office. The subcommittee deliberated and reported on dozens of administrative questions arising from the Treaty as it affected the positions of departments, including the question of the disposal of reserved services.

/162 Committee on the Provisional Government of Ireland, financial subcommittee, IF series, proceedings and memoranda, 1922. Includes memoranda which throw light on policy in regard to the transfer to the provisional government of land purchase, the Post Office and Post Office Savings Banks.

CAB 43 – Conferences on Ireland

This group documents the conferences with Sinn Féin representatives, October–December 1921, and with provisional government ministers, January–June 1922. Much of it is duplicated in the registered files (CAB 21/243–250). Again, Tom Jones, *Whitehall Diary* is an essential supplementary source.

/1   Conclusions of meetings of British representatives to the conference with the Sinn Féin delegation, SF(B) series, October–December 1921. Conclusions of meetings of the British signatories to the Treaty with Ireland, May–July 1922.

/2   Conference on Ireland: memoranda circulated to British representatives, SF(B) series, July 1921–September 1922.

/3   Conference on Ireland: memoranda circulated to British and Irish representatives, SF(C) series, October 1921–June 1922.

/4   Conference on Ireland: record of negotiations and relevant documents, 1921.

/5   Conferences of the Irish Committee with representatives of Northern Ireland and the provisional government in Southern Ireland: secretary's notes, BNS series, March 1922.

/6   Conference on Ireland between ministers of the British government and members of the provisional government of Ireland, January–June 1922.

/7   Draft Irish constitution: history of the negotiations, etc., May–June 1922.

COLONIAL OFFICE

The archives of the Colonial Office relating to Ireland in the early 1920s have had a complex, chequered career. The agency which was the provenance of a number of groups and series was the Irish Office. In February 1922 the Irish Office succeeded its former parent department, the Chief Secretary's Office, as the central bureau for the administration of Britain's affairs in Ireland. Also at this time a Colonial Office division was set up to handle matters relating to the Irish Free State. The existence of two administrative centres caused confusion until liaison arrangements were established between the two in June. In effect, the Irish Office seems to have absorbed the Colonial Office division. When the Irish Free State was established on 6 December 1922, the Irish Office, heretofore responsible to the Chief Secretary, now became responsible to the Home Office for matters relating to Northern Ireland and to the Colonial Office for matters relating to the Irish Free State. The record group which remains the major deposit of the archives of the Irish Office in its Colonial Office role is 'Irish Free State original correspondence, 1922–4' (CO 739). This consists of twenty-seven volumes of bound files arranged by year and by subject, the subjects being the Northern and Southern governments, various government departments and individuals in alphabetical order. The group, as such, is of relatively recent origin, a rearrangement of other Colonial Office groups. These other groups were apparently divided between the Colonial Office and Home Office and done away with. Also, some Chief Secretary's registered papers, removed from Dublin Castle to the Irish Office in 1922, suffered destruction due to improper storage. (See under 'Dublin – State Paper Office of Ireland'.)

Records examined in CO 739 throw light on the dispute between the Northern and British governments over the position of the Council of Ireland and other reserved services during the provisional government period; British efforts to persuade the provisional government to transfer Northern-related records to Belfast; and discussion on the position of certain services after the creation of the Free State, for example, the Quit Rent Office and Irish lights. There is also material relating to the British concern about Post Office expenditure by the provisional government over and above 1921–2 parliamentary votes. Throughout the volumes there are several duplicates of Cabinet material.

TREASURY

Under a new system begun in 1920 the Treasury organised their registered files in five subject groups: F series, finance files (T 160); S series, supply files (T 161); E series, establishment files (T 162); G series, general files (T 163); and P series, pension files (T 164). There are separate lists for the decades 1920–30 and 1930–40. In the 1920s several hundreds of these files related to the Treasury's business in Ireland. Titles of the most relevant files are here listed.

T 160 – Finance files
Few finance files were found useful for this work, although three were important sources of information on the mechanics of transferring services to Northern Ireland 1921–2.

/107/F.3997	Transfer of services to Northern Ireland: expenditure from Treasury votes, 17 December 1921–2 June 1922.
/108/F.4159/1	Irish Civil Service Committee, 19 January 1921–31 March 1923.
/220/F.8126	Deputy Paymaster for Ireland: transfer of services in Northern Ireland, 21 September 1921–25 November 1921.

T 161 – Supply files
None were found useful.

T 162 – Establishment files

The E series, the most bountiful of all the Treasury's registered file groups for this book, yielded much important information. It was especially valuable for matters relating to the effects on the civil service under the 1920 Act and the Treaty. Among the series are the key files relating to appointments in Irish departments, transfers of staff to and from Ireland, Whitley reorganisation schemes in Irish departments, and the position of staff as a result of the Treaty:

/60/E.5201   Irish departments: new appointments to pensionable establishments pending transfer of Irish services under the Government of Ireland Act, 2 April 1921–6 February 1922.

/66 [and 67]/E.5703/1 [and subseries]   Transfers to and from Ireland, July 1921–May 1930.

/85 [and 86]/9478 [and subseries]   Staff arrangements on notification of constitution of Irish Free State, 1922–7.

/87/E.9764   Ireland: schemes for transfer of staff to provisional government under article 7(i) (b); financial agreement, 24 November 1922–13 August 1924.

/95/E.11302   Reorganisation in Ireland: miscellaneous, 27 April 1921–23 May 1922.

/108/E.13539   Reorganisation of Anglo-Irish departments prior to the transfer of services, 20 January 1921–29 June 1922.

/108/E.13769   Ireland; legal departments; committee of inquiry, 23 August 1920–29 June 1921.

Several E files were vital for documenting the transfer or loan of staff to Northern Ireland:

/74/E.6968   Northern Ireland government: arrangement for loan of officers to, 31 May 1921–2 December 1921.

/74/E.7063   Reallocation of staff in various departments owing to transfer of services to Northern Ireland, 24 November 1921–10 January 1922.

/80/E.8074   Northern Ireland: officers employed on services which are being transferred to the government of Northern Ireland – recovery of salaries, 4 January 1922–11 April 1922.

Other E files yielded information on special departmental arrangements and procedures during the period:

/2/E.87/011   Authorised circulation list of Treasury circulars in Ireland, 2–28 March 1922.

/35/E.2522   Correspondence between Treasury and Dublin Castle in times of disturbance, 12–29 May 1920.

/79/E.8003   Irish Office: reorganisation of office staff, 4 February 1922–5 September 1923.

/80/E.8110   Procedure for detailed correspondence between imperial Treasury and the provisional government of Southern Ireland, 4 April 1922–26 March 1924.

/87/E.9665/01　Northern Ireland. Imperial Secretary's Department. Disposal of staff consequent upon transfer of Council of Ireland functions, 7 December 1925–23 March 1926.

/88/E.9905　Correspondence between imperial Treasury and government of Northern Ireland: procedure, 11 December 1922–24 January 1923.

T 163 – General files

Only a few files of the Treasury's G series proved useful, but these document administrative arrangements under the 1920 Act and the Treaty. To a small extent G.256/1 alleviates the loss of CSORP 2429/1. (See under 'Dublin – State Paper Office of Ireland'.)

/4/G.256/1　Administrative changes necessitated by the passing into law of the Government of Ireland Act, January–April 1921.

/13/G.687/02　Irish Free State. Agency services on behalf of, March 1922–July 1929.

/13/G.687/08　Irish Free State provisional government. Transfer of services and accounting arrangements on 1 April 1922, 2 February–26 October 1922.

T 164 – Pension files

Useful files in the P series were again few, but important. Especially valuable was P.27147A, a bulky file on the Civil Service Committee. Also useful was P.25891, relating to that committee's successor for the Irish Free State, the Wylie Committee.

/31/P.27147A　Civil Service Committee, 12 March 1921–3 January 1923.

/30/P.25891　Wylie Committee to consider compensation under article 10 of the Irish government Treaty, 12–20 October 1922.

Other Treasury record groups.

The Treasury's registry files relating to Ireland in this period should be used in conjunction with the main Treasury (Ireland) group, T 158. This consists of nine bulky volumes of out-letters in chronological sequence, written between June 1920 and October 1922, mainly by A. P. Waterfield. Only eighty-five of Treasury (Ireland)'s files are extant and form group T 192 (the Waterfield papers). These deal mainly with the Treasury's excercise of control over fresh expenditure in Ireland; some are useful for throwing light on Irish Whitley schemes. Also certain of the Niemeyer papers, 1916–30 (T 176) deal with Ireland. The main group of the Treasury Remembrancer's office, out-letters, Ireland 1669–1921 (T 14) consists of routine correspondence and was of little use.

PERSONAL PAPERS

'*The Mark Sturgis Diary*', 1920–2 (PRO 30/59) comprises five volumes of wry commentary on policy, people and events by a top Dublin Castle official.

London – House of Lords Record Office (HLRO)

PERSONAL PAPERS

Lloyd George Papers
To date this is the largest collection of any among the available papers of British prime ministers. Series F documents Lloyd George's years as Prime Minister, 1916–22. It consists mainly of in-correspondence and much official memoranda not in Cabinet records. Correspondents include Sir Warren Fisher, Sir John Anderson, A. W. Cope, Tom Jones, Lionel Curtis, General Macready, Walter Long, Hamar Greenwood, Bonar Law and Austen Chamberlain. The papers were especially important for documenting the events leading up to the reform of Dublin Castle in May 1920, the character of the new Anderson regime, and the decision to appoint an assistant under-secretary in Belfast. Documents are indexed individually. The following is a select list of the most important examined for this work.

F/31/1/32 Dublin Castle. [Report by Sir Warren Fisher and Report by Cope and Harwood on conditions in Dublin Castle], 12 May 1920.

F/31/1/33 [Report by Sir Warren Fisher, supplementary to Report of 12 May, recommending change of political character of Dublin Castle], 15 May 1920.

F/24/3/3 Ireland. [Memorandum by Tom Jones to the Prime Minister following Cabinet conference of 23 July 1920, advising conciliatory policies], 24 July 1920.

F/17/1/2 [Sir Warren Fisher to Prime Minister giving an extract of a letter from A. W. Cope, 16 June 1920 urging immediate steps to reconcile Sinn Féin nationalist opinion], 16 June 1920.

F/19/2/14 [Sir John Anderson to Chief Secretary, expressing the view that administrative reform in the Castle initially had had a positive effect on the state of the country, but that recent outbreaks were due to lack of further policy initiatives from London and that coercive measures 'should be accompanied by a declaration of policy and an appeal to moderate opinion in Southern Ireland . . .'], 20 July 1920.

F/31/1/43 [Bonar Law to Lloyd George, reporting on a discussion with Sir James Craig and expressing the view that the British should now allow the Loyalists to assume responsibility for order in the six counties, but in such a way that it would not be seen 'as if we were acting on their dictation'], 2 September 1920.

Dublin – State Paper Office of Ireland (SPOI)

CHIEF SECRETARY'S OFFICE

The British concept of 'public records' as being the records of courts and other legal records was manifest in Ireland in the Public Records (Ireland) Act, 1867.

This law established the Public Record Office of Ireland (PROI) at the Four Courts, Dublin as a repository for legal records. In the meantime the Viceroy's Chief Secretary, whose functions had evolved in the nineteenth century as those of chief executive of the 'Irish government', deposited the records of his office and subordinate departments (police, prisons, reformatories, etc.) in the State Paper Office at Dublin Castle. The distinction between 'public records' and 'state papers' was similar to the development of state papers in England where the records of secretaries of state were regarded as 'papers' – that is, the semi-private papers of the minister – rather than as government archives or public records. In Ireland this distinction was underscored by separate archival management: the deputy keeper of public records was responsible to the Master of the Rolls, the keeper of the state papers to the Chief Secretary.

The source value of the Chief Secretary's Office registered papers (CSORP) for 1920–1 would have been considerably greater had it not been for the dispersal of choice files, mainly to the Irish Office, in 1922. Although a few of these may be in Irish government offices, most have vanished and the only evidence of their existence is in the indices at SPOI. The most important for the purposes of this book would have been a subseries of 239 files (CSORP 1921/2429/1–239) dealing with 'administrative changes arising out of the Government of Ireland Act 1920'. Only thirty-nine of the less important files remain at SPOI. Most of the remainder are marked in the index as having gone 'to London' between February and July 1922. No analysis of the dispersal of CSORP has ever been carried out, but the number of files removed, at least for the 1921 period, would appear quite large. For example out of 117 files of a subseries relating to 'staff questions' (CSORP 1921/2602/1–117) only twenty-four remain; and out of forty-four files on 'civil service matters' (CSORP 1921/2964/1–44) only eleven files remain. What happened to this material? Following the author's vain search at PRO in London, an inquiry to the Foreign and Commonwealth Office drew the following sad reply:

23 February 1973

Dear Sir

I am writing in reply to your letter of 17 February about the records of the former Chief Secretary's Office at Dublin Castle.

Many of these records were sent to the Irish Office in London in 1922, when direct British rule ceased and the Irish Free State came into being. When the Irish Office was later abolished, the Home Office handed the records over to the Dominions Office. They were for many years stored in a basement cellar in a Whitehall building occupied by the Prison Commissioners. This basement, unfortunately, was liable to flooding from time to time. When the records were last examined in August of 1935, they were found to have deteriorated to such an extent by the effects of the flood water as to be completely illegible and unidentifiable. Moreover they immediately disintegrated on touch, and were so evil-smelling that I believe that the Westminster City Council sanitary inspectors were forced to order their removal and destruction on public health grounds.

Apart from those kept at the Public Record Office and at the State Paper Office in Dublin, we have no record of the present whereabouts of any other

Dublin Castle papers in which you may be interested. It is, I think, only fair to assume that those which are now wanting were among the records irreparably damaged by flood water and thus irretrievably lost to posterity. In the circumstances, I can only express my regret that this letter should bear such disappointing and frustrating news.

Yours faithfully
H. G. F. Harcombe
Library & Records
Department

The residue of CSORP at SPOI contained a few valuable bits and pieces, more especially material on the Civil Service Committee protest, the Whitley councils and the transfer of powers to the provisional government. The following is a list of the more helpful on these and other matters:

CSORP 1920
/138   Departments to which circulars are issued from the chief secretary's office.
/697   Separate grant request for five Ulster county councils.
/16963   Establishment of Treasury (Ireland).

CSORP 1921
/2429/50   Administrative changes arising from the Government of Ireland Act 1920; effect on Land Registry.
/2429/96   Administrative changes arising from the Government of Ireland Act 1920; National Education Board estimates [including circular by Sir John Anderson regarding 'expenditure by Irish departments between the beginning of next financial year and the date of transfer', 29 March 1921].
/2602/30   Loan of W. P. J. Connolly [principal clerk in Chief Secretary's Office, May 1920].
/2602/79   Government of Ireland Act: allocation of officials serving in the Chief Secretary's Office and subordinate departments.
/2638/1, 2, 5, 9, 11, 12, 15 Whitley Council reorganisation schemes, assimilation of staff.
/3864/2   Provisional government, transfer of powers.
/3866/3   Civil Service Committee.

Of more limited use among CSO records were government correspondence books, volumes for 1920–1 (VIII/B8,9), and the *'Rialtas'* papers (R series), apparently the records of that section of the Chief Secretary's Office said to be under the provisional government's authority in 1922.

OFFICE OF THE TAOISEACH

Until 1976, more than fifty years after the founding of the state, all records produced by the new ministerial departments were retained for the exclusive use of government and administration. Admittedly, the destruction of PROI during the civil war was disastrous for Irish archives. For a very long time this catastrophe was the civil service excuse for the neglect of the functions of PROI. Yet, while it may seem understandable to reduce staff for duties no longer existing by reason of the holocaust, no thought was given to the necessity of archival practices to service the executive machinery of the new state. In the mid-1970s a report of an interdepartmental committee on archives legislation was shelved and has remained ever since a state secret. It should be considered a hopeful sign, perhaps, that some departments have become aware of the existence of PROI: under pressure for space, and encouraged by PROI, a few have begun to unload their backlogs at the Four Courts. However, none of this material has been available to the public because of uncertainty about the legal position.

In 1976 the coalition government released the minutes and files of the Cabinet secretariat, 1922–44. Thus, while the government was shelving archives legislation, it succeeded in making political capital out of 'donating' certain of the state's archival material to the public. Misleadingly, this released material is sometimes referred to as the records of the Taoiseach's Office. Because the Taoiseach's Office and its predecessor, the office of President of the Irish Free State Executive Council, have acted as a Cabinet secretariat, the materials are, true enough, records of the Taoiseach's Office. However, those files released include only those cited in the Cabinet minutes. Taoiseach's Office files not cited in the Cabinet minutes, though forming the same series, are not released for public inspection. The explanation for this seems to lie in a matter of precedence. The deposit in the State Paper Office of the records of the Cabinet, as opposed to the records of the Taoiseach's Office as a whole, follows the precedent of administration under the British. The Cabinet, just as the Chief Secretary before it, is the executive of the state; and like the Chief Secretary, the Cabinet, it appears, produces 'state papers'. These are not public records, but official material which the Taoiseach as head of the Cabinet, in his magnanimity, has opened for public inspection. The recent deposits of departmental material in PROI suggest that under future archives legislation, departmental archives will be deposited there. Does this mean that the departmental material of the Taoiseach's Office, minus Cabinet papers, will also be deposited in PROI rather than in SPOI? In recent years a degree of unity in state archival management has been introduced by vesting in one person the duties of both deputy keeper of public records and keeper of the state papers. However, there remains the anomalies of both separate repositories and separate authorities. PROI and SPOI are respectively minor bureaux, the former of the Department of Justice, the latter of the office of Taoiseach. If the holy principle of civil service precedence is carried to the extreme, it will be the cause of yet another Irish archival mishap, the breaking up of the Taoiseach's Office file series, a unitary archival record group.

Thus, after sixty years of independence no ministerial records, apart from Cabinet files and minutes, are accessible to the public. In consequence, researchers in the history of Free State policy are forced to examine Cabinet policy in isolation, precluded from seeing it reflected in the action and reaction of contemporary departments and other agencies. For example, the archival resources of the sections of this book dealing with Michael Collins's Northern policy could have been richer were there public access to the records of the Departments of Finance, Education, Agriculture and others. While bearing this information in mind it is fair to state that several of the Taoiseach's Office files (S series) are of themselves rich and interesting and have much to say about the issues discussed in this book. The following were extremely helpful in documenting events of 1922, particularly the transfer of powers to the provisional government and the provisional government's relations with the Northern government in terms of administrative services.

S series – Cabinet files

S.1   Formation and allocation of departments of the provisional government, 1 January–18 October 1922.

S.2   Statement of policy of the provisional government, 16 January–13 February 1922.

S.11   Implementation of the Treaty, 16 January–20 March 1922.

S.991   Transfer of functions from the British government to the provisional government, 16 January–4 December 1922.

S.1011   North-east advisory committee, minutes and correspondence, 8 March–26 May 1922.

S.1427   Resident magistrates – termination of appointments, August 1922.

S.1730   Discussions with the Northern government regarding teacher training 8 September 1922–1 March 1923.

S.1834A Council of Ireland, 23 June 1922–12 June 1938.

S.1864   Unauthorised instruction by Lord Chief Justice Molony that Land Registry records be transferred to Northern Ireland, October–November 1922.

S.1973   Salaries and pensions of Northern Ireland teachers 1922.

S.2159   Transfer of Dublin Castle to provisional government, 1922–36.

S.3111A & B   Transfer of documents to Northern Ireland, 1922–32.

S.3124   Ratification of the Anglo-Irish Treaty, January 1923.

Other Irish government record groups

Other helpful material at the SPOI were the Cabinet minutes (G series), volumes for 1922. These are concise, much briefer than British Cabinet minutes, and normally tend to record conclusions rather than discussion. They were none the less helpful, especially in documenting the policy of paying Northern teachers. Of more limited use were minutes of the Dáil Eireann Cabinet, 1919–22 (DE 1), and Dáil Eireann files (DE 2). The following two Dáil Eireann files document what appears to be rare occasions on which the Dáil Cabinet took its rival administration under consideration.

DE 2/296   Officials and institutions of British civil government in Ireland: proposals by Austin Stack and Michael Collins for action against them, 24 June–4 July 1921.

DE 2/424   Transfer of executive power, staff and services to the Northern Ireland government (under Government of Ireland Act 1920): copies to delegates in London of two documents, that is:

(i) Dr James Gillespie, Cookstown, Co. Tyrone to President de Valera, letter 23 November 1921, and (ii) Copy, Land Commission minute about transfer work in connection with land purchase annuities; and also letter dated 15 November 1921, W. McKevitt, no. 3 section Co. Coy., 4th Batt., Dublin Brigade to Minister for Home Affairs, on the transfer of staff, which the writer holds, is a breach of the truce.

Dublin – University College Dublin Archives Department (UCDAD)

UCDAD holds the private papers of several of the ministers of the Irish Free State. Much of this consists of semi-official material. The collections used in this study were the papers of Hugh Kennedy (P 4), Richard Mulcahy (P 7), and Ernest Blythe (P 24). Relevant items were few but important.

P 4 – THE KENNEDY PAPERS

The Kennedy papers are currently in process of re-listing; however, the old reference numbers given here will be cross-referenced on the new list. The following items proved considerably useful:

/VII/23, 24 Correspondence and memoranda relating to the 'Ulster month', February–March 1922.
Note on the position of the Council of Ireland under the Treaty, n.d. [? March–May 1922].
Memorandum on the constitutional position of the provisional government and the procedure for bringing the Free State into being, 2 May 1922.
/E/1 Minute by Collins to E. J. Duggan instructing that ministers get advice on the powers of the Northern government to see that these powers remain limited and that schemes of obstruction be drawn up, 4 May 1922.

P 7 – THE MULCAHY PAPERS

The Mulcahy papers include a set of provisional government minutes from 22 February 1922. The Mulcahy papers are cited in this book as the source of Cabinet minutes in several places because when the data was collected, the Cabinet papers were not yet available in SPOI.

/B/II/242–6 Provisional government minutes, 22 February–6 December 1922.
/B/II/249 Memorandum by Hugh Kennedy on the powers of the provisional government, January 1923.

P 24 – THE BLYTHE PAPERS

/70   Memorandum [by Blythe] on policy in regard to the north-east, 9 August 1922.

Belfast – Public Record Office of Northern Ireland (PRONI)

Large numbers of record groups from all Northern Ireland departments have become available for research in recent years. At the time of research some had not yet been listed and were therefore unavailable. The most useful for this work were two Cabinet groups: Cabinet conclusions (CAB 4), and Cabinet secretariat subject files (CAB 9) which is further divided into subgroups; and one Department of Finance group: Treasury division registry files (FIN 18). The personal papers of Sir Ernest Clark proved most incisive and useful. Because of the troubled political climate in Northern Ireland in the last decade stringent criteria have been applied to civil service decisions on whether files are too sensitive for public availability. However, no file request in the course of research for this book was ever turned down at PRONI except where papers run beyond the thirty-year restriction.

CABINET

CAB 4 – Cabinet conclusions files
Photographic copies are now conveniently kept in bound volumes on PRONI reference room shelves. Memoranda and letters are often included in the files. Essentially only conclusions are recorded in contradistinction to minutes of discussions but are fuller and more detailed than those of the provisional government. Matters relating to the establishment of administrative machinery, for example, the transfer of services and staff, appointments to principal posts, Council of Ireland, reserved services, etc. are dealt with. In the autumn of 1921 Cabinet conclusions leave no room for doubt about the status of A. W. Cope in the Northern government's eyes (CAB 4/17/6, 4/19/12, 4/24/4).
/1–64   1921–2.

CAB 9A – Cabinet secretariat : Ministry of Finance
In the files of CAB 9A and 9E listed below are rich documentation on North–South relations in terms of administrative services.

/1/1   Correspondence regarding the transfer of documents relating to Northern Ireland from the Irish Free State, 1922–37.
/1/2   Correspondence regarding the transfer of documents relating to the Land Registry in Northern Ireland from the Irish Free State, 1922–48.

CAB 9E – Cabinet secretariat: Ministry of Agriculture
/3   Correspondence and memoranda in connection with the transfer of services relating to the Diseases of Animals Acts to the Northern government, 1922–3.

DEPARTMENT OF FINANCE

FIN 18 – Treasury division
The early files of FIN 18 began as files of the Chief Secretary's Office (Belfast branch) in 1920 and 1921. This shows that CSO (Belfast) was in effect the nucleus of a future Northern Ireland Treasury. FIN 18 contains the essential documentation for the establishment of Northern Ireland administration.

/1/191–2	Government of Northern Ireland: Draft schemes for departments and staff, 1921.
/1/194	Government of Northern Ireland: Museums, 1921.
/1/235	Government of Ireland Act: Summary of main provisions, 1921.
/1/238	Government of Northern Ireland: Staff, transfer and recruitment of, 1921.
/1/283	Government of Northern Ireland civil service: Recruitment prospects and conditions of service: interview with Irish Civil Service Alliance.
/1/284	Queckett, J. O. Work in connection with adaptation orders under the Government of Ireland Act, 1921.
/1/290	Government of Northern Ireland: Inland Revenue, general correspondence, staff and services.
/1/293	Government of Northern Ireland: Appointment of Comptroller and Auditor-General, 1921.
/1/294	Government of Northern Ireland: Reserved services, 1921.
/1/298–9	General correspondence with Northern Ireland government ministries, 1921.
/1/303	Government of Northern Ireland: Staff, Ministry of Finance, 1921–2.
/1/328	Steps in bringing Parliament into existence, 1921.
/1/355	Government of Northern Ireland: Staff. Transfer from executive Irish departments. Inquiry into adequacy or excess of existing staff.
/1/383	Government of Ireland Act 1920: Financial arrangements of Northern government, 1921.
/1/391	Estimates for services under the Government of Northern Ireland, 1921–2.
/1/393	Government of Ireland Act 1920: Draft general adaptation order, transfer of Irish services, 1921.
/1/423	Government of Northern Ireland: Date of transfer of Irish services.
/1/531	Government of Northern Ireland: Inexpediency of allowing government agencies, administering Northern services, to fall into the hands of the provisional government, 1921–2.
/2/314	Refusal of Roman Catholic teachers to accept salaries from Northern Ireland, 1922–3.
/2/571	Transfer of files relating to Northern Ireland affairs from the Treasury Remembrancer and Treasury, Whitehall, 1922–3.
/2/651	Irish Office: Questions outstanding with, 1922–3.

FIN 30
Unlisted at the time of research. Files containing minutes of the Civil Service

Committee, 8 December 1921–16 May 1922 are an invaluable source for documenting the history of the committee.

PERSONAL PAPERS

Sir Ernest Clark papers – D 1022
Unlisted at the time of research. Although Clark was a prolific diary writer for most of his career, he kept no diary during his sojourn in Belfast, except a very sketchy one for 1923. He later stated that he was so busy as secretary in the Ministry of Finance that he simply had not time to keep one. The most useful material among his papers were autobiographical sketches, written in his last years. (See under secondary sources.)

SECONDARY SOURCES

Unpublished Memoirs

The following three items might be regarded as a special category of secondary source because they are the personal recollections of events in this book as written down by people participating in them. Primary sources either corroborate these manuscripts, or at least do not contradict them in any serious way. They form invaluable evidence supplementary to primary sources. However, they are not of themselves primary sources for purposes of this book because they were not created out of the events of which both they and this book are accounts.

Clark, Sir E., 'Autobiographical sketches'. These are among the Clark papers in PRONI (ref.: D 1022). They may have been chapter drafts, the beginning of an autobiography. However, some of his notes would indicate that he intended these writings as a guide or notes for the use of one who would write his biography. The sketches create a fascinating scenario of the days of his Irish appointment in September 1920, and may perhaps be classed as a primary source in so far as they unwittingly reveal the tenor of Clark's political views.

Duggan, G. C., 'The life of a civil servant'. I am indebted to Dr León Ó Broin for providing me with a copy of the chapter entitled 'Chief Secretary's Office, Dublin Castle, 1919–21'. An effort was made to locate the complete manuscript among Duggan's heirs and editors, but without success.

Gallagher, M. J., 'Memories of a civil servant'. Shown to the author by Mr Gallagher before his death in 1974. Particularly relevant were chapters on the Civil Service Committee and the Whitley councils. Manuscript is now in the possession of Gallagher's son, the Rev. C. Gallagher, CC, Tallaght.

Books and Articles

Akenson, D. H., *Education and Enmity: The Control of Schooling in Northern Ireland, 1920–50* (Newton Abbot, 1973).

Berkeley, G. F. H., 'The present system of goverment in Ireland', in B. Williams (ed.), *Home Rule Problems* (London, 1911).

Bew, P., Gibbon, P., and Patterson, H., *The State in Northern Ireland, 1921–72: Political Forces and Social Classes* (Manchester, 1979).

Boyce, D. G., 'British conservative opinion, the Ulster Question and the partition of Ireland, 1919–21', *Irish Historical Studies*, vol. 17, no. 65 (1968).

Boyce, D. G., *Englishmen and Irish Troubles: British Public Opinion and the Making of Irish Policy, 1918–22* (London, 1972).

Boyce, D. G., 'How to settle the Irish question: Lloyd George and Ireland, 1918-1921', in A. J. P. Taylor (ed.), *Lloyd George: Twelve Essays* (London, 1971).

Buckland, P., *The Factory of Grievances: Devolved Government in Northern Ireland, 1921–39* (Dublin and New York, 1979).

Buckland, P., *Irish Unionism Two: Ulster Unionism and the Origins of Northern Ireland, 1886–1922* (Dublin and New York, 1973).

Callwell, C. E., *Field-Marshal Sir Henry Wilson: His Life and Diaries*, 2 vols (London, 1927).

Chubb, E., *The Government and Politics of Ireland* (Stanford, Calif. and Oxford, 1970).

Chubb, E. (ed.), *A Source Book of Irish Government* (Dublin, 1964).

Churchill, W. S., *The Aftermath: A Sequel to the World Crisis* (London, 1941).

Dunraven, Lord, *The Outlook in Ireland* (Dublin and London, 1907).

Fanning, Ronan, *The Irish Department of Finance, 1922–58* (Dublin, 1978).

Farrell, M., *Northern Ireland: The Orange State* (London, 1976).

Forester, M., *Michael Collins: The Lost Leader* (London, 1971).

Harkness, D. W., *The Restless Dominion: The Irish Free State and the British Commonwealth of Nations, 1921–31* (London, 1969).

Harkness, D. W., and Edwards, O. D., 'Cabinet papers, North and South', *Irish Times* supplement, 21 April 1976.

Hawkins, R. 'Dublin Castle and the Royal Irish Constabulary (1916–22)', in T. D. Williams (ed.), *The Irish Struggle, 1916–26* (London, 1966).

Headlam, M., *Irish Reminiscences* (London, 1947).

Hezlet, Sir A., *The 'B' Specials: A History of the Ulster Special Constabulary* (London, 1973).

Hopkinson, M., 'Collins, de Valera, Mulcahy, Liam Lynch: attitudes to the Irish civil war', unpublished paper delivered to a meeting of the Irish Historical Society, 9 September 1980.

'I.O.', see C. J. C. Street.

Jones, T., *Whitehall Diary, Vol. 3: Ireland 1918–25*, ed. K. Middlemas (London, 1971).

Kendle, J. E., 'The Round Table movement and "Home Rule all round"', *Historical Journal*, vol. 11, no. 2 (1968).

King, F. C., *Public Administration in Ireland*, Vol. 1 (Dublin, 1944); Vol. 2 (Dublin, 1949).

Lawrence, R. J., *The Government of Northern Ireland: Public Finance and Public Services, 1921–64* (Oxford, 1965).

Lenehan, T.N., 'The growth of the civil service', *Administration*, vol. 2, no. 2 (1954).

Longford, Earl of [Frank Pakenham], *Peace by Ordeal* (London, 1972).

Lyons, F. S. L., *Ireland since the Famine*, 2nd edn (Glasgow, 1972).

McColgan, J., 'British Cabinet Office records and the partition of the Irish administration', *Irish Archives Bulletin*, vol. 4, no. 1 (1974).

McColgan, J., 'Implementing the 1921 Treaty: Lionel Curtis and constitutional procedure', *Irish Historical Studies*, vol. 20, no. 79 (March 1977).

McColgan, J., 'Partition and the Irish administration, 1920–22', *Administration*, vol. 26, no. 2 (1980).

MacDonnell of Swinford, Lord, 'Irish administration under Home Rule', in J. H. Morgan (ed.), *The New Irish Constitution: An Exposition and Some Arguments* (London, New York and Toronto, 1912).

McDowell, R. B., *The Irish Administration, 1801–1914* (London, 1964).

McDowell, R. B., *The Irish Convention, 1917–18* (London, 1970).

Macardle, D., *The Irish Republic, 1911–25* (London, 1937).

Macready, Gen. Sir C. N. F., *Annals of an Active Life*, 2 vols (New York, 1925).

Mansergh, N., *The Commonwealth Experience* (London, 1969).

Mansergh, N., 'The Government of Ireland Act, 1920: its origins and purpose', in J. Barry (ed.), *Historical Studies*, vol. 9 (Belfast, 1974).

Mansergh, N., *The Government of Northern Ireland: A Study in Devolution* (London, 1936).

Morgan, J. H., 'How Ireland is governed', *Nineteenth Century* (September 1913).

Morgan, J. H. (ed.), *The New Irish Constitution: An Exposition and Some Arguments* (London, New York and Toronto, 1912).

O'Brien, R. B., *Dublin Castle and the Irish People* (Dublin, 1907).

O Broin, L., *Dublin Castle and the 1916 Rising* (London, 1970).

O Broin, L., 'Joseph Brennan, civil servant extraordinary', *Studies*, vol. 65, no. 2 (1977).

O Broin, L., *The Chief Secretary: Augustine Birrell in Ireland* (London, 1969).

O'Connell, T. J., *100 Years of Progress: The Story of the Irish National Teachers' Organisation, 1868–1968* (Dublin, n.d.).

'Periscope' [G. C. Duggan], 'The last days of Dublin Castle', *Blackwood's Magazine*, no. 128 (1922).

Phillips, W. A., *The Revolution in Ireland, 1906–23* (London, 1923).

Queckett, Sir A., *Constitution of Northern Ireland*, Vol. I (Belfast, 1928); Vol. 2 (Belfast, 1931).

Robinson, Sir H. A., *Memories: Wise and Otherwise* (London, 1923).

Seymour, J. B., *The Whitley Councils Scheme* (London, 1932).

Street, C. J. C., *Ireland in 1921* (London, 1922).

Street, C. J. C. ('I.O'), *The Administration of Ireland, 1920* (London, 1921).

Sutherland, G. (ed.), *Studies in the Growth of 19th Century Government* (London, 1972).

Taylor, A. J. P. (ed.), *Lloyd George: Twelve Essays* (London, 1971).

Taylor, R., *Michael Collins* (London, 1958).

Townshend, C., *The British Campaign in Ireland, 1919–21: The Development of Political and Military Policies* (London, 1975).

Wheeler-Bennett, J. W., *John Anderson, Viscount Waverley* (London, 1962).

White, A. C., *The Irish Free State, its Evolution and Possibilities* (London, 1923).

White, L. D., *Whitley Councils in the British Civil Service: A Study in Conciliation and Arbitration* (Chicago, 1933).

Williams, B. (ed.), *Home Rule Problems* (London, 1911).

Williams, T. D. (ed.), *The Irish Struggle, 1916–26* (London, 1966).

Wilson, T. (ed.), *The Political Diaries of C. P. Scott, 1911–28* (Ithaca, NY, 1970).

Younger, C., *Ireland's Civil War* (London, 1968).

Government Publications

REPORTS – BRITISH

1914 Cd. 7430, pp vol. 16. *Royal Commission on the Civil Service, Fourth Report, Evidence.*

1916 Cd. 8279, pp vol. 11, p. 171 *Report of the Royal Commission on the Rebellion in Ireland.*

1920 Cmd. 645, pp vol. 40. *Government of Ireland Bill. Outline of Financial Provisions.*

1921 Cmd. 1560, pp vol. 1. *Articles of Agreement for a Treaty between Great Britain and Ireland.*

1923 Cmd. 1911, pp vol. 18. *Heads of Working Arrangements for Implementing the Treaty.*

REPORTS – IRISH

1936 *Report of Commission of Inquiry into the Civil Service, 1932–5* [the 'Brennan Commission'],

1970 *Report of Public Services Organization Review Group, 1966–9* [the 'Devlin Report'].

PARLIAMENTARY PROCEEDINGS

Dáil Eireann, Reports of Debates.

Parliamentary Debates, (Hansard), 5th series.

Parliamentary Debates, (Hansard), Northern Ireland.

ACTS AND STATUTES

Parliament: Acts, Laws and Statutes, 1920–2.
Statutory Rules and Orders, 1920–2.

Contemporary newspapers and periodicals

Belfast Gazette
Belfast Irish News
Belfast Newsletter
Civil Service Journal
Dublin Gazette
Freeman's Journal
Irish Civil Servant

Works of reference

Concise Dictionary of National Biography
Cook, C. (ed.), *Sources in British Political History, 1900–51, Vol. 2: A Guide to the Papers of Selected Civil Servants* (London, 1975); *Vols 3–4: A Guide to the Private Papers of Members of Parliament* (London, 1977).
Hayes, M. J. (ed.), *Manuscript Sources for the History of Irish Civilisation*, 11 vols (Boston, Mass., 1965).
Hazlehurst, C., and Woodland, C. (eds), *A Guide to the Papers of British Cabinet Ministers, 1900–51* (London, 1974).
Hickey, D. J., and Doherty, J. E., *A Dictionary of Irish History since 1800* (Dublin, 1980).
The Records of the Cabinet Office to 1922 (Public Record Office Handbook no. 11) (London, 1966).
Thom's Official Directory of the United Kingdom and Ireland.
Ulster Yearbook.
Who's Who.
Who Was Who.
Wilson, S. S., *The Cabinet Office to 1945* (Public Record Office Handbook no. 17) (London, 1975).

Biographical Notes

Source abbreviations

BUD *Belfast and Ulster Directory*
CC Chris Cook, *Sources in British Political History*, Vols 2–4.
CDNB *Concise Dictionary of National Biography, 1901–50*
CT Charles Townshend, *The British Campaign in Ireland, 1919–21*
DIH Hickey and Doherty, *Dictionary of Irish History*
RF Ronan Fanning, *The Irish Department of Finance, 1922–58*
TJ Tom Jones, *Whitehall Diary, Vol. III*
WW *Who's Who, 1939*

Addison, Dr Christopher (1869–1951). Former professor of anatomy; Liberal MP, 1910–22, then joined Labour Party; Minister of Munitions, 1916–17; Minister of Reconstruction, 1917–19; first Minister of Health, 1919–20; Minister without portfolio, 1921; parliamentary secretary to the Minister of Agriculture and Fisheries, 1929–30; Minister of Agriculture and Fisheries, 1930–1; Secretary of State for Dominion Affairs, 1945–7, for Commonwealth Relations, 1947; Lord Privy Seal, 1947–51; Paymaster-General, 1948–9; Lord President of the Council, 1951. (CC; TJ)

Anderson, Sir John (1882–1958). Secretary, Ministry of Shipping, 1917–19; chairman, Board of Inland Revenue, 1919–20; joint under-secretary to the Lord-Lieutenant of Ireland, 1920–2; permanent under-secretary, Home Office, 1922–32; Governor of Bengal, 1932–7; Independent National MP for Scottish Universities, 1938–50; Lord Privy Seal, 1938–9; Home Secretary, 1939–40; Lord President of the Council, 1940–3; Chancellor of the Exchequer, 1943–5; created 1st Viscount Waverley, 1952. (CC; TJ)

Andrews, John Miller (1871–1956). Unionist MP for Down 1921–9, for Mid-Down and Londonderry, 1929–53; Northern Ireland Minister of Labour, 1921–37; Minister of Finance, 1937–40; Prime Minister, 1940–3; Grand Master of the Council of World Orange Institution, 1949–56. (DIH)

Antrobus, M. E. Assistant principal, Colonial Office, dealing with matters relating to the Irish Free State.

Archdale, Edward Mervyn (1853–1943). Unionist MP for Fermanagh North, 1898–1903, 1916–21; Northern Ireland Minister of Agriculture and Minister of Commerce, 1921–5, of Agriculture, 1925–33. (CC)

Asquith, Herbert Henry (1852–1928). Liberal MP for East Fife, 1886–1918; junior counsel for Charles Stewart Parnell before the Parnell Commission, 1888; Liberal-Imperialist during Boer War, 1899–1902; QC 1890; Home Secretary, 1892–5; Chancellor of the Exchequer, 1905–8; Prime Minister, 1908–16; carried Parliament Act, 1911; introduced Third Home Rule Bill, 1912; led Cabinet and country into war, 1914; formed coalition Cabinet, May 1915; visited Ireland after Easter Rising, 1916; resigned as Prime Minister,

December 1916; not returned, general election, 1918; Liberal MP for Paisley, 1920–4; devoted himself to Irish question advocating Dominion Home Rule; gave Liberal support to Labour to enable it to take office after election of December 1923; defeated at Paisley, 1924; created Earl of Oxford and Asquith, 1925; resigned Liberal leadership, 1926. (CDNB)

Balfour, Arthur James (1848-1930). Conservative MP for Hertford, 1874–85, for Manchester East, 1885–1906, for City of London, 1906–22; President, Local Government Board, 1885–6; Secretary of State for Scotland, 1886–7; Chief Secretary for Ireland, 1887–91; First Lord of the Treasury, 1891–2 and 1895–1905; Prime Minister 1902–5; First Lord of the Admiralty, 1915–16; Secretary of State for Foreign Affairs, 1916–19; Lord President of the Council, 1919–22 and 1925–9. (CC)

Barbour, John Milne (1868-1951). Unionist MP for Antrim, 1921–9, South Antrim, 1929–51; parliamentary secretary and then financial secretary to the Minister of Finance (Northern Ireland), 1921–40; Minister of Commerce, 1925–41; Minister of Finance, 1941–3. (DIH)

Barry, Kevin (1902-20). Medical student at University College, Dublin, participated in attack on British army bread-van in which a young soldier was killed, 20 September 1920. Hanged notwithstanding widespread pleas for clemency because of his youth. The hanging was the subject of the famous ballad bearing his name. (DIH)

Bates, Richard Dawson (1876-1949). Secretary of Ulster Unionist Council, 1905–21; founder member of Ulster Volunteer Force, 1912; MP, East Belfast and Victoria division, 1921–43; Northern Ireland Minister for Home Affairs, 1921–43. (Buckland, *Factory of Grievances*, p. 11)

Bell, Alan (?1855–1920). Career in RIC to 1898: stationed at Ballyconnell (Co. Cavan), Athlone, Mallow and Mullingar, traced secret Land League bank accounts during land war (?1879–82), arrested Henry George, the American journalist and land reformer at Athenry 1882; Resident Magistrate, Claremorris, 1898, later at Lurgan, Co. Armagh; transferred to Dublin in late 1919 or early 1920 with the assignment of tracing Dáil Eireann loan accounts in Irish banks. (*Freeman's Journal*; RF)

Birrell, Augustine (1850–1933). Liberal MP for West Fife, 1889–1918; president of the Board of Education, 1905–7; Chief Secretary for Ireland, 1907–16; established National University of Ireland, 1908; 'good natured but indolent', confining himself to day-to-day administration and taking no part in high policy; often accepted the advice of John Redmond and failed to realise the danger of a separatist rising; resigned after Easter Rising, 1916; 'an entertaining writer of wit and humour'. (CDNB)

Blackmore, Sir Charles H. (1880–1967). Formerly private secretary to parliamentary secretary, Ministry of Pensions, and financial secretary, Admiralty; private secretary to the Prime Minister of Northern Ireland and assistant secretary to the Cabinet, 1921–5; Secretary to the Cabinet, Northern Ireland, and Clerk of the Privy Council thereof, 1925–39. (BUD, 1923; *Who Was Who*, 1961–70)

Blake-Odgers, L. N. Home Office official on loan to Irish government (Chief Secretary's Office), 1920–2.

Blythe, Ernest (1888–1975). Gaelic League organiser, Kerry and Cork, 1905–8;

Irish Volunteer organiser, Munster and South Connaught; member of Sinn Féin executive from 1917; Sinn Féin MP/TD from 1918; Dáil Eireann Minister of Trade and Commerce, 1919–22; provisional government Minister of Local Government, August–September 1922; Minister of Local Government and Public Health, 1922–3; Minister for Finance, 1923–32; vice-president of the Executive Council of the Irish Free State, 1927–32; Director, Abbey Theatre, 1939–67. (DIH)

Boland, H. P. (b. 1876). Second division clerk, Office of Public Works, Dublin, 1895–7; Treasury Remembrancer's office, 1897–1902; various Irish offices, 1902–15; personal assistant to director-general, Ministry of Munitions, 1915–20; principal officer in Treasury, 1920–4; assistant secretary in charge of establishments, Irish Free State Department of Finance, 1924–37. (RF; Malcolm Ramsey to Sir James Craig, 15 June 1921, PRO T 162/74/E.6968)

Brand, Captain. Official of the English Board of Agriculture on duty in Northern Ireland to carry out the technical duties of the Diseases of Animals Acts. In consequence of the Treaty, this was a reserved service in the North. The arrangement was opposed by the Northern Ireland government, 1922.

Brook, Basil (1888–1974). Helped in the foundation of the special constabulary, 1920–1; senator, Northern Ireland Parliament, 1921–9; Unionist MP for Lisnaskea, 1929–68, assistant whip, Unionist Party, 1930–3; Minister of Agriculture, 1933–41; Minister of Commerce, 1941–3; Prime Minister, 1943–63. (DIH)

Brennan, Joseph (1887–1976). First division clerk, Chief Secretary's Office finance division, 1912–22; Comptroller and Auditor-General, provisional government, 1922; permanent secretary, Irish Free State Department of Finance, 1923–7; chairman of Currency Commission, 1927–43; chairman of commission of inquiry into the civil service, 1932–5; chairman of banking commission, 1934–8; governor of Central Bank of Ireland, 1943–53. (RF)

Carson, Sir Edward (1854–1935). Junior counsel to Attorney-General, 1887; QC 1889; Solicitor-General for Ireland, 1892; MP for Dublin University, 1892–1918, for Duncairn (Belfast), 1918–21; English bar, 1893; QC, 1894; acknowledged a leading advocate after Oscar Wilde's libel action against Queensbury, 1895; Solicitor-General for England, 1900–5; knighted, 1900; PC, 1905; leader of Irish Unionists in House of Commons, 1910; leader of Ulster Unionists movement during Home Rule crisis, 1912–14; offered services of UVF to war effort 1914; Attorney-General, 1915–16; First Lord of the Admiralty, 1916–17; War Cabinet, 1917–18; resigned, January 1918 on learning that Lloyd George intended to introduce Home Rule Bill for whole of Ireland; repeated his opposition to the Home Rule policy in 1920 but did not oppose the Government of Ireland Bill since its defeat would have brought into operation the Act of 1914; resigned leadership of Ulster Unionists, 1921, but always continued to watch their interests; Lord of Appeal in Ordinary, 1921–9; 'a powerful, conscientious and fearless advocate whose disregard for money compared with duty was exemplified in the Archer–Shee case (1910); at his best in cross-examination and in his appeal to the jury; a great orator of passionate sincerity; distinguished by a moral grandeur of character and a charming personality'. (CDNB)

Carter-Campbell, General. British Army, assistant GOC, Ireland, in charge of six-county area, 1920.

Chamberlain, Sir (Joseph) Austen (1863–1937). Liberal Unionist MP, East Worcestershire, 1892–1914, West Birmingham, 1914–37; Civil Lord of the Admiralty, 1895–1900; financial secretary to Treasury, 1900–2; Postmaster-General, 1902–3; PC, 1902; Chancellor of the Exchequer, 1903–5; on resignation of A. J. Balfour in 1911 he and Walter Long, as rivals for leadership of Conservative Party, stood down in favour of Bonar Law who at first relied greatly on him; Secretary of State for India, 1915; resigned after revelation of mismanagement of Mesopotamian campaign, 1917; member of War Cabinet, April 1918; Chancellor of the Exchequer, 1919–21; produced three sound budgets; Conservative leader, 1921; dissatisfaction with his support of Lloyd George culminated in Carlton Club meeting (19 October 1922) which brought coalition and his leadership to an end; Foreign Secretary, 1924–9; denounced protocol; secured signature of Locarno Pact and KG 1925; regularly attended Council of League of Nations; tried to improve Anglo-Egyptian relations; his policy of solidarity with France unpopular in many quarters; First Lord of the Admiralty in national government, August–October 1931; declined further office to make room for younger men and exercised greatest influence as elder statesman; Nobel Peace Prize, 1925. (CDNB)

Churchill, Winston (1874–1965). Fought in Boer War; Conservative MP, 1900–6, 1924–64; Liberal MP, 1906–22; President of the Board of Trade; Home Secretary and First Lord of the Admiralty before 1915; Minister of Munitions, 1917–19; Secretary for War and Air, 1919–21; Colonial Secretary, 1921–2; Chancellor of the Exchequer, 1924–9; First Lord of the Admiralty, 1939–40; Prime Minister and Minister of Defence, 1940–5; leader of opposition, 1945–51; Minister of Defence, 1951–2; Prime Minister, 1951–5; KG, 1956. (TJ)

Clark, Sir Ernest (1864–1951). Lent to Cape government, 1904–6; assistant secretary, Inland Revenue, 1919; secretary, Royal Commission on Income Tax, 1919–20; assistant under-secretary to the Lord-Lieutenant of Ireland, 1920–1; secretary, Department of Finance, Northern Ireland, 1921–5; member Australian economic mission, 1928–9; member, Joint Exchequer Board of Great Britain and Northern Ireland, 1930; governor of Tasmania, 1933–45. (CC; WW)

Clune, Archbishop of Perth. Uncle of Conor Clune, killed in Dublin Castle, 21 November 1920 ('Bloody Sunday'); attempted to initiate peace negotiations, December 1920.

Collins, Michael (1890–1922). Clerkships in London, 1906–16; active member of IRB, London; returned to Ireland, 1916; took part in Easter Rising; imprisoned for short time in England; organising genius of Volunteers and Sinn Féin movement; MP/TD, 1918–22; Minister of Home Affairs on declaration of independence, January 1919; director of organisation and subsequently of intelligence for Volunteers; on supreme council of IRB; all Irish revolutionary organisations declared illegal by British government, September 1919; responsible for raising loans for movement; one of five Irish delegates who negotiated Treaty with British government, 1901; chairman and Minister of Finance of the provisional government, 1922, faced with organised opposition to the Treaty; on outbreak of civil war, commanded Free State army; reduced opposition in Dublin; shot 22 August 1922. (CDNB)

Connolly, W.P.J. Assistant principal clerk, Chief Secretary's Office; transferred, 1920.

Cope, Alfred (1880–1954). Once a detective in the customs service; second secretary in the Ministry of Pensions, 1919–20; assistant under-secretary for Ireland and clerk of the Irish Privy Council, 1920–2; general secretary of the National Liberal Association, 1922–4; managing-director of Amalgamated Anthracite Collieries, 1924–35. (TJ)

Cosgrave, William T. (1880–1965). Sinn Féin MP/TD; imprisoned after Easter Rising; Treasurer of Sinn Féin; Minister of Local Government in Dáil Eireann, 1917–22; chairman of the provisional government, August–December 1922; president of the Executive Council of the Irish Free State, 1922–32. (CC)

Costello, John Aloysius (1891–1976). Attorney-General, Irish Free State, 1926–32; legal adviser to Irish delegation during imperial conferences, 1926, 1928, 1932; Taoiseach, 1948–51, 1954–7. (DIH)

Coyle, James Vincent (b.1864). Educated at Belvedere College, Dublin and Trinity College, Dublin; called to Irish bar, King's Inns, Dublin, 1896; entered Collector General's Office, Dublin, 1884; first class clerk therein 1892–9; principal staff officer and deputy chief clerk, Department of Agriculture and Technical Instruction, Dublin, 1900–21; chairman of Agricultural Wages Board for Ireland, 1919–21; assistant secretary, Ministry of Agriculture, Northern Ireland, 1922–30; retired, 1930; CBE, 1926; chairman of the committee of management, Peamount Sanatorium, Co. Dublin; Director, United Potash Co. (IFS) Ltd. (WW)

Craig, Captain Charles Curtis (1869–1960). Conservative MP for Antrim South, 1903–22; Co. Antrim, 1922–9; parliamentary secretary, Ministry of Pensions, 1923–4; brother of Sir James Craig. (CC)

Craig, John Herbert McCutcheon (b.1885). Educated at Foyle College, Derry and Trinity College, Dublin; entered Treasury 1908; principal assistant secretary, Treasury, 1931; Deputy Master and Comptroller, Royal Mint, and *ex-officio* Engraver of the King's Seals, 1935. (WW)

Craig, Sir James (1871–1940). Belfast stockbroker; Unionist MP for East Down, 1906–18; Mid-Down, 1918–21; in Northern Ireland Parliament, 1921–40; Treasurer, HM Household, 1916–18; parliamentary secretary to the Ministry of Pensions, 1919–20 and Admiralty, 1920–1; chief lieutenant to Sir Edward Carson in opposing Home Rule and concerned with organising means of resistance in Ulster, 1912–14; Parliamentary Secretary to the Minister for Pensions, 1919–20; Parliamentary Secretary and Financial Secretary to the Admiralty, 1920–1; first Prime Minister of Northern Ireland, 1921–40; 'restored order and introduced measure providing a new educational system, social services, improved housing, drainage, and agricultural position, and encouraging new industries'; created first Viscount Craigavon, 1927. (CDNB; CC; DIH)

Curtis, Lionel (1872–1955). Served South African War and became a member of Lord Milner's 'Kindergarten'; town clerk of Johannesburg; assistant colonial secretary to the Transvaal for local government; member Transvaal Legislative Council; Beit Lecturer, Colonial History, Oxford; Fellow of All Souls College; secretary to the Irish Conference, 1921; adviser on Irish affairs in the Colonial Office, 1921–4; Hon. Secretary of Royal Institute of International Affairs; prolific writer on imperial questions. (TJ; WW)

Cuthbertson, C. T. Treasury official on loan to the Northern Ireland Department of Finance, 1921–2.

Dale, J. A. Permanent secretary, Ministry of Labour, Northern Ireland, 1921.

Duggan, Eamon John (1874–1936). GPO 1916; director of intelligence, Irish Volunteers, 1918; MP/TD, Louth-Meath, 1919–21; Meath, 1922–33; assisted in working out details of truce, 1921; Irish delegation to Anglo-Irish conferences 1921 and signatory of Treaty; Minister of Home Affairs, provisional government, 1922; minister without portfolio, September 1922–September 1923; parliamentary secretary to the Executive Council and Minister for Defence, 1927–32; Senator, 1933. (DIH)

Duggan, George Chester (d.1969). Entered civil service, 1908; Admiralty, 1908–10 and 1914–16; Ministry of Shipping, 1917–19; first division clerk, Chief Secretary's Office, 1910–14, 1919–21; assistant secretary, Ministry of Finance, Belfast, 1922–5; principal assistant secretary, 1925; on loan to Ministry of War Transport, London, 1939–45; Comptroller and Auditor-General for Northern Ireland, 1945–9. (*Who Was Who, 1961–70*)

Fairgrieve, T. D. Scottish Office official on loan to Chief Secretary's Office and Irish Office, 1920–2.

Figgis, Darrell (1892–1925). Involved in gun-smuggling at Howth, 1914; secretary of Sinn Féin, 1917; chairman of the provisional government's constitutional committee, 1922. (DIH)

Fisher, Herbert Albert Laurens (1865–1940). Liberal MP for Sheffield Hallam, 1916–18; English Universities, 1918–26; President of the Board of Education, 1916–22; noted historian. (CC)

Fisher, Sir Norman Fenwick Warren (1879–1948). Chairman, Board of Inland Revenue, 1918–19; permanent secretary, Treasury and head of civil service, 1919–39. (CC)

Freeston, L. B. Colonial Office official dealing with matters relating to the Irish Free State, 1922–6.

French, Field-Marshal Sir John Denton Pinkstone (First Viscount French and First Earl of Ypres) (1852–1925). Served Sudan campaign, 1884–5; South Africa, 1899–1902; etc.; Chief of Imperial General Staff, 1911–14; Commander-in-Chief expeditionary forces in France, 1914–15; home forces, 1915–18; Lord-Lieutenant of Ireland, 1918–21. (CC)

Gallagher, Michael J. (1895–1974). Clerical officer, Irish civil service; secretary, staff side of Irish Whitley Council; member of delegation of existing Irish officers to Minister of Finance, Northern Ireland, July 1921; representative of existing Irish officers, Irish Civil Service Committee, 1921–2; transferred to Irish Free State; later, secretary, Inland Fisheries Commission, 1933–5; chairman, Inland Fisheries Trust, 1956–74. (Gallagher unpublished memoirs; *Irish Times*, 3 June 1974)

George V (1865–1936). King of Great Britain and Ireland and Emperor of

India, 1910–36; signed Home Rule Bill into law, September 1914; signed Government of Ireland Act 1920, December 1920; formally opened Parliament of Northern Ireland, 22 June 1921, with an appeal for peace that led to the opening of negotiations between the British government and Sinn Féin.

Gilbert, Sir Bernard William (1891–1957). Treasury career; assistant to Waterfield in Treasury (Ireland), 1920–2; later, joint second secretary, Treasury, 1944–56. (CC)

Gordon, James Scott (1867–1946). Permanent secretary, Ministry of Agriculture, Northern Ireland, 1921–33. (CC)

Greenwood, Sir Hamar (1870–1948). Liberal MP for York, 1906–January 1910; Sunderland, December 1910–22; Conservative MP for Walthamstow East, 1924–9; parliamentary under-secretary, Home Office, 1919; secretary for overseas trade, 1919–20; Chief Secretary for Ireland, 1920–2. (CC)

Greer, Sir Francis Nugent (b. 1869). Called to Bar, Ireland, 1893; England, 1912; KC, Ireland, 1918; formerly Crown prosecutor for County Meath and standing counsel to the County Councils of Meath and Antrim; parliamentary draftsman, Irish Office, 1908–22. (WW, 1922)

Gregg, Cornelius J. Born in Kilkenny; private secretary to Chief Secretary, 1920; said to have resigned, December 1920, because of the burning of Cork by Crown forces; lent to Irish Free State Department of Finance to organise civil service, 1922–4; assistant secretary, Board of Inland Revenue, London, 1924–41; chairman of Board of Inland Revenue, 1942–8. (RF)

Griffith, Arthur (1872–1922). Sinn Féin MP/TD for East Cavan and North-West Tyrone, 1918–22; journalist and editor; author of *The Resurrection of Hungary: A Parallel for Ireland*, 1904; founder of Sinn Féin, 1905; vice-president of reorganised Sinn Féin, 1917; acting president, 1919–20; head of Irish delegation to Anglo-Irish conference, October–December 1921; signatory of Treaty; President of Dáil Eireann, 1922. (DIH)

Haldane, Viscount (1856–1928). Secretary of State for War, 1905–12; Viscount 1911; Lord Chancellor, 1912–15, 1924; chaired committee of inquiry into the civil service, 1918. (CT)

Harrison, E. R. Chairman of Board of Inland Revenue, 1921.

Harwood, R. E. (b. 1883). Civil service career; principal establishments officer, Treasury, 1919; assistant secretary, Treasury, 1919–22; with A. W. Cope, carried out investigation of Dublin Castle, May 1920; deputy treasurer to the king, 1922–35; financial secretary to the king, 1935–7; governor, London School of Economics and Political Science; CBE, 1918; CVO, 1921; CB, 1924; KCVO, 1931; KCB, 1934. (WW; Lloyd George papers)

Hawtrey, Sir Ralph George (1879–1971). Served Admiralty, 1903; Treasury, 1904–45; director of financial inquiries, 1919–45; economist and author. (CC)

Hayes, Michael (1889–1976). Jacob's Factory, 1916; TD/MP, 1921–33; Minister of Education, Dáil Eireann, January–September 1922; Minister of External Affairs, August–September 1922; Ceann Comhairle (Speaker) of Dáil Eireann, 1922–32; Senator, 1933–65; Lecturer in modern Irish, UCD, 1933–51; professor, 1951–60; chairman of standing committee and national council, Fine Gael. (DIH)

Headlam, Maurice Francis (b. 1873). Clerk, Board of Trade, 1897; Treasury,

1899; private secretary to the Chancellor of the Exchequer (Austen Chamberlain), 1903–5; Treasury Remembrancer and Deputy Paymaster-General for Ireland, 1912–20; assistant secretary to the Treasury, 1920–6; British representative on the Pacific Cable board, 1923–9; acting chairman, 1927–9; Silver Jubilee medal, 1935; coronation medal, 1937; CB, 1923; CMG, 1929. (WW)

Hendricks, C. A. C. J. Private secretary to the Minister of Education, Northern Ireland, 1921. (BUD)

Henry, Denis Stanislaus (1864–1925). Barrister; Unionist MP, 1916–21; Attorney-General, Ireland, 1919–21; Lord Chief Justice for Northern Ireland, 1921; Baronet, 1922. (CT)

Hewart, Sir Gordon (1870–1943). Liberal MP for Leicester, 1913–18; Leicester East, 1918–22; Solicitor-General, 1916–19; Attorney-General, 1919–22; signed Anglo-Irish Treaty, 1921; Lord Chief Justice, 1922–40. (CC)

Hogan, Patrick J. (1891–1936). MP/TD for Galway, 1921–32; Minister for Agriculture, 1922–32; introduced 1923 Land Act; Senator, 1932–6. (DIH)

Horan, Gerald (b. 1879). Irish Bar, 1901; chairman, Kilkenny Bridge Commission, 1907; Revising Barrister, Dublin, 1912; KC, 1915; Clerk of Crown and Hanaper and permanent secretary to the Lord Chancellor of Ireland, 1915–22; Master of the High Court, Irish Free State, 1926. (WW)

Horne, Sir Robert Stevenson (1871–1940). Conservative MP for Glasgow Hillhead, 1918–37; Minister of Labour, 1919–20; president, Board of Trade 1920–1; Chancellor of the Exchequer, 1921–2. (CC)

Huggett, James. Comptroller and Auditor-General, Northern Ireland, 1921.

Johnson, R. A. Treasury official; member of Irish Civil Service Committee representing the Secretary of State for Home Affairs, 1921–2.

Jones, Thomas (1870–1955). Barrington lecturer in Ireland, 1904; confidant of Lloyd George and assistant secretary to the Cabinet, 1916–30. (CT)

Kellaway. Secretary, Post Office in Ireland, 1918–22.

Kennedy, Hugh Boyle (1879–1936). Law officer, provisional government, January–December 1922; Attorney-General, Irish Free State, 1922–4; first Chief Justice of the Free State, 1924–36. (DIH)

Kenny, J. Executive officer, Ministry of Agriculture, Northern Ireland; worked part-time on Diseases of Animals Acts administration.

Kirkpatrick, J. A. Assistant principal, Chief Secretary's Office (Belfast branch), 1920–1; private secretary to the parliamentary secretary, Ministry of Home Affairs, Northern Ireland, 1921.

Law, Andrew Bonar (1858–1923). Born in Canada, raised in Glasgow; MP for Glasgow, 1918; elected leader of opposition in House of Commons, 1911; with Sir Edward Carson, shared leadership of faction which carried opposition to Irish Home Rule to brink of civil war; Secretary of State for the Colonies in first coalition, May 1915; invited by George V to form a government, December 1916, but on failure to secure co-operation, first of Lloyd George and then of Asquith, advised king to call on Lloyd George; Chancellor of the Exchequer, 1916–18; Lord Privy Seal, 1918–21; leader of House of Commons, 1916–21; signatory of Treaty of Versailles, 1919; resigned owing to ill-health, March 1921; emerged from retirement to recommend Irish Treaty, Autumn 1921; Prime Minister, October 1922–May 1923 (CDNB)

Liddell, Sir Frederick Francis (b. 1865). Private secretary to Lord Stanmore, governor of Ceylon, 1888–90; Fellow of All Souls College, Oxford, 1891–1906; called to the Bar, 1894; first parliamentary counsel, 1917–28 (WW 1931)

Litchfield, Cecil. Permanent secretary, Ministry of Commerce, 1921.

Londonderry, 7th Marquess of (1878–1949). Conservative MP for Maidstone, 1906–15; leader of Northern Ireland Senate, 1921–6; parliamentary under-secretary, Air Ministry, 1920–1; Minister of Education, Northern Ireland, 1921–5; 1st commissioner of works, 1928–9; August–October 1931; Secretary of State for Air, 1931–5; Lord Privy Seal, January–November 1935. (CC)

Long, Walter Hume (1854–1924). Conservative MP for Wiltshire North, 1880–5; Devizes, 1885–92; Liverpool West Derby, 1893–1900; Bristol South, 1900–6; Dublin County South, 1906–January 1910; Strand, January 1910–18; Westminster St George's, 1918–21; parliamentary secretary, Local Government Board, 1886–92; President of Board of Agriculture, 1895–1900; President of the Local Government Board, 1900–5; and 1915–16; Chief Secretary for Ireland, 1905; Secretary of State for Colonial Affairs, 1916–19; First Lord of the Admiralty, 1919–21; leader of Unionist Party 1906–10; a founder of the Union Defence League, 1907; president of the Budget Protection League to oppose Lloyd George's 'people's budget', 1909; with Austen Chamberlain, a contender for leadership of the Conservative Party, both withdrawing to make way for Bonar Law; chairman of Cabinet committees on Irish legislation, 1918 and 1919–20. (CDNB)

Loughnane, Norman Gerald (b. 1883). Chief Secretary's Office, 1920–2; Colonial Office representative to the Irish Free State, 1922–4; KCB, 1924; member of financial commission of inquiry, Mauritius, 1931; principal, Treasury. (WW)

Lynch, Fionan (b. 1889). MP/TD for South Kerry, 1918–21; Kerry and West Limerick, 1921–3; Kerry, 1923; Minister of Education, provisional government, 1922; Minister of Fisheries, 1922–8; Minister for Lands and Fisheries, 1928–32. (WW)

McCloskey. Veterinary inspector, Derry port; refused to recognise Northern Ireland Ministry of Agriculture, 1922.

McDonnell of Swinford, 1st Baron (1844–1925). Indian civil service, 1864–81; Lt-governor of Indian North-west provinces and chief commissioner of Oudh, 1893–1901; under-secretary of Ireland, 1902–8; supported Land Conference which led to Wyndham Act, 1903; chairman Royal Commission on Civil Service, 1912–14; attended Irish Convention, 1917–18. (DIH; CC)

McGrath, Joseph (1888–1966). Irish Volunteers, 1913; Easter Rising, 1916; MP/TD, 1918–21; 1921; Minister of Labour, 1920, 1921–2; Minister of Industry and Commerce and Minister of Economic Affairs, 1922; Minister of Industry and Commerce, 1922–4; resigned after Army Mutiny, 1924; director, Shannon hydroelectric scheme; founded Waterford Glass and Donegal Carpets; founded Irish Hospitals Sweepstakes. (DIH)

McGuffin, Samuel (b. 1863). President of Belfast no. 12 branch Amalgamated

Society of Engineers; chairman of the works committee of the Belfast Water Commissioners; Unionist MP for Shankill Division of Belfast, 1918–22; MP, North Belfast (Northern Ireland Parliament), 1921–5. (WW)

McKevitt, W. Irish Volunteer and civil servant in National Health Insurance Commission; tried to warn Dáil Cabinet about partition of the civil service, November 1921.

MacMahon, Rt Hon. James (1865–1954). Under-secretary of Ireland, 1918–22; assistant secretary Post Office in Ireland, 1913–16; secretary Post Office in Ireland, 1916–18. (DIH)

MacNeill, Eoin (1867–1945). Vice-president, Gaelic League, 1893; co-founder, Feis Ceoil, 1894; editor, *An Claideamh Soluis*, 1899; first professor of early and medieval Irish History at UCD, 1908; article, 'The North Began', 1 November 1913 led to founding of Irish Volunteers; Chief of Staff, Irish Volunteers, 1913; used as a front by IRB whose rising in 1916 he opposed; MP/TD for Derry, 1918; Minister of Finance, 1919; Minister of Industries, 1919–21; Ceann Comhairle during Treaty debates, December 1921–January 1922; minister without portfolio in the provisional government, January–August 1922; Minister of Education, August 1922–November 1925; Irish Free State representative on the Boundary Commission, 1924–5; resigned from commission and from the government after press leak of contents of commission's report. (DIH)

McQuibban, Lewis (b. 1866). Head of secondary-schools branch of Scottish Education Department until 1913; secretary to Highlands and Islands Medical Services Board, 1913; assistant secretary to Scottish Board of Health, 1919–21; permanent secretary to the Ministry of Education, Northern Ireland, 1921–7 and civil service commissioner for Northern Ireland; retired, 1927. (WW)

Macready, General Sir Cecil Frederick Nevil (1862–1945). Military career; South Africa, 1899–1902; European War, 1914–16; director of personal services, 1910–14; Adjutant-General, British Expeditionary Force, 1914–16; Adjutant-General to the home forces, 1916–18; Commissioner of the London Metropolitan Police, 1918–20; GOC-in-C Ireland, 1920–22. (CC)

MacRory, Joseph (Cardinal) (1861–1945). Archbishop of Armagh and Primate of All Ireland (RC), 1927–45; ordained, 1885; Bishop of Down and Connor, 1915–27; Cardinal, 1929; head of Catholic Academy, Dungannon; Professor of Moral Theology and Scripture, Diocesan Seminary, Birmingham; Professor of Sacred Scripture, Maynooth. (DIH)

MacSwiney, Terence (1879–1920). Irish Volunteer, 1914; Sinn Féin and Volunteer, 1917–20; MP/TD for Mid-Cork, 1918–20; became Lord Mayor of Cork after murder of Thomas McCurtain, 1920; arrested under DORA, 19 August 1920 and embarked on a hunger-strike capturing international attention; died after seventy-four days. (DIH)

Magill, Andrew Philip. Registrar of petty sessions clerks, Dublin Castle; assistant secretary, Ministry of Home Affairs, Northern Ireland, 1921.

Martin-Jones, C. M. Principal officer, Chief Secretary's Office to 1921.

Masterton-Smith, Sir James Edward (1878–1938). Assistant secretary, War Office and Air Ministry, 1919–20; joint permanent secretary to the Ministry of Labour, 1920–21; permanent under-secretary, Colonial Office, 1921–4;

chairman of Irish technical subcommittee of the Cabinet Provisional Government of Ireland Committee, 1922. (CC)

Matthews, Sir William Thomas (1888–1968). Principal, Treasury, 1920; assistant to Waterfield in Treasury (Ireland), 1920–2; assistant secretary, Assistance Board, 1934; Principal assistant secretary, Assistance Board, 1937; civil adivser to Intendant General, Cairo, 1941; director-general, Middle East Relief and Refugee Administration, 1942; director-general UNRRA in Balkans, 1944; under-secretary, Ministry of National Insurance, 1945; under-secretary, HM Treasury, 1948; former member Administration and Budget Committee, UNO. (*Who Was Who, 1961–70*)

Megaw, Hon. Robert Dick. Irish Bar 1893; Professor of Common Law, King's Inns, Dublin, 1912–14; KC, 1921; Unionist MP for Antrim, Northern Ireland Parliament, 1921–5; parliamentary secretary, Ministry of Home Affairs Northern Ireland, 1921–5; member of senate of the Queen's University, Belfast; commissioner appointed by Ministry of Home Affairs to inquire into the administration of the Housing Acts by Belfast Corporation, 1925–6; judicial commissioner of the Land Purchase Commission of Northern Ireland, 1927–37; bencher of the Honourable Society of the Inns of Courts of Northern Ireland; Puisne judge, High Court of Justice in Northern Ireland (chancery judge), 1932. (WW)

Molony, Rt. Hon. Sir Thomas Francis (b. 1865) Irish Bar, 1887; QC, 1889; English Bar, 1900; Crown counsel for Co. Carlow, 1906–12; county and city of Dublin, 1907–12; a commissioner of education in Ireland, 1907–24; HM's second serjeant at law, 1921; a judge of the High Court of Justice in Ireland, 1915–18; Lord Chief Justice of Ireland, 1918–24; member of the Intermediate Education Board for Ireland, 1914; member of the Royal Commission on Disturbances in Dublin, 1914; member of the Royal Commission on Certain Shootings during Sinn Féin Rising, 1916; chairman of the Viceregal Committee on International Education in Ireland, 1918. (WW)

Montagu, Hon. Edwin Samuel (1879–1924). Liberal MP for Chesterton, 1906–18; Coalition Liberal for Cambridgeshire, 1918–22; parliamentary under-secretary, India Office, 1910–14; finance secretary, Treasury, 1914–15, 1915–16; Chancellor of the Duchy of Lancaster, 1915 and 1916; Minister of Munitions, 1916; Secretary of State for India, 1917–22. (CC)

Mulcahy, General Richard James (1886–1971). Irish Volunteers, 1913; Ashbourne, 1916, second-in-command to Thomas Ashe; Chief of Staff, IRA; MP/TD 1918; Minister of Defence, January–April 1919; Minister of Defence, provisional government, Irish Free State, 1922–4; resigned after army mutiny, 1924; Chief of Staff, National Army, 1922; Minister of Local Government, 1927–32; founder member Fine Gael; Minister of Education, 1948–51; 1954–7; Minister for the Gaeltacht, July–October 1956. (DIH)

Mulvin, W. G. S. Civil servant in Irish Board of National Education; Civil Service Association representative; member of existing Irish Officer delegation to Northern Ireland Minister of Finance, July 1921.

Murphy, Dr Con. Chairman of Irish Civil Service Alliance, 1921; led civil service revolt against the Civil Service Committee, December 1921; arrested by provisional government on suspicion of complicity with irregulars, July 1922.

Murray, Sir Evelyn (1880–1947). Secretary, Post Office, 1914–34; chairman, Board of Customs and Excise, 1934–40. (CC)

Niemeyer, Sir Otto Ernst (1883–1971). Assistant secretary, Treasury from 1919; deputy controller of finance, 1919–22; controller of finance, 1922–7; member financial subcommittee League of Nations, 1922–37; banker; director, Bank of England. (CC)

O'Brien, William. Principal inspector of taxes, Board of Inland Revenue, Dublin; secretary, Irish Department of Finance, 1922–3; chairman of Board of Inland Revenue, Irish Free State, 1923. (RF)

O'Connor, Rory (1883–1922). Easter Rising, 1916; director of engineering, IRA; chairman, Military Council, IRA, March 1922; led Four Courts garrison, April–July 1922; rejected Collins–de Valera pact, May 1922; executed 8 December 1922 by Free State executive. (DIH)

O'Flanagan, Fr Michael (1876–1942). Ordained 1900 for Elphin diocese; land agitator, Co. Roscommon, 1912–14; vice-president, Sinn Féin, 1917; suspended by bishop for political activities, 1918; judge in Dáil Eireann courts; Sinn Féin propagandist in USA, 1921–6; led opposition to de Valera's motion at Sinn Féin ard-fheis, that would enable Sinn Féin to enter Dáil if oath were removed; silenced by bishop 1932; went to Spain to support republicans, 1936–9; visited Canada and USA on behalf of Irish and Spanish republics; edited fifty volumes of letters of John O'Donovan. (DIH)

O'Hegarty, Patrick Sarsfield (1879–1955). Law clerk, 1895; Post Office clerk, 1897; bookseller, 1918; IRB; editor of nationalist and separatist publications; bibliographer; permanent secretary, Ministry of Post and Telegraphs, 1922. (DIH; RF)

O'Higgins, Kevin Christopher (1892–1927). MP/TD for Laois-Offaly: assistant to the Minister of Local Government (W. T. Cosgrave), 1919–22; Minister for Economic Affairs, Dáil Eireann and provisional government, 1922; Minister for Home Affairs, 1922–7; represented Free State at League of Nations and imperial conferences; assassinated, 10 July 1927. (DIH)

Petherick, Capt C. H. Assistant principal, Chief Secretary's Office (Belfast branch), 1920–1; private secretary and acting assistant principal, Ministry of Finance, 1921.

Pollock, Hugh McDowell (d. 1937). Minister of Finance, Northern Ireland, 1921–37.

Rae, Sir James (b. 1879). Principal, Treasury, 1919; assistant secretary, 1920; secretary to Political Honours Scrutiny Committee, 1923; under-secretary, 1932; KCB, 1937. (WW)

Ramsay, Malcolm Graham (1871–1946). Private secretary to Prime Minister, A. J. Balfour, 1902–5; Treasury; chairman, National Whitley Council for the Civil Service, 1919–21; Comptroller and Auditor-General, 1921–31. (CC)

Redmond, John (1856–1918). MP New Ross, 1881–5; North Wexford, 1885–91; Waterford, 1891–1918; leader of Parnellites from 1890; leader of reunified Irish Party from 1900; held balance of power in the Commons, 1910, forcing Liberal commitment to Irish Home Rule; attempted to usurp authority over Volunteer movement, 1914; tentatively agreed to temporary exclusion of six Ulster counties in an attempt to come to terms with Ulster

Unionists; pledged Irish Volunteers for service in British army, 1914–18 war, causing split in the movement; participated in Irish Convention, 1917–18. (DIH)

Robinson, Sir Henry Augustus (1896–1927). Vice-president, Local Government Board for Ireland, 1898–1922.

Robson, W. Irish civil service representative; member of delegation to Northern Ireland Minister of Finance, July 1921.

Scott, William Dalgliesh (b. 1890). Member English Bar; Board of Inland Revenue, 1910–20; Chief Secretary's Office (Belfast branch), 1920–1; assistant secretary Northern Ireland Ministry of Finance, 1921–4; permanent secretary to the Ministry of Commerce, 1924. (WW)

Shortt, Edward (1862–1935). Liberal MP for Newcastle upon Tyne, January 1910–18; Newcastle upon Tyne West, 1918–22; Chief Secretary for Ireland, 1918–19; Secretary of State for Home Affairs, 1919–22. (CC)

Sloan, Samuel. Existing Irish officer active in Civil Service Association and Whitley Council; member of delegation to Pollock, July 1921; with M. J. Gallagher, a staff representative on Civil Service Committee, 1921–2; transferred to Northern Ireland government, 1922; represented existing Irish officers on Civil Service Committee, Northern Ireland, 1922.

Smith, T. J. Head of RIC in Belfast during Ulster crisis, 1912–14; Inspector-General RIC, March–November 1920 replacing the Catholic Sir Joseph Byrne; supported by Walter Long for head of RIC, 1919. (CT)

Smyth, Col. Gerald Ferguson (1882–1920). Royal Engineers, 1906; France, 1914–18; wounded six times and lost left arm; brig.-gen. 1918; divisional commissioner RIC and police commissioner for Munster, 1920; assassinated, July 1920. (CT)

Spender, Lt Col. Sir Wilfrid Bliss (1876–1960). Served on general staff and subcommittee, Imperial Defence; retired on the Ulster question, 1913; HQ staff UVF; served First World War on General Staff, Ulster and 31st divisions and GHQ; selected by Lord Haig to organise Officers' Friend Branch, Ministry of Pensions; member of Haig's committee to form British Legion; re-raised and commanded UVF, 1920; first secretary to the Cabinet, Northern Ireland, 1921–5; permanent secretary, Ministry of Finance and head of civil service, Northern Ireland, 1925–44; member Joint Exchequer board, 1933; KCB, 1929. (WW)

Sturgis, Mark Beresford Russell Grant (1884–1949). Private secretary to Prime Minister (Asquith), 1908–10; special commissioner of income tax, 1910; joint assistant secretary, Ireland, 1920–2; assistant under-secretary, Irish services, 1922–4. (CC)

Swanzy. District inspector, RIC, Cork; assassinated in Lisburn, 22 August 1922.

Tallents, Sir Stephen George (b. 1884). Board of Trade, 1909–14; served with Irish Guards, 1914–15 (wounded); Ministry of Munitions, 1915–16; a principal assistant secretary, Ministry of Food and member of Food Council, 1918; chief British delegate for relief and supply of Poland, 1919; British commissioner for the Baltic Provinces, 1919–20; private secretary to Lord Fitzalan, Lord-Lieutenant of Ireland, 1921–2; investigated administration of justice in Northern Ireland, summer 1922; Imperial Secretary, Northern

Ireland, 1922–6; secretary to Empire Marketing Board, 1926–33; public relations officer, General Post Office, 1933–5; controller (public relations), BBC, 1935. (WW)

Taylor, Sir John James (1859–1945). Private secretary to Chief Secretary (Walter Long), 1905; principal clerk, Chief Secretary's Office, 1911–18; clerk to Privy Council and assistant under-secretary, Ireland, 1918–20; KCB, 1919. (CT)

Thomson, Sir Courtauld (b. 1866). British Red Cross commissioner, France, 1914–15; chief commissioner, Malta, Egypt, Italy, Macedonia and Near East, 1915–19; attached GHQ staff, British Expeditionary Forces, Egypt, 1916; Italy, 1918; chairman of Irish Civil Service Committee, 1921–6; chairman of several committees and commissions; trustee or other officer of several charitable institutions; dubbed a knight of several orders of hospitallers. (WW)

Tudor, Major-General Sir Hugh (1871–1965). Military career; South Africa; European War, 1914–18; Chief of Police, RIC, 1920–22; air vice-marshal and GOC in Palestine, 1922. (CC; DIH)

Valera, Eamonn de (1882–1975). Teacher and lecturer of mathematics; commandant 3rd brigade, Irish Volunteers to 1916; commandant at Boland's Mills, 1916; SF MP for East Clare, 1917–18; MP/TD East Clare 1918–59; president of Dáil Eireann, 1919–21; president of Irish Republic, 1921–2; president of the Executive Council of the Irish Free State, 1932–7; Taoiseach, 1937–48, 1951–4, 1957–9; president of Republic of Ireland, 1959–73; Minister of External Affairs, 1932–48; president of the Council of the League of Nations, 1932; president of the League of Nations Assembly, 1938–9; president of Sinn Féin, 1917–26; president of Irish Volunteers, 1917–22; TD/MP for four constituencies, 1918; fund-raiser and propagandist in USA, June 1919–December 1920; negotiated with Lloyd George the basis for Anglo-Irish Conference, July–September 1921; led Dáil opposition to Treaty, counter-proposing 'external association' as outlined in Document no. 2; founded Fáil, 1926; president Fianna Fáil, 1926–59.

Walsh, James Joseph (b. 1880). MP/TD Cork City, 1918–27; Minister for Posts and Telegraphs, 1922–7; director Tailteann games; manufacturer; president, Federation of Irish Industries; Hon. President, GAA. (WW)

Waterfield, Sir (Alexander) Percival (1888–1965). Entered Treasury, 1911; then private industry, John Barbour & Co.; re-entered Treasury, 1920; assistant secretary at Treasury (Ireland), Dublin Castle, 1920–2; Treasury Remembrancer in Ireland, May–October 1922; principal assistant secretary, 1934–9; deputy secretary, Ministry of Information, 1939–40; member of Palestine Partition Commission, 1938; commissioner for review of salaries and wages in Malta, 1958. (*Who Was Who, 1961–70*; H. A. Robinson, *Memories; Wise and Otherwise*, p. 292)

Watt, Samuel. Permanent secretary, Ministry of Home Affairs, Northern Ireland, 1921.

Whiskard, Sir Geoffrey Granville (1886–1957). Civil service career including principal, Chief Secretary's Office and Irish Office, 1920–6; High Commissioner, Australia, 1936–41; permanent secretary, Ministry of Works and Buildings, 1941–3; Town and Country Planning, 1943–6. (CC)

Whitley, John Henry (1866–1935). Liberal MP for Halifax, 1900–28; Junior Lord of the Treasury, 1907–10; chairman, Committee on the Relations of Employers and Employed (Whitley Committee), 1917–18; Speaker of the House of Commons, 1921–8. (CC)

Wilson, General Sir Henry (1864–1922). Boer War; brigadier-general, 1907; War Office, 1910; Assistant Chief of General Staff British Expeditionary Force to France, 1914; urged martial law in Ireland, 1920; MP for Co. Down, 1921; security adviser to Northern Ireland government, 1922; assassinated at 36 Eaton Place by Dunne and O'Sullivan, 22 June 1922. (DIH)

Wylie, The Hon. William Evelyn (1881–1964). Called to Bar, 1905; KC, 1914; law adviser to Irish government, 1919–20; judge of the Supreme Court of Judicature (Ireland), 1920–4; judge of the High Court, Irish Free State, 1924–36; judicial commissioner to the Irish Land Commission; chairman, Irish Free State Committee on Civil Service Compensation (Wylie Committee), 1922. (WW; PRO T 164/30/P. 25891)

Wynn, Rt Hon. Sir Henry (b. 1867). Solicitor, 1889; Crown solicitor for Cork City and Cork Co. (West Riding) and sessional Crown solicitor for Cork City, 1905–16; senior member of firm of Wynn & Wynn, solicitors of Cork, where he practised in partnership with his brother, frederick William Wynn, 1896–1916; Chief Crown Solicitor for Ireland, 1916–22. (WW)

Index

Items marked with an asterisk are references to biographical notes.